THE TRACKS OF MY YEARS

A Music-Based Memoir
by Doug Bradley

Legacy Book Press
— LLC —
Camanche, Iowa

Copyright © 2025 Doug Bradley
Cover design by Maegan Hart
Cover art by Maegan Hart
Book design by Kaitlea Toohey (kaitleatoohey.com)

Some names, locations, and identifying characteristics have been changed to protect the privacy of those depicted. As it is with all personal narratives, this one is subjective. This story is told from the author's perspective and his memories; he recognizes that everyone remembers events differently.

All rights reserved. No part of this book may be used or reproduced by any means, graphic, electronic, or mechanical, including photocopying, recording, taping, or by any information storage retrieval system without the written permission of the publisher except in the case of brief quotations embodied in critical articles and reviews.

The political views expressed in this book are solely those of the author and do not necessarily reflect the views of the publisher.

ISBN: 979-8-9905387-1-9
Library of Congress Number: 1-14716116251

ADVANCE PRAISE

"Bradley's memoir is remarkable. Through the use of music, he anchors the reader not only to the time of the narrative, but *the feeling* of the time. Few writers achieve this in any genre."

    Karl Marlantes, *NY Times* bestselling author of *Matterhorn, What It Is Like to Go to War, Deep River,* and *Cold Victory*

"There could be no better way for Doug Bradley to explore the meaning of his life than through the music of our generation. I felt soulfully connected to this book, and his compelling story, as it moved through the decades."

    David Maraniss, *NY Times* bestselling author, Pulitzer Prize winner, and associate editor at the *Washington Post*

"Doug Bradley has an incisive way of getting to the heart of the role music plays in our lives, how it lifts and supports us in difficult times and allows us to access our deepest emotions. His writing illustrates brilliantly the importance of music and how it is a universal force for good."

    Maggie Ayre, Series Producer, "Soul Music," BBC Radio Four

"Utilizing the foundational elements of melody, rhythm, harmony and timbre as his narrative hooks, and beloved songs by era-defining artists including Dylan, the Stones, and Smokey as his guiding lights, Doug Bradley takes readers on an alternately rollicking and harrowing journey through familial love, life during wartime, and the musical ties that bind. As a memoirist, Bradley sounds like your favorite radio DJ spinning one great track after another, tuned into a frequency of longing and forgiveness."

    Steven Jenkins, Director, Bob Dylan Center

"Doug Bradley's *The Tracks of My Years* is a deeply felt meditation on the power of music to bridge time, place, and experience—between past and present, war and home, memory and meaning. With a veteran's wisdom, a father's heart, and a storyteller's gift, he reminds us that the songs we hold onto don't just mark our past—they shape who we become and help us find our way forward."

Erin Celello, author, *Learning to Stay*

"A sometimes heart-wrenching, sometimes humorous, unfailingly insightful chronicle of a life lived with, in, and through music. The story of a young man working out what it means to be a son, a brother, a friend and/or lover, a husband and a father, it's at once a record of a world in constant change, its soundtrack spinning from jazz and doo-wop to Motown and psychedelic soul. Written by an award-winning music writer and dedicated veteran activist, *The Tracks of My Years* bears witness to the power of music to make sense of a world that mostly doesn't."

Craig Werner, professor emeritus UW-Madison; former member Rock & Roll Hall of Fame Nominating Committee; author *A Change is Gonna Come: Music, Race & The Soul of America;* co-author *We Gotta Get Out of This Place: The Soundtrack of the Vietnam War*

"I served as a U. S. Army nurse stationed at the 24th Evacuation Hospital in Vietnam in 1970-71. Doug Bradley was in Vietnam at the same time, but we didn't meet until the publication of *We Gotta Get of This Place: The Soundtrack of the Vietnam War,* where he and Craig Werner captured the life, energy, and critical connections music brought to our unreal existence. Then Doug's *Who'll Stop the Rain* provided similar affirmation of our more recent journey to post-Vietnam reconciliation. Now, in *The Tracks of My Years,* Doug Bradley once again uses music to transcend words as he broadens the shared view of our lives in rear-view mirrors."

Mary Reynolds Powell, Captain, U. S. Army Nurse Corps 1970-71, author, *A World of Hurt: Between Innocence and Arrogance in Vietnam*

"For nearly 20 years, Vietnam Veteran Doug Bradley has used popular music as a means of connecting with a fractious population divided by class, culture, and politics. *The Tracks of My Years* reminds us of songs and messages of unity that serve as a testament to the deep connection between music and memory."

       Jeff Kollath, Director Emeritus, Stax Museum
          of American Soul Music in Memphis

"All of us–from the 'Greatest Generation,' to Baby Boomers, Millennials, and Gens throughout the alphabet—have our own soundtracks. Whether they hum softly in the background or orchestrate our lives, they're there. Doug Bradley's particularly tight relationship with the consequential music of his era creates an intense, economical, and engaging memoir. I highly recommend it as a solo read, or as a companion to his earlier, eclectic music-filled works."

    Susan O'Neill, 1st Lieutenant, U. S. Army Nurse Corps,
    12th Evacuation Hospital, Cu Chi, 1969-70, author
      Don't Mean Nothing: Short Stories of Vietnam

"As hard as it is to imagine, there may be people whose lives do not include music. Doug Bradley is most definitely not one of those people. His entire life is a discography, each period—from childhood to adolescence to adulthood and beyond—inseparable from the songs that defined those years and times. As he describes in his honest, brave, heartfelt, and at times heart-wrenching, "music-based memoir," *The Tracks of My Years,* music guided Bradley "through all that was coming at us like a wildfire out of control." In a life examined note by note, music eased the pain of love lost or squandered, accompanied the incomprehensible loss of friends and mentors, and provided refuge from the Dickensian existential crises of imagining a Vietnam veteran's seeming inevitable place in Arlington National Cemetery. On every page, every ecstatic high, soul-crushing low, or confounding human mystery, Bradley manages to sing through it all, songs that give his life and ours an aura and context that make it all meaningful and, even perhaps, possible."

Neil Heinen, award-winning broadcast journalist; former Editorial Director WISC-TV and *Madison Magazine*

"Reading Doug Bradley's new book caused me major musical flashbacks. It was as if someone had just cued up a CD featuring the greatest hits of my lifetime. There I was in Vietnam listening to CCR, Janis, Motown jams, and the Beatles. And there was Doug relating much of what was behind many of those defining tunes. Whether you lived during the time or came along later, *Tracks of My Tears* is a magical mystery tour."

Capt. Dale A. Dye, USMC (Ret.) author, *Shake Davis Trilogy*

"With music as his backdrop, Doug Bradley writes using wit and his reporter's eye to record his own and his country's post-WWII coming-of-age stories. He adds clarity for a generation that continues to seek deeper understanding of the impacts of those tumultuous times."

Judith Gwinn Adrian, author, *From Hardship to Hope: Crossing the great divides of age, race, wealth, equity, and health*

"As a composer and Vietnam veteran, I have always used music to express my experiences in Vietnam. I have never been able to find the words that succinctly capture what that experience was like so I used my music compositions. Doug nailed it with words in *The Tracks of My Years*. He speaks from his personal experience and shows how music intertwined with his time in Vietnam. Reading his book has inspired me to compose more music to further share our story. This book is a must-read for anyone who wishes to truly understand the inner world of a Vietnam veteran as an individual, rather than as a stereotype."

J. Kimo Williams, Captain, US Army Retired (Vietnam 1970); Composer, Fulbright Specialist; Co-Founder The Lt. Dan Band

"As someone who shared the same cloistered, emotionally choked Catholic childhood as Doug Bradley, grooving to the birth of rock 'n' roll, summoned by the black hit parade artists showing us that negroes were not to be frightened of and certainly made the best music, this book is like reading my own youthful diary of the explosive Fifties. If you want to know what that era truly felt like, open these pages and become a grateful time traveler, and learn how and why music lured and guided an entire generation."

Roger Steffens, Vietnam veteran and author *So Much Things to Say: The Oral History of Bob Marley*

"We fans of Doug Bradley's writing already know that, both on his own and in collaboration with Craig Werner for *We Gotta Get Out of This Place,* he is one of our most honest, insightful, and eloquent chroniclers of the tragic complexities behind the Vietnam War, its aftermath, its veterans' experiences, and the equally complex role that music has played in those experiences. What most of us don't know yet, however, is exactly how Doug became this person – his 'origin story,' if you will. *The Tracks of My Years: A Music-Based Memoir* finally provides us with that. More important, at its heart lies a tale of someone struggling to maintain the best of his humanity in a society bent on the destruction of others, as well as itself. Thus, a book that's filled with such vivid, moving (though also at times gallows-humor funny,) and ultimately life-affirming recollections simultaneously becomes extremely relevant to our current circumstances."

Shawn Poole, Editor/Publisher, LettersToYou.net
("The Springsteen fan's companion...")

Also by Doug Bradley:

DEROS Vietnam: Dispatches from the Air-Conditioned Jungle

We Gotta Get Out of This Place: The Soundtrack of the Vietnam War
(with Craig Werner)

Who'll Stop the Rain: Respect, Remembrance, and Reconciliation in Post-Vietnam America

To all my family

"When we listen to music we are not listening to the past, we are not listening to the future, we are listening to an expanded present."

Alan Watts

"Where words fail, music speaks."

Hans Christian Anderson

DISCOGRAPHY

Overture: You've Got Your Troubles.................................1

Part One: Melody 9

    Philadelphia in Six Movements 11
    Tracks 1-2: Hit the Road, Jack; Chain Gang......30
    Track 3: Two Faces Have I...34
    Track 4: Monkey Time...39
    Track 5: Be Fair 46
    Track 6: Hello Dolly 53
    Track 7: Time is on my Side 60
    Tracks 8-9: You've Lost that Lovin' Feelin; Goin' Out of my head..68
    Track 10: I'm a Loser..75
    Track 11: Mr. Tambourine Man 82
    Track 12: I Can't Help Myself 88
    Track 13: Like A Rolling Stone 93

Part Two: Rhythm 99

    Tracks 14-15: That's The Way It's Gonna Be; Yesterday 101
    Track 16: Good Lovin 107
    Track 17: Tracks of my Tears..................................113
    Track 18: Come See About Junior 120
    Track 19: Somebody To Love.................................128
    Track 20: Double Shot of My Baby's Love 138
    Track 21: Abraham, Martin, and John 141
    Sonata: Poster Notes...147
    Track 22: The Worst That Could Happen.........161
    Track 23: You Made Me So Very Happy 167

Part Three: Harmony 173

    Track 24: Leaving on a Jet Plane.......................175
    Track 25: Rainy Night in Georgia 182
    Track 26: Fire and Rain 187
    Track 27: Yellow Submarine 193

Track 28: Dawn..198
Track 29: Kansas City 204
Track 30: Walk On By..211
Track 31: The Tears of a Clown.............................218
Track 32: Knock Three Times 224
Track 33: The Pusher 233
Track 34: Wild Horses 237
Track 35: We Gotta Get out of This Place.....247
Track 36: River..253

Part Four: Timbre...259

Track 37: It's Too Late..261
Track 38: 1-2-3..268
Track 39: Without You..274
Track 40: Key to the Highway...........................284
Track 41: On the Road to Find Out..................290
Track 42: Visions of Johanna.............................295
Track 43: Traction in the Rain.............................301
Track 44: Peace Like a River...............................308
Track 45: Ripple..312
Track 46: Thank You, Anyway (Mr. D.J.)..........318

Coda: Remember Me...328

Acknowledgements..333
About the Author..335

Overture

YOU'VE GOT YOUR TROUBLES

I played basketball with Smokey Robinson and the Miracles, walked a blind Sonny Terry and a lame Brownie McGhee on stage, sipped whiskey with Count Basie, and shared a joint with Grace Slick and the Jefferson Airplane. I held Dionne Warwick's hands when I told her Dr. Martin Luther King had been assassinated. I survived a bite on the leg from a stoned member of the Association and grooved with Sam and Dave, the American Breed, Spanky and Our Gang, and the Grass Roots. I surprised a topless Florence LaRue of the Fifth Dimension when I interrupted her wardrobe change in a locker room at tiny Bethany College, for a few years a musical oasis in the hardscrabble West Virginia hills.

And then there was the night Junior Walker and the All Stars came to campus and all the lights in the Field House unexpectedly went out…

But now, as I sift through my encounters with rock and soul royalty and the songs that defined me and an era, my thoughts settle on "You've Got Your Troubles," a minor hit by an inconsequential group named The Fortunes, and a cold March afternoon in Madison, Wisconsin, in 1982 when, ten years after returning from Vietnam and earning an MA in

English, I found myself a stay-at-home dad, my precocious two-year-old daughter Summer by my side.

* * *

For a time in the early 1980s, fatherhood was all that mattered to me. I didn't set out to trailblaze or make myself some sort of shining example, but when my spouse, Pam Shannon, and I decided to have kids, we agreed that childrearing would be a 50-50 proposition, pregnancy, labor and delivery, and breastfeeding notwithstanding.

"I want to spend as much time with my little girl as I can, learn how to be the best father I can be," is what I told those who asked why I was pulling daddy duty morning, noon, and night. Which meant not working much outside the home. Good thing I married an employable attorney. Maybe now I'd have time to knock out the great American novel on my trusty Smith Corona while my baby daughter napped.

Truth be told, I was flaunting the fatherhood badge of courage, showing off a little too much. I'd published an essay in *The New Physician* magazine about my active participation in childbirth, attended University of Wisconsin classes on child development, and was energetically involved in our neighborhood babysitting co-op. My choices drew skeptical looks from the older generation, but elicited praise, and maybe a little envy, from my peers.

Or so I thought.

But before you could say "Goodnight Moon," I found myself besieged with questions about my employment status. Worse, I stopped being invited to the "Mom's" Wednesday playgroup or being used as one of the regular backups for the neighborhood babysitting co-op when bedraggled mothers needed a break. Why had my stock fallen? Did it have anything to do with the fact I was, without thinking about it, not putting Summer in dresses?

By the time she was 17 months old, my daughter was attending half-days of preschool, supposedly to aid with her socialization. Or maybe to help with mine? I was still unemployed without any imminent career prospects. Worse, I was concluding that Summer might be better off not having me around so much. "She's too aggressive," the daycare staff informed me when I picked her up after lunch. They'd point out that Summer hung out with the boys and refused to take naps, which meant that she and I would wage a war of wills every afternoon about her sleeping routine.

One guess who won.

Try as I did to be upbeat, I grew anxious about our afternoons together. Not even music, my usual antidote to the blues, helped, possibly because Pam had dredged up a bunch of old recordings from her childhood, enriching, or infiltrating, my usual mix of rock and soul with Mitch Miller renditions of "Antoinette the Clarinet" and "Mike Malone the Slide Trombone." Some vinyl Burl Ives too. I'd spent 365 days in Vietnam, but what still gives me flashbacks is the merest mention of big Burl bellowing about a "boll weevil looking for a home."

All through that long Wisconsin winter, my afternoon ritual with my sturdy, round faced Summer, adorned with a tiny barrette in her shiny brown hair, a yellow shirt underneath grey overalls, white socks, and Stride Rite shoes, consisted of sipping hot chocolate, listening to old records, and dancing a little Hokey Pokey, followed by a story and a nap. Usually I'd nod off long before Summer did, visions of cartoon instruments dancing in my head.

Some days I just couldn't take those juvenile records anymore. So, with Pam not around to monitor the tunes, I'd slip some of my old 45 RPMs into the mix. Beat the hell out of trying to rock out to "Bobo the Oboe." Summer knew right away these records were *not* part of her usual repertoire. I suspect she suspected her mother would disapprove.

"This will be our special secret, honey," I said softly as I put on the We Five's "You Were on My Mind" or Claudine Clark's "Party Lights." Summer seemed to like the songs... or maybe she liked the fact we were doing something kind of mischievous. Regardless, she and I grooved out to those golden oldies. She didn't seem to miss Bobo or the Boll Weevil.

But there was a downside to listening to my old 45s. The songs made me nostalgic, more than just nostalgic. They sent my mind spiraling back to the early 1960s when something had happened at Thomas Jefferson High School outside Pittsburgh, Pennsylvania, that I was still trying to figure out. Music was at the center of it. And an influential, enigmatic English teacher named W. J. Kirkpatrick. Later, Vietnam made music even more vital, yet presented its own imponderables.

As I sat there with my daughter that cold March day in 1982, I conjured a younger me, a basketball-playing, girl-crazy guy who was hip and cool when the songs were popular. Gazing out at the swirling snow, I felt deceived...and humbled. Neutered. Here I was, an unemployed house-husband with no prospects, a hyperactive kid, and no other guys to commiserate with. Not even a heavy dose of the Beatles or Four Tops could fix that.

That particular Wisconsin winter went on forever. More than a season, it was a state of mind, a destination, filled with recurring sinus and ear infections. Mondays were the worst, and this particular Monday I'd gotten an earful from a daycare teacher concerning Summer's antics, and a call from a parent seconding the staff's emotion. I just couldn't deal with the prospect of "Antoinette the Clarinet."

For crying out loud, if I can survive a year in Vietnam, I sure as hell can get through this, can't I?

I didn't answer.

I put a stack of records on the turntable and sat in the corner of the couch. Summer walked across the room and sat down next to me, an earnest, concerned look on her face.

"Play 'Troubles,' Daddy."

"What sweetie?" I smiled my daddy smile at her, not sure I'd heard.

"Play 'Troubles' Daddy," she repeated.

I was stumped. What in the heck was she talking about?

"I'm sorry honey, I don't know what you mean."

At that, my clever toddler with a near-photographic memory walked over to a stack of old 45s and pulled out a copy of "You've Got Your Troubles" by the Fortunes. I didn't remember ever playing the song for her, but I put it on the turntable.

"I see that worried look upon your face/You've got your troubles, I've got mine."

The words and music shot straight through me. I'd been a senior in high school when the song was popular but hadn't given it half a thought since. Now, I could only sit, tears welling in my eyes, tears of nostalgia, of embarrassment, feeling weak and vulnerable in front of my daughter. But there Summer sat, smiling, assuring me this was our song, that everything would be okay.

"You've Got Your Troubles" would be our favorite song until it gave way to "That's All" by Genesis and eventually

"Moon River" which Summer and I would dance to, just the two of us in a spotlight on a large dance floor, at her wedding more than three decades later.

Spring finally arrived in Wisconsin. And I knew then that as long as Summer and I remained close I really didn't have any troubles worth the name. I was lucky to be at home, spending precious time watching my feisty daughter embark on life's journey.

* * *

As I write this now, Summer is in her mid-40s, a multi-talented professional with a terrific husband and two beautiful children, living just 15 minutes from Pam and me. Her baby brother Ian is thriving in Phoenix, where we live half the year, is happily married and a new daddy of two little ones himself, regularly sending me Spotify links to new songs to add to our father-son soundtrack that includes Bruce Springsteen's "Born in The USA" to which he bounced endlessly in his Johnny Jump Up; "Swing Low Sweet Chariot" which I sang to him every night at bedtime; "Shimmer" by Fuel; innumerable songs by the Dave Matthews Band; and Van Morrison's "Queen of the Slipstream" which helped bring about a much-needed détente when we were waging our own generational war.

As those songs and hundreds more spin in my mind and memory, I pull out the journal where I recorded that cherished Summer-Daddy "Troubles" moment. Then with extra time on my hands courtesy of retirement, COVID, and post-COVID, I descend to our storage locker and locate the old Garrard turntable purchased when I was a solider in Vietnam. Ready to give it a thorough cleaning, I find a bunch of old letters I'd received in Vietnam stuffed inside the turntable box. A handful are from Gina, my girlfriend at the time, a couple from my mom, the one and only letter my dad wrote me when I was overseas...and several from Bill Kirkpatrick, my high school English and Creative Writing teacher. My once-upon-a-time mentor, but also a cipher, a mystery, a question mark in my life...

A question I'm still asking.

Pondering that motherlode, cherishing those tender memories of my daughter and son, and wondering what my nearly 80 years on this planet amount to, I drop the Garrard turntable needle and trace the tracks of my years.

Part One:
MELODY

"Music was my refuge. I could crawl into the space between the notes and curl my back to loneliness."

Maya Angelou

PHILADELPHIA IN SIX MOVEMENTS

"The whole American pop culture started in Philadelphia with 'American Bandstand' and the music that came out of that city."

Daryl Hall

"There's a lot of haters in Philly...It's definitely a great city to be from...when you, like, make it out of Philadelphia, everywhere else is easy."

Lil Uzi Vert

One: "World on a String"

Inner city Philadelphia. Early 1950s. Post-World War II dads everywhere, my veteran father Jack Steele Bradley among them. And lots and lots and lots of kids. Our family compound included papa Jack, my mom Lucy "Toots" (Basile) Bradley, me, and my older brother Ron. It didn't occur to me then that we were poor, despite a gaping hole in the ceiling in the spare bedroom of the rundown row house where we lived that never got fixed. That meant Ron and I co-occupied a bedroom and a bed for my first ten years. Also meant that when it rained, we sure as hell knew it.

We shared paper-thin walls with the happy-go-lucky, beer-swilling Reillys on one side and the cussin' out Brawleys on the other, where wife beating was what usually came between dinner and dessert. The demons my father wrestled with displayed themselves when he took off his belt to discipline me and my brother the same way his father had disciplined him.

But none of that is front and center in my memory vault. Neither are the unhappy silences between my parents because they didn't have any money or because my mother's ten siblings—six brothers and four sisters—and their husbands and wives cluttered our lives. Or that Jack Bradley might leave in the morning with one job and come home in the evening with another.

No, what I do recall from those early years is music—my father singing a Tommy Dorsey or Glenn Miller tune; my mother humming Cole Porter; my Albanian-Italian grandmother playing Enrico Caruso and Mario Lanza on the Victrola at her big house; my parents clandestinely dancing in the dark in our tiny living room to "Music for Lovers Only" by the Jackie Gleason Orchestra.

Music healed the pain, held off the demons, and cast my childhood in a glow of sunshine, hope, and melody. Maybe it was that way sometimes for my music-loving parents? That might explain why they bought an expensive RCA Victor Hi-Fi in 1953. It looked like a spaceship with its large, reddish-brown wood cabinet, a huge lid you lifted like the back of a piano—my parents used the word "con-sole" to describe it—with big radio dials and an inviting turntable that could play 33-, 45- and 78-RPM records. Of course, the luxurious marvel was off limits to the rock and roll and Doo-Wop Ron liked, but every now and then my parents would let us tune into WIBG, one of the local radio stations. It sounded as if the WIBG disc jockeys were hiding *inside* the Hi-Fi, their voices louder, stronger, better than on *any* radio *anywhere* in all of Philadelphia.

I remember a sunny day in June 1953, sitting in the living room, the Hi-Fi lurching in the corner like one of my Italian uncles, dwarfing the TV and chairs. It must have been one of my father's between jobs days because we were home together. He put on his then favorite song, a 45 RPM version of Frank Sinatra's "I've Got the World on a String." My dad was in his mid-30s, his dark hair full and wavy. But he smiled less and was putting on a lot of extra weight. In a few years, the ulcer expanding inside him would nearly kill him. Music was the only thing that could give him a lift.

I sat there in a trance, trying to visualize what I knew to be a skinny Frank Sinatra holding a globe on a string, listening to the sunshine in his voice and watching my father mouth the words. Frank Sinatra wasn't the lucky "so and so" in the song. I was. My father and I were. Our little row house on 1017 South Ithan Street with the big Hi-Fi was living proof that *life is a beautiful thing*.

And then my father winked at me, walked over to the Hi-Fi and smilingly said that Frank Sinatra had just come down with a cold and was taking some strong cough medicine that made him talk funny. He switched the record to 78-RPM and out came this fast, high-pitched voice that sounded more like a chipmunk, racing to the end of "I've Got the World on a String" in record time.

We laughed, and I pleaded with my dad to play it like that again. And again. And once more please? *Anytime I move my finger/Lucky me*...Frank Sinatra's voice at breakneck speed was about the funniest thing I'd ever heard, sounding like the Walt Disney cartoon chipmunks Chip 'n' Dale. I basked in this moment with my father, the two of us smiling, singing, and giggling like teenage girls.

I couldn't wait to show off the way our Hi-Fi made Frank Sinatra sound silly, so the next day I invited my neighborhood pals Frankie and Johnny over and played the song at 78 RPMs. But when I tried to change the speed, I scratched the record. When my father came home from work that night he hit me. More than once.

And the rain poured through the hole in the ceiling in the empty bedroom...

Two: "Over the Mountain, Across the Sea"

The strains of Doo-Wop harmonies throbbed from the cramped bedroom in our rundown southwest Philly row house. The lilting ballad glided down the banister and tumbled into the modest living room where my mom and dad raptly watched *Your Hit Parade* on a small, black and white TV. What they were hearing from our tiny bedroom was *not* on their hit parade, and as they tried to tune out the soulful duet of Johnnie and Joe ("*Which one's the girl?*" I kept asking my brother), our parents grew restless.

"Ronald, Douglas, please turn that noise down! We're trying to watch television," my mother hollered up the stairs to our bedroom. Always a bad sign when mom used our full, Baptism-certified names. Our diminutive, brown-haired Albanian-Italian mother forever drew the short straw as the parent designated to bring us boys in line. But as angry as she sometimes seemed, little Lucy Bradley never really struck the fear of God in the hearts of my newly teenaged brother and me.

"You'd better turn that music down," I offered reluctantly to Ron. Being nearly five years his junior, I *never* told him to do anything, especially anything that had to do with *his* life and *his* music. How had he grown up so suddenly? One day he was just like anybody's older sibling but now he was all arms and hair and acne. Ron didn't even acknowledge I'd uttered a word. He simply smiled and turned up the volume.

The voice was louder now, the guy telling the winds to let his love pass over the mountain and be with him. Johnnie and Joe—or maybe Jo, the girl—continued to croon, and I was hypnotized. There was something about this back and forth, the rhythm of the music, its message—overcoming any barrier to be with the one you love—that had my nine-year-old head spinning.

"Darling, here I am, over the mountain," Jo tempts Johnnie. Or vice versa? I closed my eyes and envisioned a tall, handsome black man, climbing, running, and singing his way to his lover's side. Suddenly, he sees her sitting on a ledge in a white dress, high above the clouds. She calls to him. His voice, in response, grows louder, stronger. He draws close... closer. He's just about to reach out and touch her...

"Turn that crap down!" our father burst into our harmonious bedroom, his crew neck white t-shirt tucked over faded white Bermuda shorts in the heat. "What in the hell is that junk you're listening to?"

I'm scared, and a little stunned. Nothing good comes of my father raising his voice to ask questions he doesn't expect us to answer. Ron just smiles up at him and slowly, too slowly, turns down the volume. You can still hear Johnnie and Jo. Our father grimaces at the sound of two young "colored" people carrying on a conversation in *his* house. I figure his disapproval has more to do with their youth and sound than their color.

"What *is* this garbage?" he demands.

"It's okay Pop," my brother offers consolingly. "This is one of the biggest songs on the radio right now. It's what they call a hit record. You oughta listen to it."

"If it's such a big hit, then let's see what we can hit with it."

My father yanks the vinyl record off the spindle, walks to our bedroom window, and sets sail. The disc soars higher and farther than I'd imagined possible, crashing into the back of the Bianchi's row house clear across the alley. Talk about over the mountain.

Our dad stands over us, staring down at the record player. No one says anything.

It's a good thing he's standing, I realize, because my brother has just this week grown taller than he is. Ron sits there, smiling. Will he stand up and look my father in the eye? Will he apologize? Provoke him?

I'm still replaying the song, and the reverie that accompanies it, in my head—*All the mountains in the world couldn't stop your love from my heart*...But now Johnnie is my father and Joe is my brother and they're waving their arms at one another and shouting.

"Don't you ever play *that* music *that* loud in *this* house ever again," our dad threatens, underlining his relative pronouns through clenched teeth. The exchange leaves him out of breath. He exits our bedroom as abruptly as he came in.

Ron says nothing. He walks to his dresser, opens the top drawer, pulls out another record, and waves it in my direction. "Come Go With Me" by a group called the Del-Vikings.

"These cost 35 cents apiece," he says, sounding like an authority on the recording industry, "and there's millions more like them. Dad'll never be able to throw them all away. It's just a matter of time before we wear him out."

I have no idea who my brother means by *we* or by wearing our father out, but I get a strange feeling I've just witnessed the opening battle in a very, very long war.

Three: "Treasure of Love"

The rhythm changes, the songs sound sweeter, and I feel the first flip-flop of my heart. The first dance steps. The song. The voice. The music. The moment.

"*A treasure of love is not very far,*" Clyde McPhatter sings with a breathtaking quaver.

She will always be an angel in white. Pure, chaste, tempting, beautiful. Her name was Madeline—Madeline without a last name—the fetching younger cousin of my best friend and next-door neighbor, Frankie.

A beautiful spring day in April 1957. Even the dingy, cramped Philadelphia row houses sparkled. I remember it being Easter time because I was sporting a brand new, sharp brown suit handmade by my mother whose dad had been a tailor, and I'd worn it proudly to Mass on Easter Sunday. On this bright post-pascal Sunday, a nearly-ten-year-old me had invited the almost nine-year-old Madeline to my house for a "date."

I can only imagine the conversations my parents, Frankie's parents, and Madeline's parents were having. To that point in my life, "others"—my parents, Ron, the Pope, and the priests and the nuns—had directed my life. Even Frankie, the leader of our neighborhood pack, regularly told me where to go and what to do when I got there.

I'm not quite sure what got into me, but for some reason I'd decided to do something on my own and to try to act proper and grown up. What I really wanted was to hold a girl in my arms like William Holden held Kim Novak in *Picnic* and Robert Cummings did every week on TV in *Love that Bob*. Inviting Madeline to my house on a Sunday afternoon in April 1957 was my way of taking a big, adult step.

Why Madeline? Probably because she wasn't from our neighborhood, because she was an unknown, somebody without a story everyone already knew. Maybe it was a way to get a leg up on large and in-charge Frankie? There was no way he'd dance with his own cousin, cute as she was. And she sure was cute.

Madeline and I sat across from one another in my parents' clean, well-lit living room, unaware how the music we were listening to could shape our, or at least my, take on the world. We'd never be this young and innocent again, never have another real first date.

Madeline was pure alabaster. Her all-white dress—her first communion dress I wondered—was a perfect contrast to the curly black hair that fell on her dainty shoulders. She smiled like an angel. Shiny patent leather shoes adorned her feet and white ankle socks covered just the bottom of her skinny legs. I don't know why, but I was obsessed with those legs and those socks. Seventy years later, I still see them clearly.

My heart beat so fast, and so loud, that I placed both my hands over it, worried that my mother and Madeline's mother could hear it. Wearing my natty brown suit, I sported a white shirt, a chocolate-colored tie, and slightly oversized "grown up" shoes, wing tips I'd swiped from Ron's half of our shared closet. There I was—dressed-up, nervous, expectant, for what I wasn't sure, but I knew we had to dance to *the* perfect song. I was suspended between "It's Not for Me to Say" by Johnny Mathis and "Treasure of Love" by Clyde McPhatter. Just before our date/dance, I started to panic a little, wondering if my choice of song would somehow affect my entire future. And Madeline's too? Maybe we'd end up naming our first child Johnny or Clyde?

Eventually, I decided that the Johnny Mathis song was just a little too romantic, and, well, older, which is probably why it was a favorite of my mother's. Okay then, I was ready. I held my breath, waiting for the rest of my life to start. I could hear Clyde's voice telling me that some things were stronger than diamonds and worth more than gold, my heart beating, our hands touching, the smell of her hair, the light in the room, the two of us shuffling back and forth, my hand on her slight hip, albeit staying in one place, our heels clicking on the wood floor.

"This is a treasure that never grows old..."

My palms were sweaty, my mother was there, somewhere in the room. What was she thinking? But my eyes were fixed on Madeline. The singer sang only to us and for the first time in my life, I knew joy. Bliss. A girl, a song, a touch, a dance. A genuine treasure of love that could only be found in my arms.

The part of me that is always ten remains forever in that room, with the voice of Clyde McPhatter whispering in my anxious ear, telling me to seek the treasure in my heart.

Four: "Bad Boy"

By the end of fourth grade, I'd started getting a handle on people, at least the ones who inhabited my southwest Philadelphia world. I clustered them into categories, and for the most part they acted accordingly: moms and dads, older brothers, aunts and uncles, cousins, best friends, grandmas, bullies, weirdos. Basic stuff, but it helped me navigate my world.

There was one outlier among the groups: the nuns who were my teachers at The Transfiguration of Our Lord Catholic School. They weren't really women or girls—most of them were angular giants, Amazons from another galaxy, covered head to toe in dark blue "dresses." They described themselves as "Brides of Christ" which sounded like a horror movie on *Chiller Theater* late on Saturday nights. They exuded power and control, wielding immense, blondish rulers that came *thwap* out of nowhere to command your attention. And they were experts at pulling your hair or banging your head against the blackboard. With either hand.

The nuns were scarier than *The Creature from the Black Lagoon,* and they knew how to leverage that fear, especially among us boys. Up until this point in our lives, we'd been able to charm older women with good manners and cute smiles. Not the nuns. They seemed to dislike us because we *were* boys, as if their main purpose in life was to keep us in line and knock us down to size.

Their secret weapon was words, specifically the words of the *Baltimore Catechism,* which we were forced to submit to during class time every day. Lord have mercy (trust me he wouldn't) if you were called on and got nervous or choked and blew the response to the *"Why Did God Make You?"* The correct answer being: *"God made me to know Him, to love Him, and to serve Him in this world and to be happy with Him forever in heaven."* Note the repetition of the masculine pronoun (grammar was something else the nuns taught us), which I'm sure must've pissed off the "Brides of Christ" to no end. It was, as James Brown would remind us later, a man's world after all.

One day, Danny Brogdon blew the answer to that question. We'd just come in from a spirited game of "Buck Buck" on a hot September afternoon, and Sister Mary Elise, one of the less threatening Immaculate Heart of Mary nuns, asked Danny, *"Why Did God Make You?"* The poor kid was so gassed from spending the entire recess under the heft of Tubby Carter and Fats Williams that he forgot where he was and burst out "God didn't make me, my parents did."

Poor Danny would spend the rest of the month in the cloakroom, which as far as we knew had never harbored a single cloak. Coats, scarves, hats, nameless shadows, yes. But a cloak? Sister Mary Elise hung a sign outside the door reading, "Danny is a bad boy."

The nuns saw things that way, black and white, cut and dried. We were bad boys or good boys. Nothing in between. And no redemption either. A bad boy like Danny, who had an angelic voice, a beatific smile, and was maybe the best altar boy ever, would never again be a good boy. Never.

Maybe that's why he and I, when the nuns weren't around, would harmonize to a song by a Doo-Wop group called the Jive Bombers, called, appropriately, "Bad Boy." It didn't tell a story like some songs, but there was something crazy and carefree about the way the lead singer would trill *"la-la-la-la-la-la"* and more *"la-la-la-la-la-la"* before telling us he was all dressed up in fancy clothes, not bothering to take the trouble to *"blow my bubbles away-ay-ay."* He and his fellow Jive Bombers made it seem like being a bad boy wasn't all that bad.

So Danny and I kept on singing. And obeying, most of the time, trying to figure out how the world we inhabited with our parents and siblings and friends had anything to do with good and bad, with the world of the "Brides of Christ" and the *Baltimore Catechism*. After lunch recess one sunny afternoon, Sister Mary Elise told us in her quiet, soothing voice to put our heads down on our desks and listen as she read us a book about a young rascal named Pompey Briggs, a boy a little older than we were, from a book called *The Good Bad Boy*. Sister Mary Elise didn't so much read the story as perform it for us, and those 20 minutes after lunch recess became the best minutes of our fifth grade lives. I loved listening to the trials and tribulations of young Master Briggs. Even the girls in our class wanted to grow up to be Pompey Briggs.

The Good Bad Boy was written in a diary format which lent itself quite nicely to our daily rendering. Often, we'd beg Sister Mary Elise to read just one more excerpt, both because the story was enthralling and because we didn't cotton to the alternative—having to recite the *Baltimore Catechism* all afternoon. For weeks, we were lost in *The Good Bad Boy,* following Pompey Briggs through his eighth-grade year at Holy Cross Catholic School, reliving his ups and downs from September to graduation in June. We got to know his family and friends, cheered him on during basketball games, laughed at the antics of his club known as the "Beaver Chiefs," and agonized with him over algebra exams.

Meanwhile, Danny Brogdon, on parole from the cloakroom, joined me in a cheery chorus of "Bad Boy." But were we really bad boys? I mean Pompey Briggs sure seemed like a bad boy, but the book was titled *The* Good *Bad Boy*.

And then came the last diary entry. The simple, surprise twist at the end of the book was that Pompey Briggs who was telling us his story as an adult was now **Father** Pompey Briggs. Meaning, I guess, that there was hope for all of us so-called bad boys.

I felt betrayed by that twist at the end, like I'd been set up somehow. As I looked around the classroom at all the crucifixes and Catechisms and pictures of Jesus and Joseph and all the guy Saints, I felt sorry for the girls in my class. Even the nuns. As hard as they might try, they'd never be a good, or even a bad, boy.

Five: "16 Candles"

I didn't consider my brother Ron my friend. Brothers were just brothers, and friends, well, that was different. Besides he was nearly five years older, a teenager in Philadelphia which had to be one of the coolest things ever, a generation-defining experience that separated some of us from the rest. Cars or girls, hairstyles or clothes, my brother and his teenage pals were at the epicenter of everything new and cool and copied.

Especially the music, their rebellious rock and roll. Ron and his crowd were so far up the popularity food chain that they were too cool to go on Dick Clark's *American Bandstand.*

"Only the squares show up there because they can," Ron observed icily one afternoon.

Lucky for me, during those few times when my brother didn't find me totally annoying or ignore me, I could bask in that adolescent glow a little myself. Sometimes he'd let me reply to something said by one of his buddies, receive a pat on the head from one of their breathtaking, bouffant-ed girlfriends, listen to them rehearse their own Doo-Wop songs, or snap my fingers to Elvis, Jackie Wilson, and all the "race" music he played by groups with bird names like Orioles and Flamingos.

As far as I could tell, the only things keeping my brother's life from perfection were our mother and father, the ballast to his high wire act, tugging him back to earth. Sometimes they pulled too hard or yanked him in the wrong way. Not much of the generational back and forth involved our mom. She might not have been cool, but since she was a mom and did mom things like cook great meals and sign our report cards and give us our allowances, she usually got a pass.

It was different with our dad who had to act like he was the boss and tell us what we could and couldn't do. I don't think he liked playing the role, but it came with the fatherhood territory so when he was around, he took it on. If we didn't comply, well, this was the 1950s so the consequences, which usually involved his belt or the back of his hand, were severe.

That's why we almost always complied.

But for every cool thing going on in my brother's life—from the perfect wave in his hair to the souped-up cars he rode around in with his buddies to the songs he was writing and singing—there was a corresponding downbeat in my dad's life. His thinning hair, an obsolete automobile that barely made it around the block, and his intolerance for rock and roll music because it wasn't HIS music. He was always—*always*—turning down the volume on our tiny record player.

These disparate worlds, on a collision course, collided spectacularly on Ron's 16th birthday, January 23, 1959. It was a cold winter Saturday. My mom made Ron's favorite dinner, lamb chops, and his favorite dessert, lemon meringue pie. The pie wouldn't hold 16 candles, so we sang happy birthday with the kitchen light on.

No sooner had my brother wolfed down a huge piece of pie then he was out the door with Jimmy Porter, Tommy DeFelice, and three girls. Their destination was PAL, the Police Athletic League, where the coolest teenage Philly kids would be. Danny and the Juniors were scheduled to perform a song or two *live* there that night. According to my brother, Danny and company were going to switch to Dick Clark's Swan Record label with the release of their brand-new single.

And all of this was happening on my brother Ron's 16th birthday. How can one guy be so lucky?

Meanwhile, back at our house, poor little 11-year-old me was ordered to bed immediately after *Gunsmoke*, my dad's favorite TV show. Maybe part of him wanted to be Marshall Dillon? I went off to sleep with dueling visions of guns blazing and teenagers dancing.

Hours later, I awakened to the sound of screeching tires, shouts and giggles, and car doors slamming. I crept to the top of the stairs to see my dad confronting my brother in our tiny vestibule, blocking his way into the house. My mom was standing a little further back, looking like she wanted to hide behind something that wasn't there.

Ron looked like a million bucks in his bright white shirt sporting a perfectly knotted striped tie. His charcoal vest had a bright red rose pinned to the left side. He was twirling a 45-RPM record in his hand as my dad shouted stuff I had a hard time hearing. It didn't help my dad's mood that my brother was smiling the whole time.

Playing the role of referee, my mom slid between the two of them, pleading with my dad to let my brother explain why he was late.

His words came cascading, he almost sang them, and all I could remember hearing was "16 Candles, 16 candles, 16 candles." As I watched his testimony, followed by my father's cross-examination, I kept hearing that song by the Crests in my head.

"Happy birthday/Happy birthday baby..."

In a casual voice sure to raise our father's hackles, Ron repeated that his girlfriend Peggy had dedicated "16 Candles" to him at the PAL dance and given him a copy of the record. The two of them had held hands, embraced, and danced arm in arm.

My brother and his girlfriend. In Philadelphia. At the Police Athletic League dance. Just the two of them. In a spotlight. And all this on Ron Bradley's 16th birthday. I truly believed that my brother's life could only go downhill from there.

Dad would have the last word, as 1950s dads would. He grabbed the copy of "16 Candles," looked at it as if it were kryptonite, and threw it down on the vestibule floor, telling my brother in no uncertain terms that that he would never go to another PAL dance. In fact, since he was seriously flustered, what my dad actually said was "You'll never go to another PAL dance on your 16th birthday."

My brother smiled as he passed me at the top of the stairs on his way to our bedroom, whispering low enough so my parents couldn't hear.

"Hell, I just did."

<u>Six</u>: "Smoke Gets In Your Eyes"

There weren't very many secrets growing up in those inner-city row houses. The walls were too thin, the voices too loud, the families too big. Even all the dogs and cats we called ours drifted back and forth from house to house, as I realized when my neighbor Frankie referred to the black cat we called "Smokey" as "Blackie." Of course, being a cat, Smokey/Blackie didn't respond to either name.

So, it was left to me and Frankie to fashion our own private confidences.

Frankie sported a slick pompadour in his jet-black hair and rolled up his white t-shirt sleeves way before it was cool. We invented games with the infinite packs of cigarettes that inhabited our households. His parents smoked Lucky Strikes and Pall Malls while mine favored Raleighs and Camels. Raleighs mainly because of the coupons on every pack and the four extras you got in a carton. My folks would save up the coupons to buy toasters and waffle irons that usually didn't work. Frankie's parents joked that you could use the Raleigh coupons to buy the iron lung you'd need from smoking so many cigarettes.

Our World War II veteran dads, long cigarette ashes dangling dangerously from their lips, loved the old standard "Smoke Gets in Your Eyes." My father favored the version by Nat King Cole while Frankie's dad, Frank senior, preferred Peggy Lee. When we tried to tell them that a new recording group, the Platters, had made a hit record of the song, they refused to listen. Maybe the smoke filling their homes got in their ears as well as their eyes.

Before we ever started sneaking and smoking their cigarettes, Frankie and I speculated on what the L. S. M. F. T. letters printed on the packs of Lucky Strike meant. "Lucky Strike Means Fine Tobacco" was the sanctioned answer, but we substituted "loose shits mean floating turds," and laughed uproariously. "Okay smart guy," Frankie posed a Perry Mason-like question one day, "what does *In hock senior vank-ees* mean?"

"Huh?"

"It's here on the pack of Pall Malls." Frankie pointed at the phrase *In hoc signo vinces.* Not yet altar boys, we didn't recognize the words as Latin. "What does *that* mean?"

"I'm in hock for buying these ciggies?"

"Nah," Frankie dismissed me proudly. *"'In this sign you will conquer.'"*

"Come again?"

"'In this sign you will conquer,'" he repeated.

"What sign and who's conquering?"

"How should I know? I don't buy the damn things. I'm just telling you what my folks say."

But as far as we two pals were concerned, the best cigarette game was the one my brother Ron taught us about a pack of Camels.

"If you're stuck in the desert," he put to us, pointing to the front of the brownish-yellow cigarette pack with C-A-M-E-L spelled out in big bold letters and a one-humped creature next to two pyramids and three palm trees." If you're stuck out here in the desert, where's the best place to be?"

"Under the palm trees?" Frankie guessed.

"Nope."

"Under the camel?" I volunteered.

"Naaah."

"Inside the pyramid?" We said in unison.

"Wrong again." And then, with a sweeping "ta-da" gesture, my teenager-in-love brother would flip over to the back of the cigarette pack.

"No, spaz, you and your thirsty camel should go around back and check out the Casbah."

Frankie and I laughed, oblivious to what a Casbah was. Later, we'd play the game ourselves for hours, reversing roles as we went. We even gave it a name—the riddle of the Camel and the Pyramid.

Eventually, Frankie and I grew tired of each other and our silly games and being best friends. He became something of a trendsetter, smoking and swearing and feeling up girls while I lagged far behind. The distance between us, physically just a porch railing and paper-thin wall, grew. Our dads didn't hum "Smoke Gets in Your Eyes" anymore.

One day, I announced across the railing that separated our two porches that we were moving to Ohio because my dad was getting transferred. Frankie, a grown-up-looking 12-year-old, exhaled smoke from a Camel, put it out on his shoe, and said he and his family were moving too.

"Right next to Fairmount Park." Frankie seemed puffed up. "Best place to be if you're stuck in this fucking desert," he snarled at me, as if we'd never been friends.

The road out of Philadelphia was paved with hard feelings and empty packs of cigarettes. Next stop, the wasteland known as Ohio.

Tracks 1-2:

HIT THE ROAD, JACK; CHAIN GANG

June 1959. The sheltered familiarity of Philadelphia faded in our rear-view mirror as we four Bradleys set out seeking fame and fortune, or at least a new start, in Youngstown, Ohio. General Foods, Inc. had rewarded my dad with his first-ever promotion—his talent for selling Maxwell House, Sanka, and Yuban coffees catapulting us from our noisy, inner-city row house life into the unknown hinterland of eastern Ohio. For all we knew, Ohio could just as well have been North Dakota or Nebraska—there wasn't an inch of Philly soul or atmosphere to be found. While it was tough for my mom to detach from the crucible of her extra-large Italian family for the first time in her life, it was worse for Ron, yanked from his teenage Mecca and dropped into no man's land.

But as Ray Charles reminded us, *we had to pack our things and go*. We hit the road, with Father Jack at the wheel.

Thank god for Ron's record collection and Boots Bell, a DJ on Youngstown's pop radio station WHOT. Boots wasn't in the league of Philly radio legends like Jerry Blavat ("the geater with the heater"), Hy Lit, Joe "Rockin' Bird" Niagara, or Georgie Woods, but he'd do in a pinch, and man were we ever pinched. Who cares if he played Joe Jones's "You Talk Too Much" and Bobby Lewis's "Tossin' and Turnin'" every hour? It was *our* rock and roll music, so Ron and I would close our eyes and pretend to be back in Philly, he at the coolest dances with the cutest chicks and me relieved that he could be his old, happy-go-lucky self as long as the records were playing.

On the other hand, 12-year-old me was oblivious to the bumpy transition my folks were experiencing in their relocation, and their marriage, not to mention the enormous pressure of my dad's demanding new job and the nonexistence of familiar faces. I'd found safe harbor with a big, sprawling Italian family, the Poppas, who lived down the street from the tiny apartment we were renting in Hubbard, Ohio, as we awaited the availability of a new house in a nearby development. Like my mom's passel of Basiles, there were 11 Poppas in all, including one a year older than me (Bobby) and another my age (Danny). There were even a Poppa or two around Ron's age, including a couple kinda cute girls, and a seminarian among the older boys. Life for me inside their family bubble didn't just feel like home, it *was* home. Most nights I'd be seated at their dinner table—"what's another mouth to feed" a short, smiling Mrs. Poppa would laugh—while the walls of our nearby apartment were closing in on the rest of my family.

After we moved into our brand-new house, my dad still wasn't singing much, not even in the shower, and my folks weren't putting romantic records on the Hi-Fi. Ron was having a hard time at Ursuline, Youngstown's catholic high school, and, with the Poppas now way across town, I joined in our Ohio misery. Ron added insult to misery by forcing me to trudge through a foot of snow, not once, but twice, to the record store in the nearby shopping center to buy new records he just had to have.

"I'm going nuts," he directed at me one of those snowy winter days, "and I gotta get the hell out of this damn place." He looked serious, and, well, a little defeated. "And you're coming with me or I'll beat the crap out of you."

It turned out those Arctic escapades were worth the trip—"You Got What It Takes" by Marv Johnson kept us smiling all the time crooning *"You got what it takes to set my soul on fire..."* And then there was "Money" by Barrett Strong. We didn't know Berry Gordy from Benny Goodman and Motown wasn't on anyone's radar, but the song knocked us over. The jangly, funky piano intro, the crazy lead guitar, the chorus, the rapid drum beat that sounded like an Indian pow-wow ceremony...and that incessant demand *"I need money. That's what I want."* Didn't we all?

* * *

In the summer of 1960, we once again "hit the road" with Jack, taking a long car trip back to Philly to reunite with my mom's family. Dad was pretty stressed the whole time, but Mom and Ron were happy, so I think that was enough for him. On the return ride, the car was silent, none of us eager to be back in Ohio any time soon. My dad must've sensed this, because when we neared Pittsburgh, he tuned the radio to a station that was playing rock and roll. He gave us a nod in the rear-view mirror, not saying a word as he drove, windows down, his dark brown hair in the breeze, Camel cigarette hanging from the left side of his mouth, as our music played.

Ron and I exchanged a big smile. Just before the Pennsylvania-Ohio border, a new song by Sam Cooke came on, and we listened intently. So raw and real. Different. The oohs and ahhs and groans and sound of metal hitting pavement, of rustling chains.

"What's the name of that song?" my dad turned toward us in the back seat miles later as we exited the turnpike.

"What song, Dad?"

"The one with the moanin' and groanin'." We were still a little baffled. "The oohs and aahs, the metal banging."

"Oh, you mean 'Chain Gang,'" Ron volunteered.

"That's it," my dad smiled.

"It's by Sam Cooke, a really cool singer," Ron added.

Our dad smiled all the way to our Ohio home.

It wasn't until weeks later he told us how "Chain Gang" had made Jack Bradley the hit of the coffee salesmen's summer meeting. Seems they referred to their supermarket customers as "chains," so when he played "Chain Gang" as scores of General Foods coffee guys walked into the meeting, the sound and the lyrics spoke directly to their thoughts about working the highways and byways, frowning their lives away on their own corporate chain gang.

Ron and I beamed when Dad told us that story, proud that our music had helped our father who sure as heck needed a lift. Music had brought us back together as a family. And it would keep us together as we navigated those two years in Ohio, a pit stop en route to Pittsburgh where so much awaited: college for Ron, high school for me, menopause for Mom, another firing for Dad. My first teenage romances.

And W. J. Kirkpatrick.

Track 3:
TWO FACES HAVE I

One day I woke up a teenager in 1960s America, truly believing I'd died and gone to heaven. All that was hip and cool and genuine—from clothes and cars to comic books and color TV—seemed to revolve around us. Our music broadcast our independence, anointed our individuality. Music on the radio, from records spinning on the tiny RCA 45-RPM record player I shared with Ron, music constantly in my head, in the hallways, everywhere. Connecting me to my body, my feet, to every other kid walking down the halls of Thomas Jefferson High School.

My first two years at TJ included the requisite new kid in town ups and downs—learning who was cool and who wasn't; joining the right clubs; skipping CCD classes; making the JV basketball team; enduring taunts, glares, and punches from greasers who didn't like my looks; feigning sickness to avoid school; jumping out of the window of my locked bedroom; driving my worried parents crazy…

But strutting down the TJ halls on this perfect, sparkling spring afternoon in May 1963, I exhaled. All the bad stuff was behind me. As I wrapped up my sophomore year, my grades were good, my jump shot pure, my record collection the highlight of parties and dances. I even had the attention of several of our class's foxier females. And I'd held my own in a bare-knuckles brawl with Kenny Stout, my designated tough-guy tormentor, meaning I'd finally passed muster with the greasers and hard asses. Maybe now they'd leave me alone.

This particular day was a Lou Christie day, Luigi Alfredo Giovanni Sacco as part-paisanos like me knew him. Something about his voice, the haunting falsetto, his playfulness. Exhibit A was "Two Faces Have I," ringing in my ears and on my lips that May afternoon. Lou starts off the song as if he's miserable, but when he jumps into a chorus of those catchy falsetto "*yayayayaya, yayayayayays*," you're happy and you're hooked. Maybe it was my mom's Italian heritage or Ron's Philly falsetto that had me enjoying the hell out of Lou's song that afternoon, unaware of its other, darker meanings about the danger in living a lie.

I smiled my Lou Christie smile on the way to my locker after seventh hour, high on life and status and music. Ron was away at a small state teachers college, so I had complete jurisdiction over a motherlode of great tunes. I pulled in a little income spinning the platters at sock hops and mixers and never missed an opportunity to bring my record collection to a girl's house for talking, dancing, and necking. Yes indeed, life was a whole lot more fun near the top of the high school food chain. I dressed the part too, the sleeves on my white shirt turned up just so, my black, peg pants perfectly tapered, sharp black loafers on my feet. Or I should say

Ron's black loafers, which I'd catch hell for wearing if he knew. But man, I was feeling good, in charge, as hip as any almost 16-year-old high schooler can feel with his hair just right and a "Two Faces Have I" strut.

"Yo, Dube, heads up man." I heard a familiar voice calling me by my nickname which had something to do with a brand of basketball Ron liked. "Hey, over here dumb ass."

Larry Jackson waved me in his direction. I'd hung out with him during ninth grade since his house was near mine, but by tenth grade he had been deemed less than cool, meaning I couldn't be bothered. Larry persisted, oblivious to that unwritten rule of the high school caste system.

"Dube, come here man!" Smiling broadly, his garish plaid shirt with a collar so pointy it could put a hole in the ceiling, Larry motioned me across the hall.

"What's up Jackson?"

"Have you met Mr. Kirkpatrick yet?" Larry looked like he was harboring a major diplomatic secret. "Have you?"

"Have I what?"

"Met Mr. Kirkpatrick?"

"Can't say I have."

"Man are you ever missing out!" Larry's words seemed to be in a bigger hurry than he was. "He's our newest English teacher. Been Miss Livingston's sub since she bugged out. He's cool and funny and knows everything that's going on. The guy is a major riot."

Larry stood there, waiting for a reaction. Getting none, he rushed on. "You wouldn't believe how smart he is. And fun! And he's r-e-a-l-l-y young."

One of the points on Larry's collar nearly poked me in the eye.

"You don't say," I responded, nonchalant and tuned out.

"I do say," his voice went up an octave, almost cracking. "Forget that AP English shit you've been stuck with all year. Mr. Kirkpatrick is where it's at." He shot me a big smile. "And he's supposed to teach a bunch of sections of 11th grade English next year so we're all going to have him."

Imagining "having" a teacher conjured a vision of Mrs. Vernon, our sultry Spanish teacher. Maybe I should drop French and switch to Spanish so I could look at her every day? Lost in my spicy reverie, I registered Larry's freckles looking like dots on the big European map in Mr. Lowenstein's AP History classroom.

"Larry, buddy, whoa man, slow down."

And suddenly there he was. I did a double take, stunned that this, this "kid" was actually a bona fide high school English teacher. Mr. Kirkpatrick reminded me of one of the douchey freshmen who dressed up for picture day in loud, checkered coats and non-matching ties. His black hair was cut short atop a small, near-scrawny body. The things that stood out most were his big, black-rimmed glasses and a blotchy, red birthmark on the right side of his face.

"Mr. Kirkpatrick hey, Mr. Kirkpatrick…Over here. Yo, Kirkpatrick." Despite Larry's entreaties—I'd never heard a student call a teacher by his last name as if they were best buds—his new favorite teacher never turned toward us, continuing his conversation with a handful of other students. Larry couldn't control himself, and in his excitement, he grabbed Mr. Kirkpatrick by the arm and tried to spin him around.

"For crying out loud, Mr. Kirkpatrick, there's somebody here you gotta meet."

Refusing to turn, or be turned, Mr. Kirkpatrick stood his ground. Larry looked like he was about to burst a blood vessel.

"Hey, chump," he hollered, "chump!"

At that, Mr. Kirkpatrick wheeled around, cupped his right hand in a way that could only mean one thing, and told Larry to "Chump on this."

That putdown was loud enough so that laughter rained down the halls. Poor Larry turned beet red and bolted. For a moment, I was a little star-struck. I'd never heard a teacher put somebody down like that in public, especially in such a raunchy way. And damn if this wiry little guy with big glasses wasn't simply dissing Larry, he was, in effect, telling him to, well…

As I looked away, I caught a glimpse of Larry making a beeline down the hall, muttering about Mr. Kirkpatrick's being an asshole. I stood there politely, directly across from my locker where an unread copy of *Silas Marner* sat on the top shelf. I could hear a couple of girls mimicking the *One to laugh and one to cry* chorus from the Lou Christie song. I turned and extended my hand for my proper student-teacher introduction.

Mr. Kirkpatrick was nowhere in sight.

I reached into my locker, grabbed the copy of *Silas Marner,* slammed the door shut, and walked down the hall in the same direction a humiliated Larry had scrambled, harmonizing with Lou Christie all the way. Had I just witnessed a "Two Faces Have I" moment between Mr. Kirkpatrick and an adoring student? Was one of them, or maybe both, living some kind of Lou Christie lie?

Track 4:
MONKEY TiME

My chance encounter with Mr. Kirkpatrick, or the decision whether to enroll in his 11th grade English class in the fall, were the furthest things from my mind the summer of 1963. That's because Robbie Black, the star basketball player on the JV team and one of the older guys in our class, already had his driver's license. You had to be cool enough to be part of Robbie's vehicular circle, and my saving grace, besides my b-ball credentials, was knowing the words to all the songs on the radio. Even though that was something girls were usually good at. The guys who'd cram into Robbie's little Corvair joined in when I snapped my fingers to "So Much in Love" by the Tymes or proclaimed "two girls for every boy" at the beginning of Jan and Dean's "Surf City." You'd have thought I was blessing who we were, what we were doing, and where we were headed.

Case in point: "Monkey Time" by Major Lance. As soon as those big, brassy horns surfaced from the radio, I knew there was "a place right across town…"

"Are You Ready?" came the call from me/Major Lance.

"Are You Ready?" echoed Curtis Mayfield/my pals.

And off we sped, singing "Monkey Time" at the top of our lungs.

It seemed every time we hopped in Robbie's car that special summer, "Monkey Time" was playing. "Boys, that's our song," observed Dan Turkel, a tall, lanky, good-looking kid who lived at the top of my street in the Pittsburgh suburbs. Some days we'd meet halfway for Robbie's drive-by, and Dan had an uncanny sense of knowing exactly when the tiny emerald chariot would arrive. Meaning he'd always call "shotgun" in advance. And sure as hell, there'd appear Robbie's dirty, noisy, leaky Corvair with Major Lance belting out "Monkey Time."

Most of the time, Dan and I were accompanied by two, three, or four others—Joe Jackson, Ben Murphy, Mike Carpenter, and Pete Starr. Dan's shotgun call placed him up front next to Robbie, so the rest of us sardines packed into the back seat, bitching about whose knees were in whose face and whose hands were on whose balls or up someone's ass. Robbie stepped on the gas and Major Lance reiterated, *"Are You Ready?"* and in unison, we sang "Well you get yours, 'cause-a I got mine..."

For those brief musical minutes, life was more than good.

Sometimes Robbie would only be going to get gas, pick up something for his mom at the store, or drop the car off to his older sister. Didn't matter. Everything was new and different from inside an automobile. Life moved faster. You could leave behind the crap you wanted to leave behind in an instant. The world was one, big, high-speed freeway, going, going...going anywhere you wanted.

Robbie choreographed the conversation from the front seat, telling Dan or whoever was next to him to turn the radio up or down depending on what song was playing—Bobby Vinton got the hook a lot that summer—as he lectured us on the mysteries of the female anatomy. Usually his Corvair sermons had something to do with Jennifer Furrey, a very cute classmate and how far they'd gotten the night before.

"Man, you can't believe how hot she was, how fucking great it was," Robbie leered into the rear-view mirror. "My fingers were on her you know what and…"

Howls and a chorus of "Holy shit," "you can't be serious," "you did what?"

Back seated me never could grasp the details, and I wasn't sure why whatever he and she did was better than listening to rock and roll. So, I pretended to be impressed with Robbie's progress, while I sat in the backseat singing along with Major Lance.

If I was lucky, I'd have my license by August, light years away. In the meantime, I lived for that moment when the green Corvair came barreling down Bruceton Road and dipped into the tiny slope in front of our house across the street from the Arboretum. A plume of dirty smoke, loud voices, and "Monkey Time" preceded the car's arrival. When I sprinted from our front porch to the Corvair, I felt like I was running for the winning touchdown or chasing the holy grail. By the time I got to the car, the insults and put-downs and Robbie's bragging were in high gear, but all that was music to my ears. The blessed trinity of rock and roll, sex, and friendship came together in Robbie Black's Corvair.

Later that summer, I'd watch wistfully as the Corvair screamed past our house, the smoke and voices and music still inside. But never stopping. Never. Sometimes Pete Starr or one of the other guys would raise his middle finger in the direction of my house, but that was the extent of any recognition. Robbie's Corvair never paid me or my house another visit.

And no one ever told me why.

My heart was in my throat the rest of July and all August. With no wheels myself, I was stranded. If our paths crossed at the Dairy Queen or baseball diamond, they all pretended not to see me. One time Joe Jackson gave me the coldest, meanest stare. What in the hell had I done to produce that kind of look from one of my best friends?

I decided my blackballing may have had something to do with ratting out Matthew Weiner, a preppie kid who went to private school but whose parents had a big house and a pool and were always away somewhere, making his place *the* destination for carnal escapades. Still, "Matthew," never Matt or Matty, wasn't anybody's favorite, so when TJ's hard-ass greasers threatened to kick my butt if I didn't throw them a bone, I tossed them Matthew. Apparently, if I did that to him, I could turn on one of the other guys too.

Or maybe they all just got sick of my singing along to all the songs. Was my knowing all the lyrics too girlie? One day I was the Major Lance maestro in the backseat of a car driven by a fellow high schooler, the next I was on the outs. The far, far outs. A Thomas Jefferson High School untouchable.

I burrowed deep inside my isolation, let it surround and engulf and define me. "I'm the guy everyone hates" was how I introduced myself to Jody Pulaski at the local pool in July. She just laughed, asking me "who's *everyone*?"

The worst was knowing my parents were watching, shaking their heads, and saying nothing. Ron was gone as usual—summer school or work or getting laid—so I'd get a daily dose of pitying, parental looks that made me feel shitty for letting them down by being such a loser. They didn't ask me what was wrong because they didn't want to know. But they watched with wet eyes and heavy hearts.

I spent the rest of the summer walking our little black poodle Monty, going to baseball practices and games, watching *Where the Action Is* on afternoon TV, and hitting golf balls into the arboretum. I spent a lot of time listening to the radio and playing records, too. Every time Major Lance came on, I'd turn it off. Luckily, the DJs had moved on to "Easier Said Than Done" by the Essex and Little Stevie Wonder's "Fingertips." But I couldn't quiet the echoes of "Monkey Time."

I remembered Pete Starr bragging "my brother says that Major Lance had three professional fights. Look at that nose—sure as hell it's been busted a couple times at least."

I missed those conversations. Hell, I missed any conversation. The ones I liked best were when we'd tease Robbie about what a piss poor car the Corvair was. A couple of the guys' dads were engineers at U.S. Steel, one of them worked in plant safety, and they'd warned their sons about the dangers of the Corvair's engine being in the rear of the car and the bad swing-axle rear suspension, and the heating system that pumped out noxious fumes.

"The straw that broke the camel's back," Carl Fuller quoted his engineer father once, "was that Chevrolet even offered a gasoline-burner heater in the front trunk of the Corvair. Talk about pouring fuel on a fire," he grimly concluded.

I laughed along, even if I didn't know anything about car engines or camel's spines. But the potential danger only made riding in Robbie's Corvair more exciting. Would this be the day it exploded? Would Robbie be impaled on the single-column steering wheel? With him gone, who would be left to flick Jennifer Furrey's switch?

But I wouldn't be around for any of those conversations. I'd been blackballed.

Now I had to steer clear of my parents' pitying glances, avoid the whispers in the bleachers at the baseball games, and pretend the phone calls from solicitors were really somebody from school calling for me.

By summer's end, all the guys now had their driver's licenses and invariably one of them would drive past my house with a carful of their pals and cute girls. Joe Jackson's convertible was the best of the lot. And the worst too since with the top down, I could hear him and his fellow passengers screaming, "Fuck you, Dube!"

I finally got my driver's license in late August, after flunking the test the first time and having a huge argument with my father about laziness, responsibility (my lack of), preparation, and appreciation for the money he'd spent on private driving lessons. Just what I needed. Even with my driver's license, I didn't have anywhere to go for fear I'd run into somebody who'd ignore me or whisper behind my back or give me the finger.

By the time we returned to school that September, Robbie's Corvair belonged to his older sister. It was rumored she'd gone on a couple dates with Mr. Kirkpatrick. Robbie and Jennifer had broken up, and supposedly now he was pursuing Sandy Styles who had access to a car they could use for their carnal escapades.

"How in the hell am I going to get through this?" I asked myself.

And in my lonesome and solitary wondering, I found a way out of my misery.

I began to write about it.

Track 5:

BE FAIR

Thomas Jefferson High School had morphed into Dante's eighth circle of hell, the dark cavern of ditches reserved for fraudulent people like the guys who'd turned on me. Not a single one of my 11th grade classmates would so much as give me the time of day, fearing the wrath of my blackballing betrayers. It was as if Doug Bradley had disappeared.

My parents were off in their own world, having given up on me during the summer, and Ron was once again back at California State Teachers College doing his college thing. He'd come home for Labor Day weekend, and I'd told him about the blackballing. He shrugged it off with a "fuck them." Easy for him to say. How was I going to survive two years of high school without any friends?

With more time on my hands, I listened to the radio around-the-clock, but quickly grew tired of Bobby Vinton, Kyu Sakamoto, and the rest of the Top 40 pablum on the "popular" Pittsburgh stations. Walking my no-man's land, I turned to the oldies/R&B/Doo-Wop station, WAMO, to keep me going. I couldn't get enough of WAMO's best known DJ, Porky Chedwick, who often referred to himself as "the daddio of the raddio," "Pork the Tork," or the "Bossman."

Without Ron to introduce me to new songs, I relied on Porky to help me navigate the differences between the East Coast and West Coast sounds, Italian American Doo-Wop, and "negro" Doo-Wop. I'd listen intently to "Drinkin' Wine" by Vernon Green and the Medallions, "Island of Love" by the Sheppards, "White Port Lemon Juice" by the Four Deuces, and "Florence" by the Paragons. An occasional pop song like "Our Day Will Come" found its way into Porky's mix. What you wouldn't hear was any of the ripped off, white bread stuff by the likes of Pat Boone and Bill Haley. Rumor had it Porky had even rebuffed Col. Tom Parker, Elvis Presley's manager, who wanted him to play some of the King's music. Porky thought Elvis was "too country," so for years the only "Hound Dog" heard on his show was "Big Mama" Willie Mae Thornton's original.

That miserable fall, "Be Fair," a sad, Doo-Wop classic by the Gallahads became my song sung blue. Porky seemed to be playing it all the time, a heartbreaking tale about a blind kid whose girlfriend is cheating on him with his best friend because the kid can't see the deception. "Be Fair, darling be kind. It's no fun when you're blind," the poor guy implores her at one point. I figured he was talking for me.

By the end of September, I'd mastered the role of social outcast—vacant look, downcast eyes, dumpy clothes, scuffling walk, stocking cap pulled down on my head when going to and from school. Of course, I ended up in Mr. Kirkpatrick's 11th-grade English class. Even with a handful of my major detractors in the room, Kirkpatrick's class was a place I could shine, academically, if not socially. Shakespeare and Steinbeck couldn't put anything over on me—hell, I was on my second or third reading of *Catcher in the Rye*. And Mr. Kirkpatrick's impish ways and teenage tendencies gave Room 107 a party-like atmosphere. As sullen and separated as I was, Room 107 gave me a home, if only for 50 minutes every day.

My survivor skills were basketball, writing, and music. But even those avocations had taken a hit—if I was to make the jump from JV to Varsity b-ball, I'd have to be teammates with Robbie and Ben and the others, and I wasn't sure I could handle it—or if they'd even pass me the damn ball. Musically, my blackballing meant I was spinning the platters at fewer parties and gatherings outside of official school sock hops and mixers.

Writing helped. Every day I'd scribble in my high school notebooks in between, and sometimes during, my classes. Poems about despair and loneliness. Imitations of songs like Danny and the Juniors "School Boy Romance" and the Heartbeats "A Thousand Miles Way." At night, right before bed, I'd enter my final thoughts in my journal, replaying the day's slights and injustices to certify my anger. My pain.

Given my sad, solitary state, "Be Fair" hit me hard. I didn't know what a Galahad was, but that haunting plea by the group's lead singer, assuming the role of a blind man being dumped by his girlfriend, became my melancholy anthem. "*Be fair,*" I wanted to shout up and down the halls of Thomas Jefferson High School. *Give Doug Bradley a break for Christ sake. Be fucking fair*!

Things got so bad that I stopped joining pick-up basketball games after school. With no girls around who'd risk talking to me and my homework always done, I was bored with a capital B. Having my driver's license offered no salvation since the only car I had access to was my parents' green Ford Falcon.

I hated the Falcon. Not the kind of car you drove if you wanted to pick up hot chicks. Joe Jackson's convertible always had a cute girl in it next to him. Ditto for Tim Gates's GTO. Doug Bradley's borrowed Ford Falcon looked like something from outer space, belching a smoke screen of burning oil. To top it off, my folks made me keep the original owner's brochure, the one with Charlie Brown and Lucy from the *Peanuts* comic strip, in the glove box.

Mom and Dad loved that disaster of a car. They'd purchased two of them after the model was first introduced. My dad sang the praises of Robert McNamara, JFK's Defense Secretary and a fellow World War II vet, who ran Ford before he joined the administration. "The father of the Falcon" was how Jack Bradley referred to McNamara whenever he appeared on TV or was mentioned in the newspaper. McNamara was on TV a lot lately, usually with a big pointer in front of a map of Asia, warning about "Communist aggression" in faraway places the broadcasters never pronounced the same way twice.

"Screw McNamara," I said aloud, cursing the defense secretary for his role in creating my lowly mode of transportation. Communist aggression was the last thing on my mind. Being liberated from my blackballed Siberia was priority number one. Not even WAMO and Porky Chedwick could help me with that.

At the beginning of October, Mr. Kirkpatrick assigned a character sketch, short story, scene from a play, a poem…

anything that could display our writing chops. This was my chance, and I dove in headfirst. Too deep. The short story I concocted was way too autobiographical. But I couldn't help myself, so I kept going and going, writing and rewriting as if my life depended on it.

"The Outcast" centered on a young man, conveniently named J. C.—I would have been better off if I'd never read *The Red Badge of Courage.* When the community discovers he's mixed race, he's branded an outcast. J. C. ends up falling down a mine shaft, and no one in the whole damn town bothers to rescue him. I knew it was too raw and too honest, but turning my predicament into a fictional story made me feel better.

The assignment was due Friday.

It usually took Mr. Kirkpatrick a week or more to get our papers back to us—he was a stickler for detail and correcting everything in red ink and adding extensive comments in the margins. So, I wasn't holding my breath to hear back from him.

The following Monday, sitting in my second period study hall, I looked up to see Mr. Blakemore, one of the harder-ass TJ teachers, approaching me with a hallowed hall pass in his hand.

"Bradley, get your butt to Room 107 pronto," he waved the pass at me, smiling as if we were in on some sort of secret.

My heart stopped for fear I'd done something terribly wrong. Maybe the guys who were blackballing me had enough clout to get me kicked out of school? My current state of paranoia knew no bounds. In my panic, I totally forgot that Room 107 was Mr. Kirkpatrick's. I peeked through the window in the door, catching a glimpse of him gesturing wildly as if he were in a sword fight, all the students laughing. Figuring there'd been some sort of mistake, I turned to head back downstairs to my study hall when I felt a tug on my arm.

"Dube," Mr. Kirkpatrick had a hold of my right arm, squeezing it ever so lightly.

When I turned around and saw that he was holding "The Outcast," I started to choke up.

"It'll be okay," Mr. Kirkpatrick whispered as he moved me away from the door. "Honestly, I didn't know how bad it was. I'm sorry. If you want to talk, or just need a shoulder to cry on, let me know." His words were so quiet and comforting I couldn't stop whimpering. In the three months since my banishment, no one had consoled me about my pain and hurt, and here was this young English teacher I hardly knew making me feel cared for.

Mr. Kirkpatrick handed me a white handkerchief from his sport coat, gently squeezing my arm. "See you in a couple hours," he smiled and turned back toward his classroom. "You can keep the hanky."

My heart lifted a little until I started to worry Kirkpatrick might say something about my confessional story to the class or ask me to read a portion of it as he sometimes did with assignments. I wouldn't be able to get through "The Outcast" without breaking down. The more I worried, the worse it got. Hadn't Kirkpatrick dated Robbie Black's older sister last summer? Shit, he was at their place once or twice when we guys stopped by. He had to know all about my outcast status. Was he just playing a cruel joke on me?

Chagrined, and unhinged, I barely made it through the rest of the school day. I decided to avoid any additional embarrassment by skipping the school bus and walking the three plus miles home. I was singing "Be Fair" to myself as I left the high school grounds: "It's no fun when you're blind," I recounted.

A horn beeped, and I looked up to see a white Plymouth almost on top of me. Behind the wheel sat Mr. Kirkpatrick, looking like a high school kid who'd just got his driver's license.

Track 6:

HELLO DOLLY

The lights dimmed. The Pittsburgh Civic Center crowd hushed. A band played "Hello Lyndon" in the vein of Louis Armstrong singing "Hello Dolly."

> *You're lookin' swell, Lyndon*
> *We can tell, Lyndon*
> *You're still glowin'...you're still crowin'*
> *You're still goin' strong*

The crowd started singing along as if this was their guy, this long tall Texan who was nothing like the president he'd followed, the one who'd captured our imaginations, our hopes and dreams. But the fella he was running against scared the crap out of everyone. So, yes, President Lyndon Baines Johnson was our man.

A bunch of us TJ students were among the Pittsburgh area high school kids seated in the Civic Arena audience to hear the President of the United States. While everyone else around me was caught up in the political moment, I was feeling the vibes of a recent "Porky Chedwick Groove Spectacular" where Jackie Wilson, Bo Diddley, the Drifters, and other R&B royalty had serenaded me in this very building.

Tonight was different. It was the eve of a presidential election that was going to determine our futures. Who cared if we couldn't vote? We TJ seniors had car caravanned from Pleasant Hills with our parents and teachers to show LBJ we believed in him and his message. Whatever that was...

Just before the President took the stage, the crowd serenaded him again with that stupid "Hello Dolly" take-off. I covered my ears, wishing they would've adapted "Do Wah Diddy Diddy." The singing went on and on as LBJ waved and smiled. He addressed us as "boys and girls," droning on about his modest upbringing and bestowing a verbal kiss on the ass of every Pennsylvania Democrat running for office.

I kept trying to catch a glimpse of Kirkpatrick, who was on the premises somewhere, no doubt puffed up because he was one of the TJ chaperones. I'd made the trip here with Mr. Sawyer, my old JV basketball coach, surmising Kirkpatrick had driven down with fellow teacher Kay Justice and students Will Beale and Shirley James, the cooler—in a certain odd way—kids he spent most of his time with. Or if not all of them, at least with Will. Definitely not with me, which bothered me for reasons I couldn't explain.

And that got me to thinking about how far we'd come, me and Kirkpatrick, and where we might be headed...

* * *

So much had happened since that day last year when Kirkpatrick drove a distraught Doug Bradley home from school.

He parked his car at the top of a small knoll of gravel and dirt above our driveway where my dad usually deposited one of our two Ford Falcons. I wasn't sure how long we sat there, but I remember crying most of the time as Kirkpatrick consoled me.

"You'll get through this. I've been where you are now and believe me, if it ended for me, it can end for you too. Take my word for it, one day it'll all be over and you'll forget how miserable you were."

"But I'm miserable," came my sobbing response. "And I don't have any friends. Not one."

"I'm your friend," Kirkpatrick said softly. In that moment that was more than enough.

For the rest of 11th grade and into 12th, Mr. Kirkpatrick was my friend, my confidante, a soul mate who understood my teenage trauma.

"I've been there," he kept reminding me about his own difficulties at Clairton High School, and early on at college. Didn't matter that he was my teacher. From the ride home that afternoon to the solace he offered the school after the JFK assassination to his turning us kids on to the Beatles and his stewardship of *You Can't Take It With You*, the Junior Class play for which he fearlessly named me one of two student directors. Not to mention the two dozen very long letters he wrote me that summer as he began work on his Ph.D. at Ohio University. Letters that opened my eyes to literature, professors, and poetry; letters that boosted my confidence, reaffirmed I mattered. And forced me to write about my feelings, my despair. W. J. Kirkpatrick was Doug Bradley's one-person rescue and recovery operation.

Back to here and now, 1964, this fall, senior year, he'd spend countless Saturday and Sunday mornings with me in my family kitchen, sipping coffee with my parents and making fun of me. Not once did my parents ask why he was there or what our relationship was really like. Never. Not even when the two of us visited his alma mater, West Virginia Wesleyan, in Buckhannon, West Virginia, so I could get a feel for college life and meet some of his old friends and professors, knowing I'd be spending the weekend with him. Jack and Lucy trusted Bill Kirkpatrick. And they trusted their son too.

My brother Ron was different.

"So, is Kirkpatrick like a perv or something?" he asked me when he was home from college one weekend.

"Whaddya mean?" I was taken aback by Ron's directness. And by how much he'd changed while he was away. Physically more imposing, grown up, his dark brown hair grown out, untamed. His wispy goatee made him look like Maynard G. Krebs on the *Dobie Gillis* show.

"I mean, doesn't he ever hang out with anybody his own age?" Ron added. "I've only ever seen him with you and your buddies, or in the kitchen with Mom and Dad. Seems pretty weird to me."

"Kirkpatrick's not weird," I rose to his defense. "He hangs out with lots of people his age. He's dating Kay Justice, one of the TJ teachers, and he spends a lot of time with Don Strand, another English teacher, and…"

"Don't flip your wig," Ron interrupted me. "I was just curious is all."

That made two of us. But with Kirkpatrick my main, and only, confidante, there was no one else I could talk to about my feelings for my friend, my teacher.

* * *

LBJ was still kissing up to the crowd. Ever since JFK's assassination, Kirkpatrick had made no bones about his dislike for Lyndon Johnson. Not that he was a Goldwater guy. He just didn't trust LBJ. He asked our Creative Writing class if they thought it was a coincidence that LBJ was a gun-toting Texan and JFK had been killed in Dallas. He'd driven all night from Clairton to Washington D. C. to stand in line for hours and hours so he could walk past the slain president's coffin. Okay, so he loved JFK. He hated LBJ. Big fucking deal. Get over it.

The Democratic event planners had sandwiched us high school kids in every corner of the Arena. Those whose daddies were big deal Democrats or were rich or had union ties or whatever, got to be down on the floor next to the President's platform. Less influential others, like me and the rest of the TJ crowd, were seated in the Arena's cavernous upper reaches. I could barely see the tips of LBJ's big ears from where I stood, but I sure as hell could hear him droning on and on about how great JFK was and how well Pittsburgh had bounced back—from what I wondered—and how out of touch his Republican opponent was.

As LBJ rambled on, I kept tilting my head back to check out the retractable roof, the first major arena in the world with one. Carl Fuller, Glenn Bright, and the other guys whose dads worked for U. S. Steel informed us that the hydraulic jacks, the ones supposed to open the roof, weren't for shit. So far, the roof had been opened only once, when my mom's favorite comedienne Carol Burnett performed. The U. S. Steel middle managers also liked to boast that the Civic Arena was built with 3,000 tons of our very own Pittsburgh steel. The kids of the really big shots were probably down on the floor near the President.

I was sitting next to Stacey Augmon, one of the brighter, street-smart kids in our class. Stacey was one of the few girls in my class who'd give black-balled me the time of day, but ours was more of a friendship than a love affair. I was still trying to find Kirkpatrick in the crowd, so I flinched when Stacey squeezed my arm.

"Did you hear that?" she asked in a loud whisper.

"Hear what?"

"What the President just said about Viet-nam." She seemed agitated.

"I didn't hear him say anything like V-et-nam," I added gusto to the word since I didn't want to admit I wasn't sure who or what in the hell "Viet-nam" was.

"I swear I just heard him say something about Viet-nam," Stacey insisted. "That's what Kirkpatrick has been talking about in Creative Writing, why he's got us reading *A Farewell to Arms* and *All Quiet on the Western Front*. He's afraid you guys will be drafted and sent there."

I patted Stacey's arm and placed my other arm around her shoulder. "Don't worry about us," I said, squeezing her shoulder. "We'll be fine. We'll all be fine," I repeated. "LBJ is going to win the election. Goldwater's a warmonger. Johnson will keep us out of trouble." Stacey threw me a look that said I was crazy as the crowd burst into another chorus of "Hello Lyndon."

The rest was a blur—noise and balloons and a long walk back to Mr. Sawyer's car, and an even longer ride home. The evening was a major letdown. If politics was sitting and standing around and applauding when you're told and singing on cue, I wanted no part of it. Maybe I should have taken a ride with Kirkpatrick? I bet he and Will and Shirley and his fellow teacher Kay were having a whole lot more fun than I was. Or maybe they were talking about me.

"*Now, don't sit around here and wait until they start playing a patriotic song and you go to packing up your boy's suitcase. Step in here...*" those words of the president came back to me as I sat in the backseat. Stacey would be pleased to know I had been listening.

"*That is your—job—to pick the person that you want to lead you,*" LBJ had wrapped up. "*You won't have another chance after next Tuesday. It will be four long years, and there are a lot of things that are going to happen in the next four years.*"

True. In four years I'd be a senior in college. But all I could think about right now was that damn roof at the Pittsburgh Civic Arena. Wouldn't it be something, I thought as Mr. Sawyer pulled up to my house, if the Arena's roof had opened tonight and JFK himself had floated down, grinning his boyish grin. Maybe he'd tell us that the past year had been one big practical joke. Even if the joke was on us.

Track 7:

TIME IS ON MY SIDE

I held my breath when I opened my locker and saw the word *"Doug"* typed on a slim white envelope taped inside the door. Not the usual *Dube* or *Duber* nickname, just plain ole Doug. Not a good sign. I knew it was from Kirkpatrick because nobody else would leave a typed letter in my locker. I couldn't open it now, not out here in the open, in the halls of TJ. I didn't want to ever open it, because I knew what it would say. I got the signal in Creative Writing earlier today—the total avoidance—and then the look, *the* look, the one that said he'd had had it with me. I'd crossed a line, gone too far, royally pissed him off…

My heart sank. When was I ever going to catch a fucking break in this place? What was I doing so wrong? Mick Jagger's voice on "Time Is on My Side" played in my head, the anger, the swagger. "But you'll come runnin' back," Jagger snarled. I seconded that emotion. "But you'll come running back Bill Kirkpatrick."

Or would he?

Why wasn't I as self-assured as Mick Jagger? No sooner did I want answers than I started feeling guilty. Of what exactly? Trying too hard? Demanding too much of Kirkpatrick's time and attention? Being too possessive, jealous? Had I done something to bring on this rejection? "*Think*!" I ordered my brain, "you must've done something…"

* * *

There was that one perfect spring Saturday last year when I was spiraling out of control, desperate for a friend or a date or a nod, some indication I even existed. As he often did on Saturdays, Kirkpatrick had stopped by our house to hang out with me and my parents in our kitchen. I wished it was just the two of us, but my folks enjoyed his company almost as much as I did.

Suddenly, Kirkpatrick jumped from his chair, grabbed me by the arm, and begged me to go outside.

"It's spring. Dube. Spring!" He looked possessed. I glanced at my parents.

"Go ahead you two, have a ball," was my father's broad-minded blessing.

And so, we two, teacher and student, took a long walk in the arboretum across from our house. The only other time I'd set foot in the arboretum the three years we'd lived here was the winter after we'd moved in when a bored Ron took me tobogganing down the steep, snow-covered hills. Today was completely different—the space was bursting with bright colors and intoxicating smells. Kirkpatrick's encyclopedic knowledge of nature took me by surprise as he pointed out the dogtooth violet and early buttercup, the limestone bittercress and something called a Virginia spring beauty. He even talked about Walt Whitman and the damn grass! I was enthralled, and a little overwhelmed.

"Give me odorous at sunrise a garden of beautiful flowers where I can walk undisturbed," he recited, and then something Wordsworth wrote about the periwinkle and wreaths and flowers, and finally a few lines from his idol Percy Bysshe Shelley:

> *I am the daughter of Earth and Water,*
> *And the nursling of the Sky;*
> *I pass through the pores of the ocean and shores; I change,*
> *but I cannot die.*

Shelley's words hung in the sweet spring air.

"Welcome to the world, Doug Bradley," Kirkpatrick turned to me with a sly smile, his large, black-rimmed glasses hidden under a crazily plaid sunhat. "This is where you should come every day. This is where everything you need to know exists."

Was he still stuck in his nature-lover mode? His poetic trance? I couldn't quite follow, but by now was becoming terrified somebody would find us here, alone, just the two of us…

"Life in all its beauty and mystery is here, right here," he reached down and grabbed a flower and a clump of grass. "Here!" he stuck it in my face. I backed away.

"Don't let all the petty high school crap cause you to overlook all this!" He spread his arms out as if he owned the entire arboretum. "Nature, beauty, poetry, SPRING! It's all here and it's all yours, Duber. Just across the street! This is what really matters, not whether Robbie or Pete or Diane likes you. What's important 'tis here, not there."

I don't think I said a dozen words that entire afternoon, but something happened to me. I felt a change from the invigorating odors and dazzling colors. Or was it the beguiling words of the poets? Or maybe because after Kirkpatrick finished his soliloquy, he rested his hand on my knee? Just resting. The two of us sitting there…

Later, after Kirkpatrick had gone home, my mom mentioned that while he and I were communing with nature, a bunch of my fellow 11th graders, including a few of my black-balling nemeses, had stopped by our house. My mom seemed pleased by the fact they'd come to see me. Were they welcoming me back into the fold, she wondered? Or had they spotted Kirkpatrick's car parked near our driveway? Whatever the case, when they came to the front door to ask if I was home, my naïve, obliging mom told them Mr. Kirkpatrick and I were "across the street in the arboretum."

"Jesus, Mom, you can't be serious. Did you really say that?"

"What's wrong with that?" she asked, clueless. "And don't swear."

"You told the guys who stopped here that I was in the arboretum with Mr. Kirkpatrick, just the two of us?" I don't think I'd ever been madder at my mother.

"Did I do something wrong, honey?" She looked distraught.

"What did they say?"

"Nothing."

"They didn't say anything? Think, Mom, what did they say?"

"Nobody said anything really. Just a lot of hooting and hollering as far as I could tell."

"Jesus Christ, Mom!"

"I told you not to swear," she turned heel and left.

* * *

I don't know why I was so defensive, or so offensive, with my poor old mother and why I didn't want my high school classmates to know I was alone with Kirkpatrick. Was I feeling something for him I didn't want to admit? What exactly was it? Kirkpatrick would be the only person I could talk to about this, but since it was about him, there was no one I could confide in.

I'd made sure nobody else knew about our weekend together at West Virginia Wesleyan. But now with all my classmates making jokes about Walter Jenkins, the guy LBJ fired because he was a "fairy," I got scared. I made a point of diverting attention to Kirkpatrick and Will Beale, pointedly asking them about their trip to some college they'd taken over the weekend. Brought it up to the whole class in Creative Writing, oblivious to how much that would piss Kirkpatrick off.

Once home, I retreated to the basement, plunked down on our ugly, sticky, orange plastic sofa, and put on the record that had been filling my head all day, "Time is on my side."

"Yes it is," I shouted. Damn, I wanted to be that sure.

And then I opened the envelope.

"*Dear Doug*," the typed, single-spaced, two-page letter dated November 17, 1964, began. "*I want you to know that your statement on the stairs today did not fall on blinded ears. In one stinging sentence, you lashed out at me and the blow landed. I can barely collect what I want to say, but I will try...*

Jesus, did something I'd said in jest really land a blow? Must've, because from there Kirkpatrick went on in full Shakespeare mode to let me have it, both barrels. I was "*selfish, jealous, conceited, and mentally unstable,*" among other things. "*I have given, given, given, so tell me why you are being mentally and spiritually sick if you envy Will for my friendship or attempt to deny him of it?*"

This rant went on for nearly two pages, and then he closed with "*I do not have time to give to someone so small, so conceited, and so ill-mannered. I have proven over and over again my love of you and my desire to be a friend to you. You'd better wise up.*

You have two shoulders, son, and you'd better make room for someone besides Douglas Bradley!"

He signed the blistering note "*Yours sincerely, Holden Caulfield,*" typing and writing out the name of the narrator of *Catcher in the Rye* in ink. For once, I didn't punch anything or cry or run out of the house. I calmly re-read the letter from Kirkpatrick. Then, I read it again.

What the hell? Had I struck a nerve about his relationship with Will? *Holden Caulfield*? Was there some hidden message there? Wasn't Kirkpatrick more like Mr. Antolini, Holden's teacher in *Catcher*, than Holden Caulfield? Or, like Holden, was I misinterpreting everything about my favorite teacher?

Too many questions. Maybe I'd even expected this would happen when I poked him about Will? Hoped for this result? Whatever, I'd done it, and now I had to live with it. Without Kirkpatrick.

When my mom opened the door to the basement and started downstairs with the laundry, I stuffed the two pages under one of the sofa pillows. Hiding it. Why I wasn't sure. My hurt? My embarrassment? But moms always know when you're hiding something.

"Whatcha got there?" she asked, smiling.

"Whaddya mean?"

"There, under the pillow," she pointed. "Who's that letter from?" She hadn't missed a damn thing.

"Ah, well, ahem, well…" I couldn't stall any longer. "It's from Carla." She was my girlfriend of a few weeks, a cute, smiling brunette who lived on the poor side of town and was taking so-called "vocational" classes at TJ.

"Typed?" my mom was not persuaded.

"Yeah," I was delaying, trying to recover. My mom was an expert card player, mostly pinochle and Canasta, so it was hard to get the upper hand with her. "Carla's in this advanced typing class where she has to send out a bunch of sample business letters, and she wanted me to proofread some of them."

"Good for her," my mom smiled. "If you need me to take a look, I can. I took typing in high school myself. And wanted to be a teacher too."

"That's okay," I took the letter out from under the pillow and waved it at her. "I'm good at this sort of thing. You taught me well," I smiled my innocent, "I'm your little boy" smile.

"I sure did," she turned and headed into the laundry room.

"You'll come running back… " Jagger was trying to turn the tables on his adversary. It sure felt as if Kirkpatrick had broken up with me. But he's a guy, a guy seven years older than me. Nothing was going on between us…was it? He tousled my hair a lot and occasionally put his arm around me. Gave me a hug. And the moment in the arboretum…Did I like it? Welcome it? Return it? Were he and Will Beale doing that too? Doing something more than that?

The song kept repeating and it merged with the letter, and I couldn't tell the difference. Who'd come back to whom?

And when? Jesus, I wished I was done with all this high school crap. And what would Holden Caulfield make of all this? Probably call everybody a phony. Add Kirkpatrick to that list. Sure, he'd helped get me through my heartache and humiliation, but he was just like everybody else. Piling on.

"Time is on my side " I sang into the basement.

Turn off the record player. Turn over a new leaf. I had Carla. I was applying to colleges. I was writing up a storm in English and Creative Writing. Who needed W. J. Kirkpatrick anyway?

Tracks 8-9:

YOU'VE LOST THAT LOVIN' FEELIN; GOIN' OUT OF MY HEAD

Kirkpatrick's breakup letter gave me blackballing flashbacks, hurting where I was most vulnerable, my desperate need for approval and attachment. As much as I liked Carla and wanted more from her, physically at least, what I had with Kirkpatrick was different. Scary, but special. Unchartered territory.

I knew better than to respond to his note or try to get back in his good graces, so I sucked it up and pretended everything was okay, playing it cool daily in Creative Writing class and weekly at Key Club meetings where Kirkpatrick served as faculty impresario.

The tall, cool, angular Will Beale was Key Club president. He exuded aloof, sporting a tie with his pure Perry Como blue cardigan sweater. He wasn't part of the blackballing crew, but he wasn't my friend. His allegiance was to Kirkpatrick.

Kirkpatrick maintained a "go f-yourself" demeanor with me while our Creative Writing class waded waist-deep in war and death and dying as he maneuvered us from *All Quiet on the Western Front* to *A Farewell to Arms*. That only made carnal extracurriculars with Carla more appealing. Neither of us was well-versed in wanton foreplay, but we tried our best, or at least I tried my best to figure out how to unhook her bra with one hand. Hell, if we're all gonna die, why not go down smiling? Who needed Kirkpatrick preaching some D. H. Lawrence bull about men loving men as well as women and likewise women loving women? Much too weird…

No sooner than you could say *Johnny Got His Gun*, my already less-than-perfect world came crashing down. Miss Carla Bonner of the school's sweetest smile, intoxicating innocence, and breathtaking beauty…Carla Bonner, TJ Homecoming Queen of 1964, my girlfriend for several glorious weeks was gone.

And I had no Kirkpatrick to turn to.

* * *

"Thank you, Jesus, Mary, and Joseph," I'd repeated at Mass every Sunday that fall, giving divine thanks for Carla's existence, and her beauty, starting with her lush, jet-black hair fashioned in an under-control beehive, her bangs always perfect. Expressive deep brown eyes. Killer body filled out perfectly in all the right places. Wholesome, friendly, innocent, constantly smiling. "World without end. Amen."

Carla lived in the part of town where the fathers worked like dogs inside the steel mills, so our worlds outside high school rarely collided. Didn't cross-pollinate inside either because she was taking the vocational track so we didn't have any classes together. My earliest recollection had to do with her helping with makeup for the Junior Class Play. I did a double take, realizing just how desirable she'd become. I probably would have noticed her sooner since she was a member of the cheerleading squad, but the dopes made her the Jaguar mascot. Why would you bury such a beauty in a Jaguar suit for Christ's sake?

When Carla fully blossomed senior year, she took my breath away, in or out of a Jaguar suit. She was beautiful, fun, and, apparently, unclaimed.

And I made Carla laugh. Even in my misery, I made a lot of people laugh—it was my chief survival skill—but Carla seemed to genuinely get a kick out of me when we had a study hall together our senior year. She'd giggle at the nicknames I made up for the teachers and staff—"Just-in Sider" for Mr. Snyder; Whet Fartz for Mrs. Whetland; and Barb Wire for Miss Weir. She laughed even harder when I described student hairdos—Jerry Douglas's aircraft carrier flattop, Ronnie Severino's frozen Jell-O pompadour, and Eileen Stewart's pigtails resembling two very sick garter snakes. With such an alluring, receptive audience, I kept the jokes coming.

Study hall gave me and Carla an hour a day to talk, laugh, and flirt. Enough time for me to get my hopes up about asking her for a date. But I figured she had to be going out with one of the tough guy greasers from Clairton or West Elizabeth. Lust or no lust, I sure as hell didn't want to get my ass kicked by some brute named Buzz or Rico.

Things probably wouldn't have progressed if Carla hadn't been nominated for homecoming queen. Of the five nominees, the house money was on long-standing Pleasant Hills hotties Sandy Styles or Sharon Oliver. Carla was an afterthought, a dark horse, a gesture to the scores of girls in our class headed nowhere. But for the Thomas Jefferson High School Homecoming Queen election of 1964, those of us who lived on the right side of the tracks had it wrong. Sandy and Sharon split the white-collar vote and Carla won in a landslide. She definitely had my vote.

Just before her coronation, Carla confided in me that she had to have a male appendage for the Homecoming Dance. At first, I figured she wanted me to help her decide who to ask or maybe even help with the asking. Never dawned on me that this was her way of asking *me* to be her date. But when I jokingly offered, "Miss Bonner, if you aren't otherwise engaged, may I represent the male TJ student body and run interference for you at the Homecoming Dance?" She smiled her big, bright, beautiful smile, squeezed my arm, and whispered, "Yes. Thanks."

And then we tumbled hard and deep and totally into teenage love. It happened so fast we hadn't even decided what "our song" was. We laughed a little less, kissed and cuddled a lot more, and began to explore our bodies. More unchartered territory for me.

We didn't get very far. But we spent many a fall night steaming up the windows in my dad's Oldsmobile F-85— he'd finally gotten rid of those ridiculous Ford Falcons. Being head over heels in love made life brighter and lighter, the blackballing and the Kirkpatrick fall-out tolerable.

But then my big mouth got the best of me again. One night at her house, where her mother always eyed me warily, I joked that next year I'd be attending some school titled the U of A while Carla would be a checkout girl at the A of P. "He jokes around too much," I overheard her mother console a crying Carla.

The joke was on me. A humiliated, angry Carla broke up with me the day before Thanksgiving.

***

I was devastated. And no Kirkpatrick for support. Not having anyone to hold and caress was one thing, not having anyone to talk to about my heartbreak, to describe how I was feeling, to tell me how to get through this, was even worse.

My brother Ron, home from college, tried to cheer me up by taking me shopping at the big department stores in downtown Pittsburgh the Friday after Thanksgiving. "There'll be some fine-as-wine chicks in those stores," he promised. My heart sank even further. What if I saw Carla? What if I saw her with another guy? My heart was racing and my head was aching, and this was only the third day of our breakup.

The worst thing my brother did that day was to buy two new 45-RPM records at the National Record Mart. Not your usual Motown dancing in the streets. No fun-fun-fun from the Beach Boys. No John, Paul, George, and Ringo feeling fine. No, he purchased "Goin' Out of My Head" by Little Anthony and the Imperials and the Righteous Brothers' "You've Lost that Lovin' Feelin'." And he played them over and over and over that interminable weekend.

My heart didn't just hurt when I heard the Righteous Brothers sing "We had a love, a love, a love you don't find every day." It was even worse when Little Anthony reminded me that I was indeed "goin' out of my head." Nothing had ever ached like this. Was it because I'd squandered Carla's love? Or that I didn't swallow my pride and apologize and beg her to take me back?

Didn't matter. It was the longest weekend of my life. I didn't sleep. Couldn't eat. Out of my head, love slipping away. Even after Ron took the records back to college with him, there was no respite with the Pittsburgh radio stations playing them incessantly. Even WAMO, the R&B oldies station, played them. I'd lose it at the first modulation of Bill Medley's bass, the first glide of Little Anthony's falsetto.

So, what's a lovesick, despondent teenager to do? Contemplate suicide, the Quentin Compson-Sylvia Plath dreamy state that we Creative Writing students found so appealing? According to my *Baltimore Catechism* education, suicide was a mortal sin, and I'd spend eternity in hell. We had a short story assignment due after Thanksgiving, and my break-up with Carla became the focus. I knew the story I wrote was better than "The Outcast." No obvious references to Jesus or St. Sebastian at least. I wrote honestly about a kid whose girlfriend had just broken up with him, who decides to commit suicide by getting hit by a car. Written in flashbacks. With *italics*.

My short story needed just the right title, so I thumbed through my parents' *TV Guide* and, voila, there it was on Monday night on ABC's Ben Casey: "*Kill the Dream but Spare the Dreamer.*" Pitch perfect.

The songs kept playing but they didn't hurt quite so much anymore. Let Carla and Kirkpatrick "*criticize little things I do*," I could write my way through the tears and pain. I could get back on my own two feet.

I'd written "Kill the Dream but Spare the Dreamer" out of pain and loss and despair. It didn't help me get Carla back.

It brought back Kirkpatrick.

He returned our class papers right before Christmas vacation and put a big scarlet "A" on mine, commenting that "*the title is superbly integrated into the story.*" Chalk one up for *TV Guide*. He added in the margin that he wanted me to come in to talk to him about my story. Did he know I was goin' out of my head? That the protagonist of "Kill the Dream but Spare the Dreamer" was contemplating something drastic?

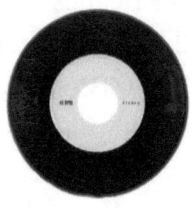

Track 10:
I'M A LOSER

If I'd learned anything from Kirkpatrick over the last few years, it was that "words matter." So I poured my heart and soul into a letter. "Kill the Dream, but Spare the Dreamer" had thawed the ice, but I still needed to apologize to him directly and honestly. Poetically, even, through our preferred channel, a personal letter.

But first I had to get my bearings. I was still reeling from the combo of Kirkpatrick's November broadside and the Carla breakup. It didn't help matters that "I'm a Loser," an uncharacteristically bleak, confessional song from the just-released *Beatles '65* album was stuck on repeat in my head, had me wondering what I'd done to deserve such a fate. Those lines were pounding like a jackhammer gone berserk.

Yet another of the other things I'd learned from Kirkpatrick—to love the Beatles.

★ ★ ★

"Listen carefully to the Beatles" he instructed us when the group first arrived on the scene in early 1964. "They're the Beach Boys and the Everly Brothers and Chuck Berry and Little Richard all rolled into one. They're not just fun and '*yeah, yeah, yeah.*' They are choice."

As much as I valued Kirkpatrick's opinion, it took me a while to join the Beatles fan club. At the time they arrived, I was grounded in Pittsburgh grit and grime, songs like "Working in the Coal Mine," "Mama Loochie," and most everything else my platter pushin' papa Porky Chedwick sent out from WAMO. Soul, lots and lots and lots of soul. And black. Very, very, black.

But truth was, the Beatles had almost single-handedly resurrected America, white America anyway, from the depths of JFK's assassination. We'd been a mess—I'd never seen so much public weeping in my life, and it just kept on going. How much crying could one school, one community, one city, one nation do? As the days got shorter and the skies darker it felt like our faith had been broken by the death of our young, charismatic president.

Music on the radio wasn't helping much. The Singing Nun was topping the charts, and I turned off the radio with disgust every time I heard "Dominique." Even Pork the Tork was in a funk, playing way too many depressing Doo-Wop ballads. The mixers and sock hops were canceled, and I quit the basketball team because the guys who'd blackballed me wouldn't give me the time of day or pass me the damn ball when I was wide open in front of the basket.

Kirkpatrick took the assassination hard. He'd firmly believed in the promise of Kennedy's Camelot. He drove nonstop from Pittsburgh to Washington D. C. to see JFK's body lying in state. Stood in an endless line, choking back tears. When he reached the front, he made his peace, turned around, and drove straight back. The next day in English class, he looked bleary-eyed and defeated as he told us about his visit to our dead president and recited lines from Tennyson:

> *Willows whiten, aspens quiver,*
> *Little breezes dusk and shiver*
> *Thro' the wave that runs for ever*
> *By the island in the river*
> *Flowing down to Camelot...*

We all started crying again. It was hell. Something told me that only music was going to save us. But how long would that take?

Thanks to the Beatles it didn't take all that long. In early January 1964, Kirkpatrick put a record on the turntable at the front of the classroom.

"Nobody's heard this yet," he exclaimed as if he'd just discovered a cure for cancer. "It's called 'I Wanna Hold Your Hand' by the Beatles."

"The whats?" we asked him.

"The Beatles," he smiled. "Wait until you see their haircuts!"

I listened to that song over and over, its sweet harmonies, its energy, its optimism. Jesus, these guys were so happy, they were making me happy, they were making all of us happy. That long winter of our discontent would soon be over. It was time for us to sing and dance and bounce our way into a future where we would all hold hands…well, maybe nobody would hold mine, but the Beatles made me think even that was possible.

* * *

That Beatles' history didn't explain my current fixation with "I'm a Loser." It was more than the obvious "loser" reference. It was how the song was different from the other Beatles' songs. It was as brutally honest and unsparing as I'd felt in "Kill the Dream, but Spare the Dreamer." Whatever the case, "I'm a Loser" was stuck on repeat in my head. With the two people in the world I cared about the most having abandoned me, I sat down to write my letter of apology, to explain myself to Kirkpatrick, and to myself.

The writing came in fits and starts. I listened to the *Beatles '65* album, the first Beatles album I'd bought with my own money, for inspiration, but I could only do that when my parents weren't home. Ditto using my dad's typewriter which I would have to fetch from his office in the basement. Why was this so damn difficult?

And then the stars aligned, my fingers started flying across the keys, and off I went into the wild blue yonder, jet fuel courtesy of *Beatles '65*. "No Reply," "Baby's in Black," "Mr. Moonlight," and, always, "I'm a Loser."

The breakup with Carla was in those songs, but Kirkpatrick more so, the first actual Beatles fan I knew. He'd gone to see the lads just this past October when they performed in Pittsburgh, declaring it the best concert ever. For me, one of the last "not sold on the Beatles" holdouts, *Beatles '65* had totally brought me around. If I told Kirkpatrick how much I liked them, maybe he'd forgive me for my trespasses?

I wrote draft after draft, finally deciding on the version seemingly written by the kid who contemplates suicide in "Kill the Dream, but Spare the Dreamer." It was the shortest and contained the fewest "I'm sorrys." When I re-read it, I was struck how much my writing had gone to some other place.

Pure and unfiltered, fluid. Would Kirkpatrick realize that was his doing? As hard as the letter was, I enjoyed writing it.

Putting my fate in the hands of the U. S. Postal Service and mailing the letter to his home address, I held my breath and crossed my fingers. Even blessed myself and uttered a lot of prayers. Now here it was December 18, the last day before Christmas vacation, and "no reply" from Kirkpatrick. Not a clue from his behavior in Creative Writing class either. He must've received the letter by now. Or had I sent it to the wrong address?

Christmas without Carla would be bad enough—I couldn't stop thinking about her, especially after I saw her and Tim Bates cozying up by her locker. Like a dumb ass, I'd call her house daily and hang up when her mother or brother answered the phone. I even drove past her place a couple times, hearing the Beatles somewhere in the back of my head reminding me that I'd seen her walking with another man, "hand in hand in my place."

I missed her hair, her voice, her eyes, her smell, her body…but Christmas without Kirkpatrick would be a whole 'nother lump of coal. I knew how disappointed my parents would be not to see him, especially my mom. Any minute now she'd start peppering me with questions: "When's Mr. Kirkpatrick stopping by," "Why isn't Mr. Kirkpatrick here?" and on and on. Christ, she'd even knitted a winter cap for him as a Christmas present…way too much for my fragile adolescence to withstand. I'd be a loser in her eyes, too.

Not a sound or a word or eye contact from Carla. And the Beatles kept on singing that damn song. Alright, already, I know I'm a loser, but I've learned something about myself in the process. Isn't that worth something?

Just as I was about to give up all hope, I discovered a slim note from Kirkpatrick tucked inside the essay I'd written about "The Death of the Ball Turret Gunner." I was too nervous to read the note in class, so I waited until the next period. What if he didn't forgive me? What if my letter had had absolutely no impact? Zero? This would be the worst Christmas ever.

"Dube, your letter today was beautifully written, and I shall always cherish it," the handwritten note opened. *"It's easy to see that it was written with a lot of feeling."*

I breathed a major sigh of relief.

"It is time that I see a lot of Will," he went on and my heart momentarily sank. But then he added, *"especially because I've developed an interest in his sister!"*

Holy shit! I nearly shouted out loud. So that's it. Kirkpatrick likes Will's sister. How come I hadn't known or suspected it? Why had I jumped to conclusions about him and his relationship with Will?

After the revelation, Kirkpatrick got to the heart of the Will Beale-Doug Bradley dynamic, explaining that I made Will nervous, that the two of them could sense my possessiveness and jealousy, and so on. Much like in his last letter, but without the nastiness and "fuck off" feel. They were still pissed about my telling the Creative Writing class about their college visit, and my shouting to Kirkpatrick on the stairs.

Maybe he was right. Maybe I wasn't being fair to either of them, especially Will. And now his sister was in the act? I owed Will Beale an apology…but there was a phrase in Kirkpatrick's note that unsettled me. *"Will gets the impression you are unwilling to allow anyone else to enjoy the affections I've given you."*

I paused to catch my breath. What the hell? Just what *affections* had Kirkpatrick given me? Does everyone else know what's going on between us, whatever it was? Had I forgotten about that afternoon in the arboretum when the guys stopped by my house? Just where in the hell had I been?

There was more, there was always more in a Kirkpatrick letter, but it was as if a major fog had lifted after two years, and I could see myself as others did. It wasn't pretty—insecure, distrustful, hypersensitive, isolated, helpless. Violated? By Kirkpatrick and Will and everyone else who thought Kirkpatrick and I were up to something? How had I let all of this happen? Was there any way out? What a loser. I never should've written that damn letter.

* * *

Our ugly yellow kitchen telephone rang on Christmas Eve. My mom answered, her voice so very warm and cheery. I knew who it was.

"Doug, phone call," she sang from the kitchen. "It's Mr. Kirkpatrick."

Track 11:

MR. TAMBOURINE MAN

If I got caught playing *Bringing It All Back Home* on my parents' Hi-Fi, I'd catch holy hell. Even in 1965, their high-status stereo was still a forbidden zone for my music. At least when they were in earshot. But I couldn't play albums on my portable 45-RPM player, and I just had to hear how this strange Bob Dylan song, "Mr. Tambourine Man," sounded on a quality stereo. Kirkpatrick had introduced us to Bob Dylan a year or two ago, and while I wasn't a big folk music fan, I'd heard the kids with guitars strumming and reciting lyrics to "Blowin' in the Wind" and now "Mr. Tambourine Man." One particular line kept nagging at me—"ain't no place I'm goin' to." Damn if that didn't sum up my life with the blackballing, impending graduation, and anxiety about running headlong into an uncertain future.

My parents were in the back of the house, so I put on the album, careful to turn down the volume until the needle dropped on the "B" side. Dylan's voice had changed. I wasn't sure how. The third time through the song, I looked up and was startled to see Kirkpatrick's shaken, ashen face at the front door.

"Dube, we have to talk." His words entered the house before he did, and I knew something was wrong.

"Sure thing." I could tell this was serious, but with my parents, two of Mr. Kirkpatrick's biggest cheerleaders, somewhere on the premises, it was going to be hard to navigate the rapids. They had a sixth sense when it came to Kirkpatrick's comings and goings.

"Ho, ho, look who's here?" my dad belted out as if he were greeting a regular at the neighborhood pub. "If it isn't the world's best English teacher!" My mom entered beside my dad, smiling her welcoming smile.

Kirkpatrick returned a sheepish grin and a mild "Hi," and gave my mom a quick hug, a first. My parents stood there, grinning approvingly, maybe recalling their own favorite high school teachers from 30 or more years ago. The mutual affection the three of them shared forever left me puzzled.

"Would you like a sandwich or a cup of coffee?" my mom always acted as if she ran an all-night diner.

"No thanks, Mrs. B., I just ate."

Shrugging her shoulders, my diminutive, apron-appareled mom took this minor setback in stride. "Maybe one of my homemade cinnamon buns a little later," she winked. Kirkpatrick again forced a smile.

"So, what's news?" My dad was decked out in his customary weekend outfit, blue Perry Como sweater with the bottom button unbuttoned, yellow shirt with an open collar, black corduroys, wide white belt, and bright white tennis shoes. He was eager to strike up a conversation, unaware of the "stand back" vibe enveloping Kirkpatrick, still wearing his pea coat.

"I have to help your son with his college preparations," Kirkpatrick lied, flashing me a quick "please help me out here" look. At the mere mention of college, my dad, a high school dropout, would head for the hills. For him, college was a distant planet, a world he couldn't comprehend and didn't want to.

"Go right ahead," my dad made a sweeping hand gesture in my direction, "he's all yours."

Jesus, I could hardly believe my father said that. Then again, it was true to form. My folks had never uttered a single cautionary word about a 23-year-old, awkward, youngish-looking, single man hanging around their 17-year-old son. They trusted me, trusted us, and that made all the difference in the world, the one Kirkpatrick and I inhabited. Maybe I'd sensed that all along, but I finally saw it in that moment. Armed with my parents' trust, I could deal with whatever was bothering my mentor.

Kirkpatrick and I descended the stairs to the cave-like basement that doubled as my dad's office and my Don Juan lair where I tried, unsuccessfully, to seduce Carla. Rain or shine, winter or summer, that tiny basement on Bruceton Road in the Pittsburgh suburbs was cool, dark, and private.

Kirkpatrick's deep blue eyes filled his huge, black-rimmed glasses, something I didn't remember noticing before. Those glasses, and the birthmark on the right side of his face were his distinguishing features. No, what truly set him apart were the words that came out of his mouth. He was wearing his usual Navy pea coat, but everything about him seemed different…foreign…frightening.

"What's going on?" I asked.

"I tried to off myself," Kirkpatrick looked lifeless when he spoke. "I had the rifle in my mouth, I had everything ready to go and…and…"

I jumped from the sofa, shaking. I wanted to do something—go back upstairs? Listen to Bob Dylan? Hug my teacher? Close my ears? Something. But all I could do was stand there, trembling and bewildered. Were my parents listening? Was all this really happening?

"Kay Justice came by just as I was about to…" he paused. I waited. Kay was a Thomas Jefferson phy ed teacher. She seemed like more of a sister to Kirkpatrick than a potential love interest. Some of my classmates thought otherwise.

"I just couldn't go through with it, not with her at my front door," Kirkpatrick was out of breath, close to tears. "Isn't that crazy? If I'm dead, I'm dead. It's over. But somehow, I felt like Kay's being there would make her an accomplice, that she'd spend the rest of her life feeling guilty and responsible."

I wasn't quite following, but Kirkpatrick kept on explaining, patting the seat next to him for me to sit down.

"I stopped. Answered the door and let her in. She could see something dire was going on, so I broke down and told her what I was going to do. She screamed and cried and called me a coward. Then she slapped me and stalked out."

I felt woozy, as if I too had just been punched. I couldn't sit still and listen. I paced back and forth, wanting to burst out of the basement. Or just go back a couple hours. No, let me think. Mr. W. J. Kirkpatrick, the Thomas Jefferson High School Class of 1965's beloved teacher, my only true friend and confidante…suicide? With a rifle? Just like Hemingway?

Kirkpatrick paused. "Please, sit down and I'll give you the whole wretched story," he situated me next to him on the burnt orange vinyl sofa. "Besides Kay, you're the only one who'll know anything about this. Ever."

Over the next half hour, Kirkpatrick related all the grisly details of his aborted suicide attempt. I felt like we were inside one of those phantasmagoric Dylan songs. I was surprised how composed and unemotional Kirkpatrick was, as if he were telling a story about someone else. In a way he was, because despite all the particulars about his last meal and final sips of coffee and the location of his father's rifle and how he carefully wrapped the heavy-duty string from the rifle to his trigger finger so he could fire the fatal shot, Papa Hemingway style, he revealed nothing about why he was doing it. Did he assume I knew? Given our own breakups, my missteps with Carla, and my ongoing outcast status, shouldn't I be the one contemplating suicide?

I was completely clueless as to why the smartest person I'd ever known, the guy who'd opened worlds of ideas and words and feelings to me and my classmates would even consider killing himself. But in that moment, I was too damn scared to ask…and now I was in on his deep, dark secret. I was his accomplice.

* * *

Kirkpatrick eventually left but I couldn't remember if he was any better than when he arrived. After he'd gone, my folks asked if something was bugging him. I simply said "girl trouble" which stopped their questioning. Maybe they were even relieved Kirkpatrick might have a girlfriend.

I returned to the basement and plopped a stack of records on my 45 RPM turntable. But what I really wanted to do was listen to *Bringing It All Back Home,* loud, on my parents' Hi-Fi. Listen hard enough to understand "Mr. Tambourine Man" since it was still running through my head. With the aroma of Kirkpatrick's attempted suicide lingering, the song's words seemed even more fatalistic. Suicidal? Kirkpatrick *was* the tambourine man, I thought, spinning, swinging, skipping. Haunted. Disappearing, far from all the pain, mine, his, the crazy reach of twisted sorrow.

Now what? Would Kirkpatrick be the same person the next time I saw him? Or would he go back home and finish what he started? Should I do something? Call somebody? Go after him?

I just sat there, doing nothing, reciting lines from Bob Dylan, over and over and over again.

Track 12:

I CAN'T HELP MYSELF

With so much to look forward to, I didn't want to spend time looking back at the last four months. But Dylan and the Beatles took me back to Kirkpatrick, "High on a Hill" and "We Belong Together" conjured Carla. Major Lance my blackballing. Up and down and all around…

Less than a month from graduation, a new song brought me back to life, making me feel a joy I hadn't felt since last fall when Carla and Kirkpatrick had been in my corner. The Four Tops' "I Can't Help Myself"—"Sugar Pie, Honey Bunch" as some of us called it—pulsated with everything upbeat and carefree about being a teenager in America in the spring of 1965.

My road to the song, the joy, was a strange one. From Kirkpatrick's suicide confessional that day in my basement when he didn't kill himself to yet another break-up… Jesus, I'd broken up more with him than I had with any of my girlfriends.

Kirkpatrick proclaimed this latest separation our last, sealing it with a scathing, no-holds-barred, tongue-lashing via a three-page typed letter in late January. Just what I'd done to piss him off this time was immaterial. Kirkpatrick seemingly just wanted to be done with me. So, he let me have it again. Both barrels. In the classic Aristotelean arc he'd taught us.

An opening salvo of *"Your basic problem is that you are a real misfit. You just aren't human"* to **rising action** with *"You stick out like a sore thumb anywhere a group of normal, well-adjusted kids gather together"* to a **climax** of *"You are out of the class of people worthy of my best attentions and interest. Please just stay put"* with a **denouement** of *"I still love your parents but don't expect I'll be seeing much of them now."* Three fucking pages.

I'd grown numb to all the snubs, putdowns, and verbal abuse, so I didn't spend a lot of time thinking about it. In fact, I stopped, simply stopped, fretting. Instead, I listened to lots and lots of music; wrote poems; played records at the mixers; got accepted to all the colleges I'd applied to, including Notre Dame—every good Catholic boy's dream—and was offered a scholarship and financial aid package from tiny Bethany College in nearby West Virginia. I was savoring basketball again, playing with a playground, pick-up crew of outcasts and misfits that was winning games in tournaments. Recovering from my blackball status. Reuniting with Carla.

She showed up at the St. Patrick's Day dance where I was spinning the platters in the midst of a blizzard. The week before, she'd given me a senior class picture with "I'm sorry" and "I wished we'd never broken up" sentiments scrawled on the back. That got my 17-year-old heart racing, but I was careful to calibrate it. Still, seeing her there that night, dressed all in green and looking so damn foxy, I had to catch my breath. When she beckoned me down to the dance floor when I played "Chapel of Dreams" for a lady's choice, I kinda lost it. Walked her home through piles of deep, fluffy snow. Shared a brief kiss, and I was back in love.

Carla and I were tighter, literally, than ever. I'd forgotten how having a girlfriend gives you equilibrium. We explored our way through the rest of that spring, talking more about what awaited me in college than what she had to look forward to. About why her mother seemingly couldn't stand me. And how we'd love one another for eternity.

When I wasn't with Carla, I hung out with a cadre of guys I'd always thought either weren't cool enough or else were beneath me, but turned out were just as anxious and nervous and clueless about girls and college and the future as I was. Carl Fuller, Tom Clifton, and I drove around in Tom's Dodge Dart, listened to music, played pool in his basement, and talked about, well, girls and college and the future. Tom's older brother was in the Army, so the subject of Vietnam came up a couple times, but none of us knew where he was stationed or what the hell he was doing or where in the hell Vietnam was. We'd seen LBJ on TV and McNamara with his pointers, but our asses would be saved, we hoped, because we would go to college and not be drafted.

None of us knew what was going to happen after graduation, but one thing we did know was that, according to Thomas Jefferson High School tradition, we would be celebrating our one and only "Senior Day" that May. It would mark my final performance as a high school DJ.

The TJ Senior Day routine included an approved late arrival at school, a long lunch in the cafeteria, minus all the underclassmen, the Junior-Senior basketball game, closing with post-game hijinx away from the school which usually involved drinking and smoking. Cigarettes and beer we'd swiped from our parents. But this wasn't just another Senior Day. Thanks to some heavy-duty lobbying by Kirkpatrick and a couple of his fellow English teachers, the school's administration, including James Brock Knoll, TJ's commanding, first vice principal, had agreed to let me take charge of the music during the lunch "hour." On top of that, some of the teachers who were chaperoning our time in the cafeteria encouraged us to get up and dance. They had no idea we would dance and dance and dance to the same damn song over and over and over.

This was the Senior Day when the Thomas Jefferson High School seniors went off script, refusing to vacate the cafeteria as we kept on singing and dancing to "I Can't Help Myself/Sugar Pie Honey Bunch." For those 20, 25, or 30 minutes, we were rebels. Not because we'd ducked out on school or had had a huge food fight in the cafeteria. No, because Mr. Knoll, with all his authority and position—and sheer size—couldn't dislodge us from the cafeteria. We, and he, were under the spell of pure Motown soul, hopped up on dancing and freedom.

I must've played "I Can't Help Myself" 12 or 13 times in a row. Eventually, Mr. Knoll stopped trying to tell us to leave and pulled the plug on my record player, ending the singing and dancing mayhem. His large, round face bore down on mine as he pitched his words at me like darts.

"You…will…never…violate…THE RULES of this calf-er-tier-e-ah again!"

"I already did," I smiled, flashing back to those same words my brother tossed at my father in 1959. I grabbed my records, my turntable, and darted down the hall to the gym to take on the Juniors.

As we made our way to the gymnasium, with Mr. Knoll in hot pursuit, we came upon Kirkpatrick, handing out hall passes to every one of us. "*I come a runnin' to you*" we all sang in unison, hustling out from under the glare of James Brock Knoll and into the bright lights of the TJ gymnasium to beat the crap out of the hapless 11th graders.

Later, when I looked at the Hall Pass Kirkpatrick had given me, I saw he'd written "Dube, let me sign your yearbook" with a smiley face at the bottom.

I'd bounced back alright. And was bouncing forward. Toward what, I wasn't sure.

Track 13:

LIKE A ROLLING STONE

"Freedom! Hot damn. Dube, man, we're done with high school. We are so fucking outta here."

I wasn't sure whose voice that was in the back seat of Tom Clifton's Dodge Dart. Or was it a chorus of liberated senior-class voices? The reality for us members of the Class of 1965 was that high school was over, period. No more assemblies and mandatory pep rallies; no need for hall passes and gym classes. We were going to the finest schools alright, or at least the ones that had given us the best financial aid packages. For the summer, we were on our own.

That second semester of senior year felt like the last two minutes of an NFL game. Live action, Mach speed, a blur… then timeouts and slowdowns and commercial breaks. High highs and low lows. Then it was over. Mine had opened with that "I tried to off myself" moment with Kirkpatrick followed by his "I'm finished with you" letter. And yet, I'd rebounded. Big time. Part of that had to do with music, and with my fellow seniors relaxing my blackball status. We were all about to jump off the edge of the earth into tomorrow, so why stay pissed at one another? And a lot had to do with getting back with Carla. No matter how hard I tried, I'd never, ever, understand what it was that was so different, mysterious—just plain better—about members of the opposite sex. I just knew it to be gospel.

There were times I wished I had Kirkpatrick's counsel about Carla and the college selection process and my dad's unemployment and the lyrics of The Beatles' "Ticket to Ride" and Dylan's "Like a Rolling Stone" masterpiece. But we kept our distance, even though I had several roles in the Senior Class Revue that he, Will Beale, and Shirley James had written and produced. I figured this extravaganza had been Kirkpatrick's way of cementing his relationship with Will, whatever the hell it was. They'd been working on it since last fall. How Shirley figured into it I wasn't sure, but I relished being on stage and in the spotlight, so I enjoyed what there was to enjoy and forgot about the rest. It seemed strange that I'd had more of a connection with Kirkpatrick last summer when he was away at graduate school. I occasionally re-read the letters he'd written, but I resigned myself that any future relationship was never to be.

That was until he grabbed my yearbook. He didn't hand it back until the following afternoon in Creative Writing class. He'd filled the entire inside front cover with a pitch-perfect reminiscence about adolescence and friendship and growing up and memory and moving on. Music even, saying I had a "ticket to ride" to many college acceptances. He ended it, with typical Kirkpatrick flair, *"So, someday a long time from here, when you open this old yearbook and read these words, remember what it was like once to be young and to dream and to hope and to learn and to be sad and to be joyous – and hold on always to all these memories that we made together. They are just that and things not worth much to anyone but us – but we'll always have them. Thank you. Thank you for being there, Dube. Stay there – for me and you and time. Yours always, W. J. Kirkpatrick."*

I teared up when I read it, believing Kirkpatrick could never be that earnest and intimate, if only in words, with anyone else. No one else at Thomas Jefferson had this kind of tight connection with such a unique, romantic soul. More than one of the kids who signed my yearbook later, including Carla, commented on the space Kirkpatrick had taken up and the power of his words. Jesus, the guy could write.

But special bond or no special bond, I steered clear of him and Will because of what had happened last January. And because of that afternoon when he'd scared the shit out of me with the suicide story. Maybe I was afraid if I got too close to him, he might tell me he'd tried it again? Or maybe I'd catch the suicide bug myself? Was it contagious? I didn't want to find out...

Eventually, Kirkpatrick caught up with me at a cast party after the Senior Revue to say he was sorry and he was wrong and that I was a great kid, blah blah blah. He touched my arm while he talked and hugged me after he'd finished. Carla was watching and she looked, well, kind of nervous. Did she wonder about me and Kirkpatrick because he and I were tight again?

I figured it was only a matter of time before Kirkpatrick would stop by some Saturday or Sunday to have coffee and my mom's cinnamon buns, just like old times. My parents would be happier about that than I would, and they needed a lift since the two of them were caught in my dad's downward employment spiral. They weren't paying much attention to their college-bound son now that he had a girlfriend and friends and disappeared most nights to God knows where before dragging himself in two minutes before curfew. For them having Kirkpatrick back for coffee would be more reassuring than any of the good stuff I was experiencing.

"Freedom! Hot damn!" the voice sounded again, and here I was riding shotgun in a fellow senior's car, hearing that snare drum pop and Bob Dylan asking us how it felt to be on our own. We sang along at the top of our lungs.

It hit me that night, one of the first nights after high school graduation, that this was what the entire summer of 1965 would be like. Driving around endlessly, aimlessly, listening to Dylan, or digging Keith Richards' manic guitar on "Satisfaction," or the Supremes saluting me and Carla with "Back in My Baby's Arms Again." Music, cars, baseball, pranks, smoking, boredom, Carla, and beer, not necessarily in that order.

The best nights were the ones hunkered down in the back seat of my dad's Oldsmobile F-85 with Carla as Terry Lee's "Music for Young Lovers" late-night radio show reminded us how young and innocent we were and how little time we had. Things between us got hotter and heavier, but we stopped short of making love. Maybe we were both a little scared? Too inexperienced? Both? For whatever reason, it didn't seem right to go any further, so we didn't.

Carla was going to keep working as a checkout girl at the local A&P and I was going off to Bethany College. Didn't help our chances that Carla's mom never was in my corner.

She was a very pretty, older version of Carla, and her age had accented her French features, and thickened accent. "Z is not zerious," she would pretend to whisper to Carla, ignoring the fact, or intending, that I could hear her clearly. Never mind that I was seriously in love with her daughter. Or maybe she'd decided I wasn't man enough for her daughter? But I guess her mom knew better than we did that our relationship wouldn't last the summer after graduation.

But what about my renewed relationship with my former soul mate? I thought about that in the car as Dylan reminded us there were frowns on faces and that it was no good letting others get our kicks for us, whatever the hell that meant. Damn, Kirkpatrick had been there for me, even if he'd given me stiff arms last fall and winter. Maybe I'd had it coming. Now that I thought about it, maybe I'd brought about the blackballing too. Not the extent and length of it, maybe, but because I was acting too high and mighty sophomore year just before things came crashing down? Maybe I was beginning to grow up, maturing since I was having such unselfish feelings?

And then a nervous flicker about darkness and suicide. Another line from Dylan, a song about a vagabond rapping at your door. Had I really done nothing to help Kirkpatrick, to save him? Had he expected me to do something risky because I was in on his secret? How many teachers tell their favorite students that they tried to commit suicide? And why? All of that was too much for my *"summertime, summertime/ sum- sum- summertime"* brain to unravel.

Whatever the case, I decided then and there that I would reach out to Kirkpatrick before the 85 days of summer were over and I was off to Bethany. I'd make it a special invite, just the two of us, not a communal thing with my folks around our kitchen table.

"Like a Rolling Stone" reminded me of Kirkpatrick, but it turned out it wasn't just me. I remembered Pete Starr growling one night that "he wasn't where it's at," the hatred in his voice scared me, warning anyone who'd listen that he'd meant those lines for Kirkpatrick. "He took from us everything he could steal," Starr sneered. Puzzling.

Had Kirkpatrick stolen anything from any of us? I thought he'd given me way more than he took, but Pete obviously felt different. And I thought he liked Kirkpatrick.

Come to think of it, I wasn't so sure Carla liked Kirkpatrick either. What about Will Beale? What about the guys I was with tonight in the car?

I started to feel worse that I hadn't talked to Kirkpatrick since that first graduation party, the one where he looked like he was about to cry, after Shirley James's mom had whispered something to him and he left. Maybe he doesn't have any more secrets to conceal after he confessed his suicide attempt…

I decided to call him first thing tomorrow. "It's the least I can do," I said aloud, rehearsing the line I'd use later to explain to Carla and everybody else why I'd sought out my true best friend.

I never made that call. The summer was what it was, a whole lot of beer and cigarettes and music. Next thing I knew I was Carla-less, away at Bethany College, and Kirkpatrick was gone from Thomas Jefferson, back at Ohio University full time. Both of us figuring how it felt to be on our own, with no direction home.

Part Two:

RHYTHM

"Music is your own experience, your thoughts, your wisdom. If you don't live it, it won't come out of your horn."

Charlie Parker

Tracks 14-15:

THAT'S THE WAY IT'S GONNA BE; YESTERDAY

My arrival at Bethany College in September 1965 triggered an avalanche of firsts. First night without any parental oversight, first keg party, first hangover, first all-nighter, first homecoming, first protest, first (near) conjugal bliss, first campus campaign and election… Classes, conversations, and confessions. Girls blossoming into women; boys being boys. Losing religion, purchasing condoms. Conjugating verbs, cutting classes. Giving the grown-up world the finger, keeping my other fingers crossed for luck with girls, grades, and (not) going off to war.

And, always, music.

A couple of hours after my folks deposited me and my things at Cochran Hall that September Saturday in 1965, I attended my first folk music concert. The Mitchell Trio—three guys named Mike, Joe, and John—at Bethany's Rhine Field House. As I watched and listened to their soft guitars, sweet harmonies, and disturbing words, I found myself fixated on their warnings about war and peace, government and race.

One of their songs, "That's the Way It Is," asked whether the good times were gone. I hoped mine were just beginning. Would music help us keep our heads high, guide us through all that was coming at us like a wildfire raging out-of-control?

In that moment, I realized that my main man Porky Chedwick and his Doo-Wop oldies on WAMO, along with my sock hop DJ-ing and ladies' choice slow dancing to sentimental ballads like "High on a Hill," were behind me, relics of my high school past.

I had a clean slate. No blackballing. No Carla.

No more Kirkpatrick. Though that would take a while longer.

For now, it was time to *sing my song to the sky* as three guys named Mike, Joe, and John were advising me.

* * *

My other notable firsts were my first semester of honest-to-goodness college classes and my first-ever non-relative roommate.

"Hi, I'm Doc," a tall, lanky, young man with a firm handshake and slight Southern drawl introduced himself. We were standing in the doorway of a tiny room on the second floor of Cochran Hall. Mason "Doc" Neville hailed from the great state of West Virginia. He'd gotten his nickname because he was going to be a doctor like his father and grandfather.

Doc seemed more worldly and self-assured than the rest of us freshmen. He'd already unpacked, laid claim to the bottom bunk, and was preparing to head off to the student union with a group of guys from the floor. As we exchanged banalities, I decided we didn't have a whole lot in common—his pedigree, course selections, and taste in music for starters. Still, I hoped for the best, or at least not the worst, since the two of us would be sharing a cubbyhole cramped with the bunk bed, two beat-up desks, a dresser, and a radiator.

Given my economic status and loan/tuition commitments, my first semester was shaping up to be beyond daunting. Besides the 6:30 a.m. three-mornings-a-week dishwasher job in the women's dining room, I was taking 15 rigorous credits, including three Saturday classes. No other freshmen in Cochran Hall had more than one Saturday class, but I had Chemistry at 8, French at 9, and British Studies at 10. How in the hell was I going to have any kind of social life?

The remaining bit of my time was consumed with my dream of playing college basketball. I hung around Bethany b-ball practices and shoot arounds, trying to get the coach, a no-nonsense bowling ball of a guy named Edward Martine, to add me to the team since college freshman at this low level of college of basketball—Lew Alcindors we were not—were eligible to play all four years.

The newfound freedom mixed with occasional homesickness, loads of good-looking girls and coat-and-tie professors, and 3.2 beer and fraternity rush parties…all going by "like a bat-out-of-hell" as my brother Ron would've described it. At times the speed left me teetering, holding on for dear life to a desk or a book or discarded dormitory dish, or a song—Dylan, the Beatles, and, thanks to the Mitchell Trio's concert, a little more folk via Joan Baez and Peter, Paul, and Mary. Their takes on "Farewell Angelina" and "Early Mornin' Rain" expanded my repertoire and helped me to keep on keeping on.

And then there were the letters from my one and only long-time, if erratic, supporter now at Ohio University full-time, one W. J. Kirkpatrick. He was employing a variety of pennames ("Sir William," "Sandy," and "the Campus Wit") in his twice-a-week missives. When the first one arrived, I was so damn homesick I nearly cried.

"*I require nothing of you except the quest for some kind of eternity,*" he wrote in his second letter dated September 12. "*I need a forever.*" I figured from the way he wrote it that I was his *forever*, but why me and what did that even mean? Of course, he also wrote at length about his classes and professors and all the grad school rigor. But it seemed to me he was spending too much time with the TJ kids who were freshmen at Ohio U—Nancy Travis, Les Willinger, Ronnie Severino, and Dee Burnett—which struck me as kinda ass backwards since he disparaged TJ up and down in his letters.

Maybe I was just envious of the Kirkpatrick attention they were getting.

Before I could figure anything out, he went back down that dark hole he'd been in the year before when he'd contemplated suicide. His favorite group, the Beatles, were topping the charts with "Yesterday," which sure seemed to be where Kirkpatrick's head was at, even if he'd argue otherwise. Hell, he wasn't half the man he used to be, and he definitely had a huge shadow hanging over him.

"*I have just passed through the emotional crisis of my life,*" he wrote, "*brought on by the conglomeration of three years of sadness and disgust...the man you once knew is dead.*"

Had TJ really killed him? No more Kirkpatrick? Maybe that's where the pseudonyms came from? All I could think was that the guy was losing it, and my feeble 18-year-old heart wasn't up to dealing with it. I had my own trials and tribulations, albeit more pedestrian, and while I tried in my letters to cheer him up, I couldn't invest too deeply. After all, this was the same damn guy who'd battered my heart two or three times in the past year. I had to focus on my college experience, not his. I felt bad—he was obviously careening out of control—but what could I do? I started to sense a distance in the letters, one far greater than the less than 200 miles that separated Athens, Ohio, and Bethany, West Virginia.

* * *

The more I got my bearings in the dorm and the classroom and fraternity rush parties, the less sure of himself Kirkpatrick sounded. *"I will be damned disappointed if I reach 40,"* he wrote on October 12. *"The past three years mean nothing to me, they were wasted... You were the most constant source of inspiration to me and although my ship was wrecked, you kept my eye on the star."*

How do you respond to that?

I didn't. Which explains the letter I got on October 24, 1965.

"I'm curious as to whether I'll ever hear from you again," Kirkpatrick worried. *"Could this be the end? I hope not. The decision is yours."*

"Now I long for yesterday" is what I kept thinking. Even with our ups and downs, we'd had some good times at TJ. Hell, we laughed. A lot. But now? I was feeling as if we'd switched roles...I was the one counseling him to keep his chin up, not to give up, to persevere. An 18-year-old doing that for an almost 25-year-old was backwards. But what helpful life advice could I give him? It wasn't like I'd figured anything out.

I saw him briefly at Thanksgiving. It was beyond awkward. As much as Kirkpatrick adored my parents—proclaiming in one of his Bethany letters *"Of all the parents I met in three dastardly years, they were the only <u>real</u> people, meaning the only unpretentious people"*—he refused to set foot in our house. If he needed a place to hide away, wasn't it here, tonight, with me and my folks?

We stood outside at the top of our driveway on a cold November night, a light snow falling, leaning against his car. He talked over and over about how unhappy he was.

"Dube, I don't know what to say," he kept repeating. And he looked like shit—he hadn't cut his hair since he'd left TJ so it was curling and sprouting all over. He smoked the whole time, sometimes lighting a Winston from the one in his mouth. His voice was robotic. No energy. No enthusiasm. No nothing.

"Dube, I don't know what to say."

Neither did I.

Track 16:

GOOD LOVIN'

"Why don't you do a radio show?" my roommate Doc asked me point blank in early February. We'd survived our first semester, and Doc, a card-carrying electronics geek, was spending time as a studio engineer at WVBC (**W**est **V**irginia **B**ethany **C**ollege), our brand-new campus radio station that had just gone live.

"Come again?"

"You like music—you're always humming some tune or listening to some album—and you've got pretty good taste…"

Doc's questioning made me realize that my old habit of singing along to the songs on the radio must have followed me to college. I'm not sure why I did it, but knowing all the words to all the songs made me feel like I was in control of the stories. I knew all about the people on "The Last Train to Clarksville" and what would happen in the "Five O'clock World," and who Nancy Sinatra's boots were walking on.

"Are you with me? What do you think?"

"Me, a radio DJ? I don't think so?"

"Au contraire," he grinned. "I've got the perfect slot for—you—Monday and Wednesday afternoons from 3-5. And just so you'll be calm and more relaxed, I'll serve as your studio engineer."

Doc had obviously planned this whole thing out. He smiled even more broadly, before adding, "And I can pair you with Kenny Miller."

I knew Kenny from TJ where he'd graduated two years ahead of me. He was smooth and cool and struck me as mature and sure of himself. I was preparing my rebuttal when Doc interrupted.

"In fact, Kenny requested you personally to be his co-DJ," he smiled. "So, it's a deal then?"

I'm not sure why I didn't say no, or at the very least ask more questions. My second semester course load included a whopping 19 credits, so how in the hell could I devote four hours to a college radio show? On top of that, I was president of my Alpha Sigma Phi pledge class, still had the scholarship work commitment—at least waitering in the men's dorm turned out to be better than dishwashing in the girls dorm—and continued to hang around the basketball program.

Not to mention I was head over heels for a bright, popular, and likely unattainable, sophomore, Penny Pratt. Notice I said unattainable. As the only freshman in a rigorous British Studies lit class, I was lucky enough to have the alluring Miss Pratt sitting next to me. But, alas, even though she smiled so sweetly and laughed at my jokes and even studied with me once in a while, Penny was going out with a junior tennis player from a much cooler fraternity. Why even harbor hopes? Or go on the stupid radio for that matter?

Maybe Doc knew how to appeal to my ego. For sure, Kenny Miller was one of the more established guys on the Bethany campus and everybody liked him. But the kicker to my agreeing to do the show was the hope that Penny would listen, and I'd dedicate a song to her some afternoon and she'd fall in love with me. What were her favorite songs? I'd sure as hell try to find out. Maybe Marvin Gaye, or the Beatles, or the Mamas and the Papas held the secret to her heart.

So, with motives behind the music—and taking a page out of the Porky Chedwick oldies concert labels—the "Bradley-Miller Groove Spectacular" was born in late February 1966...

* * *

Meanwhile, back at the *Ballad of the Sad Café,* several unanswered Kirkpatrick letters were gathering dust on my desk. Every time I picked one up and started reading, I'd come across a line like *"I'm just glad I used to be sane and was able to help you when you asked"* or *"And the clock unwinds and I unwind with it."* The poor guy was spiraling out of control, but I couldn't help him, didn't want to help him, because, well, it would just take too much damn energy. I guess that's why I blew him off at Christmas—all the TJ kids were back home from their respective schools with upbeat college stories, so the last thing I wanted was to have to deal with a huge lump of coal name of Bill Kirkpatrick.

Of course, my mom would miss having him around. My dad was spending most of this time back east trying like hell to get a job, and Ron and I were both away at college, so little Lucy Bradley was definitely lonely.

"Don't you ever hear from Kirkpatrick?" she asked me just about every day over Christmas vacation. Ron would shake his head and roll his eyes, but I'd explain that Kirkpatrick had stayed at Ohio U. so he could complete his Masters and start on his Ph.D. Tossing around higher ed terms would sometimes throw Mom off the scent, but she was relentless. Finally, I promised to call Kirkpatrick's home, only to have her stand next to me at the kitchen phone while I surreptitiously held down the receiver so she wouldn't know that the alleged conversation I was having with Kirkpatrick's sister was phony.

"Can't you call him at Ohio U? You have his address, don't you?" she paused, looking a little frightened. "I'm worried about him."

I hated to do it, but I lied and told her I'd lost his address. Maybe she was right to be scared about him. Maybe I was worried too. But I had my own college thing to get together, so I headed back to Bethany without so much as a by your leave.

Kirkpatrick's letters were where I'd left them. A few more trickled in over the winter. But I would never write, nor receive, another letter from W. J. Kirkpatrick the rest of my days at Bethany.

* * *

The "Bradley-Miller Groove Spectacular" played Motown, James Brown, and British hard rockers, no Frank Sinatra or white bread stuff like Paul Revere or Gary Lewis and the Playboys. With Doc in the engineer's booth and Kenny's smooth DJ banter, the show was in the groove alright, with a lot of requests and dedications.

What song would win the heart of Miss Penny Pratt?

With final exams approaching, we'd be going off the air pretty soon, so I was hearing a clock ticking loudly. Maybe that's why "Good Lovin'" by the Young Rascals was such a welcome relief. I had the fever, alright, and Penny had the cure. Kenny and I played the heck out of that song, show after show, hour after hour, that entire spring. The lyrics didn't make much sense, but the song was so catchy it didn't matter. "Good Lovin'" was the song Bethany students requested most that 1966 spring.

Was it too risqué to dedicate to Penny Pratt? Maybe. Would "Did You Ever Have to Make Up Your Mind?" by the Spoonful do the trick? Nah, that was pushing the point. If Penny was forced to choose between me and her Beta boyfriend, she sure as hell wouldn't choose me.

When my moment of truth arrived, I choked. Kenny was kind enough to set me up—I'd confided in him about my Penny infatuation—so one afternoon in May he leaned into the microphone and smiled. "My fellow top jock, Mr. Bradley, has a very special song he wants to dedicate to a very special someone. All I'll say is, are you ladies at the Zeta house listening?"

The clock was running and the turntable was turning and Doc was drumming his fingers and Kenny and our listeners were waiting. Dead time on a student radio station was a no-no. In my panic, my R&B roots took hold of me, and I hollered into the microphone—"Sending out the latest hit record by the very popular group the Contours to all the girls at Zeta Tau Alpha. 'Can You Do It!'"

Kenny burst into laughter—his mic was off—and Doc shook his head as he quickly found "Can You Do It" in our stack of possible tunes to play. Had I just asked all the girls in the Zeta Tau Alpha sorority, Miss Pratt among them, if they could *do it*? Holy Edward R. Murrow! My radio career was over, and with it any minute chance of winning the heart of Penny Pratt.

"Well," Kenny flashed a condescending grin. "You should have stuck with the Rascals. For sure you've got the fever, but you ain't got the cure."

Doc guffawed in the control room. They were probably in stitches at the Zeta house too.

Track 17:

TRACKS OF MY TEARS

My parents moved back east at the beginning of my sophomore year. Since I'd yet to set foot in their new apartment in the Philly suburbs—and with Pleasant Hills and Pittsburgh now just place names on a map—Bethany was home. What really made it home was music. I'd brought along a bunch of my old albums—*Going to a Go-Go, Help!, The Beach Boys Today, The Temptations Sing Smokey,* some Moonglows and Flamingos Doo-Wop—and they became my havens when I needed to smile, reflect, and remember.

I'd been assigned to an upper-class dorm that fall, but I spent most of my time at the Beta Theta Pi house where something always seemed to be happening. Pool. Cigarettes. Beer. Girls. Singing. Fall Greek rush was on, and it was hard to believe that just a year ago I'd been elected president of my Alpha Sigma Phi pledge class, only to de-pledge and sign on that spring with the much cooler Betas. A dangerous move on a small campus. But, like the Miracles said, I was going to a go-go. Some of the Alpha Sigs hated me for bolting, and it seemed like everybody on campus knew what I'd done. I couldn't tell if that was good for my reputation or not.

I was still a waiter in the men's dining room, still harboring hoop dreams, still lusting after Penny Pratt…still a virgin. For some strange reason, I'd decided to be a Chemistry major like my brother Ron, so I was saddled with five hours of Organic Chem, including two three-hour labs a week, not to mention nerve-wracking Calculus and Stoichiometry. My head was spinning, and my grades were dropping faster than a Wright Brothers airplane.

The Bradley-Miller Groove Spectacular was no more, but I was helping with WVBC broadcasts of the Bethany football games, meaning I got to travel with the team to away games in exotic places like University Heights, Ohio (John Carroll U.) and Greenville PA (Thiel College). Not exactly the big time, but the team went undefeated and won the President's Athletic Conference championship.

The beat went on, accelerating. I started writing a weekly music column, "Wax Stax," for the campus newspaper, represented my dorm on the campus's social committee, and joined the staff of CLEW, Christian Living Emphasis Week, mainly because Penny Pratt was the president. Oh, yeah, and drank too much beer. Way too much, even if it was watered-down 3.2 beer. I was making up for the freshman 15 pounds my last year's body hadn't amassed.

"Wax Stax," my weekly column about the mind-blowing music of 1966, became my respite from the overwork. Ranking the tunes every week gave me a type of pied piper power, as if I was some kind of goddamn Dick Clark. But my list was better than his—"96 Tears," "Cherry, Cherry," "Black is Black." No "Cherish" or Petula Clark songs on my hit parade.

The downside was that my heightened musical acumen got me worked up about what the Social Committee was, or wasn't, doing. The committee chair called the shots and was usually some tone-deaf sleeper from an unhip dorm who'd been on the committee the longest. These guys offloaded all the Bethany concert choices, booking, promotion, and the rest to a mediocre talent agency in Pittsburgh that sent us rejects like the Critters, who I'd seen—for free—at a party in New Jersey. Hell, if little Washington & Jefferson College up the road was hosting Miss Dionne Warwick, why not us?

I started to ask pointed questions at committee meetings. Some of the fraternity and sorority reps agreed with my critique. Turns out my old radio partner Kenny Miller had spent some time on the Social Committee and had likewise left frustrated. No sooner than you could say "I'm a Believer," the college announced a campus-wide election for social chairs. Kenny and I teamed up on one ticket; the other included my friend and Alpha Sig pledge comrade Bill Jarman and another upper classman named Miller.

Too many Millers for one election, but what the hell?

There wasn't much campaigning. All Kenny and I did was repeat our lone campaign pledge—if elected, we would bring the Miracles to Bethany. A promise. A guarantee. Cross our hearts and hope to die, which we might have to do if we reneged.

I remembered the Miracles records among those on our tiny RCA turntable, stacked under Ron's favorites, Sam Cooke and Jackie Wilson. The Miracles were my guys.

Smokey Robinson's voice was at times happy, warm, and friendly, at other times yearning and just a bit sad. I felt better when I listened to "Shop Around," "Bad Girl," and "Got a Job."

My crush on the Miracles grew when they became Smokey & the Miracles—"What's So Good about Goodbye," "You've Really Got a Hold on Me," "Mickey's Monkey," and more. They'd helped get me through TJ, cemented my relationship with Carla, and provided a fallback when I DJ-ed mixers and sock hops. No better numbers for a ladies' choice than "Ooh Baby Baby" and "Tracks of My Tears."

Our campaign pledge probably won us the early February election. Senior Ken Miller and sophomore Doug Bradley were the first campus-wide elected social chairs in the history of Bethany College.

And then it actually hit me.

"Kenny," I asked warily after our victory, "how in the hell are we going to get Smokey and the Miracles to come to Bethany."

"*Take a good look at my face,*" he tried to mimic Smokey. "*If you look closer…*" Then he gave my shoulder a pat and smiled. "It's a done deal."

* * *

"*Alright, is everybody ready?*" William "Smokey" Robinson, Jr., was shouting the intro line from "Mickey's Monkey." But he wasn't delivering it to a gymnasium full of Bethany College kids. No, he was talking to me and his three fellow Miracles—Ronnie White, Bobby Rogers, and Pete Moore—as the four of us squared off for a game of two-on-two basketball.

Shooting hoops close to midnight with my all-time favorite group on March 5, 1967, in tiny, remote Bethany, West Virginia? How was that even possible?

Kenny never did reveal the secret of how he pulled it off, but on that Sunday evening, he and I took a limo from Bethany to the hotel in Pittsburgh where the Miracles were staying. Kenny would transport Smokey and the Miracles in the limo to Bethany, while I'd drive down in a van with guitarist Marv Tarplin and the rest of the band. It was going to be a very, very long night, but I was ready to do anything to shake hands with Smokey, Bobby, Ronnie, and Pete. And shake hands I did, in the lobby of the Omni William Penn Hotel in downtown Pittsburgh, watching Smokey smartly remove his gloves and grasp my outstretched hand. His was soft and warm.

"Hi, I'm Smokey," he said in his sweet voice, and that was that.

Smokey and the Miracles sang all their biggest hits that night, bringing coeds to tears with extended versions of "Ooh Baby Baby" and "Tracks of My Tears," and premiering "The Love I Saw in You Was Just a Mirage." Maybe not the greatest Miracles' song, but it has a special place in my heart because that's the first time I ever heard it.

The guys—Claudette Rogers-Robinson wasn't with them that night—decided to do one long set rather than two shorter ones with an intermission, so the show wrapped up just before 11 instead of midnight. Their dressing room was the boys' locker room, so after the crowd cleared out, Kenny and I waited for them on the bleachers as they changed clothes. I watched as they walked slowly, single file, toward us across the gym floor that just minutes ago had been filled with a thousand adoring fans. They still looked damn good, even without the sequins and sparkles of their stage outfits. Marv Tarplin and the rest of the band seemed eager to make an early exodus and quickly packed up their equipment.

A basketball backboard and hoop were stationed behind and above the bleachers where Kenny and I were sitting. I noticed Pete and Bobby glancing up at the hoop as they headed in our direction. By the time they reached us, Pete spoke up: "Man, I would love to play some ball right now. I haven't shot any hoops for a long time." I thought he was joking, but when I saw Bobby and Ronnie nodding their heads, I turned toward Kenny and Smokey to see what they thought. Smokey waved at us.

"Go ahead and knock yourself out," he laughed. "I'm gonna sit right down and write myself a letter."

He sat down next to Kenny who wasn't eager to join in. Thrilled by the prospect, regardless of what time it was, I raced to the locker room and came back with a new Wilson basketball. We collapsed that section of the bleachers, displacing Smokey and Kenny, and squared off. Pete and me against Ronnie and Bobby.

"Alright, is everybody ready?" Smokey sing-songed and the match was on.

Our dress shoes sounded out of place on the hardwood floor, and we slipped and slid a little too much. But inner-city playground basketball genes eventually took over, and the next thing I knew we were all in t-shirts, sweating, dribbling, shooting, hustling, and talking trash.

We played games to seven by ones and split two games. Bobby was taller than the rest of us and was killing me and Pete on the boards, tipping in missed shots and grabbing rebounds. As we geared up for the rubber match, Smokey's voice, not as lilting and sweet as before, rumbled across the gym.

"Game over. Time to head back."

We dutifully retrieved our shirts and jackets and began to head out. I looked behind to see Bobby waving at me to throw him the basketball.

"You gotta make your last shot," he smiled as he caught my pass and banked in a short jumper.

"Ooo, baby!" I shouted. They all shook their heads and smiled. I swished a layup myself for good measure.

With Marv, the band, and the van long gone, I caught a ride back to the Omni William Penn Hotel in the limo with my idols. It was way past midnight, and no one spoke as we listened to a gospel music tape playing on a cassette deck. As I took in those soulful hymns, it dawned on me where all those "*ooo babys*" came from…church! The place that Smokey, Pete, Bobby, and Ronnie called home

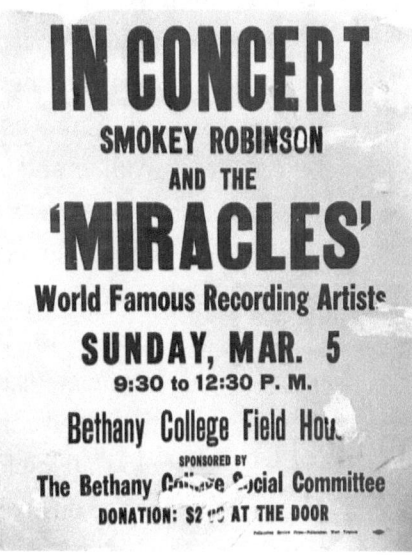

Track 18:

COME SEE ABOUT JUNIOR

Tonight, September 25, 1967, was the night. My coming out party as Bethany College social chair*man*. Singular, because my co-chair and partner-in-crime, Kenny Miller, had exited stage left swiftly and abruptly. He'd let me know that during a long phone conversation over the summer, but all I could concentrate on now was making sure that everything was set for Junior Walker and his All Stars.

Last year's booking accomplishments had been more Kenny's than mine thanks to his numerous contacts, savvy negotiations, and contract acumen. Now all the follow-through rested on my bony, 20-year-old shoulders, beginning tonight with Junior Walker and the All Stars kicking off a fall schedule that included Count Basie, the Jefferson Airplane, Ian and Sylvia…not to mention having to deal with the insufferable agent of Miss Dionne Warwick, who'd already canceled two Bethany concert dates.

If I screwed up tonight, I was in big trouble. That was a lot of pressure for a white kid from Pennsylvania and a black saxophone player from Arkansas. Junior didn't know what he didn't know. I knew what I knew, and it gave me butterflies in my stomach the size of footballs.

Luckily, a couple of my fraternity brothers and a few folks from the Social Committee had stepped up to help out with posters, publicity, and tickets for non-Bethanians. The old Rine Field House sparkled in the dimmed floodlights. Sound and lighting had been a major cause for concern going into this evening, and I still wasn't happy with the equipment we'd rented. But somebody said there was a huge limo and a big bus pulling up outside the Field House, so off I went…

* * *

My current anxiety notwithstanding, it was good to be back on the Bethany campus where I was known, liked, and respected, where I was somebody. I'd felt anonymous and out of place the past summer in the Philly suburbs where my parents were struggling day-to-day. I'd worked 50 hours a week in the blistering heat at a low-paying construction job. At summer's end, my dad landed a job with the U. S. Post Office so at least his paychecks wouldn't bounce. But living again with the two of them in a tiny apartment was less than ideal. The only person I knew my age who lived nearby was my cousin Steve, but he was spending as much time as possible down at the New Jersey shore water skiing and chasing girls.

What made matters even more unsettling was my brother's wedding that August. I was anxious about my best man speech which I wanted to be pitch perfect for my big brother Ron and his fiancée Carol. I was kinda nervous, too, about how my folks would conduct themselves at a fancy wedding in Forest Hills, New York—Carol was based there as a United Airlines stewardess—especially after the possibility we'd get stuck in the Holland Tunnel or lost trying to cross the wrong Big Apple bridge.

Or maybe I was just being anxious to be anxious?

I would've asked for Kirkpatrick's advice all that summer, but for all I knew he was communing with Percy Shelley in merry old England…or who knew where? Maybe he was dead even? So, I spent the summer rehearsing my best man lines multiple times daily at my crummy job. And paying more attention to the war in Vietnam which was inching closer and closer. Jesus, where *was* Kirkpatrick when I needed him?

Upping the Vietnam ante that year was an aptitude test known as the **Selective Service Qualification Test**, or the "Sending Your Ass to Vietnam Exam" as we called it. While we Bethany men, along with millions of our peers at colleges and universities across the country, cherished our very own get-out-of-jail-free card—a **2-S** draft deferment for postsecondary education—the war in Vietnam was escalating, and the U.S. Army needed more recruits.

Lots.

Guys with connections like Kenny Miller were joining the Reserves or National Guard, so it was a pretty good bet that LBJ wouldn't ask them to fight in Vietnam. To meet their monthly quotas, the U.S. military began to draw from two other pools: inner-city kids with shaky qualifications and college guys like me. If my Bethany buddies and I were going to keep our student deferments, we'd have to achieve a certain class rank, or else pass the Vietnam exam. If you didn't score well, your ass could be drafted.

My academic standing hadn't been helped by my brief stint as a Chemistry major. I'd struggled to make a C average first semester sophomore year. And while I immediately bolted the sciences for safer academic ground—English—which helped improve my grades and class rank, I still had to take the goddamn test.

It was early on a damp April morning, just a few weeks after the Smokey & the Miracles concert. We were huddled in masses, almost like we were already in the Army, except for the beards, mustaches, sideburns, and slovenly dress.

"Piece of cake," I heard Stan Vincent, one of the guys ahead of me in line shout. "Nobody's gonna have any problem passing this thing. Hell, you could take it with your eyes closed."

Heads nodded from the guys who were half awake. I buttoned the top button on my Pea coat and tried not to listen. I bummed a cigarette off Bob Runkle—was this my last smoke?—and tried to focus. I was NOT going to sleep through this test or treat it like a joke.

"Get out of town," I heard a shout from behind me. I turned to see a couple guys jump back from a big dude in a Sigma Nu sweatshirt puking his guts out. "Gross," came the shouts and catcalls. The puker clamped down on the ground and shivered.

As we made our way into the building, I overheard two guys talking as if they were in a Philosophy class.

"This is a Christian school, isn't it?" the taller of the two bearded guys asked the other.

"Damn straight, son. Bethany was founded by the Disciples of Christ."

"Amen, brother," the tall guy smiled. "So, our professors will do the Christian thing about this, won't they?"

"Whaddya mean?"

"I mean, if they hold our futures in their hands, can't we count on them to do the right thing, professionally and spiritually?"

"Huh?" his friend wondered. Like me, I think he'd decided it was too early in the morning for such a heavy conversation. But the tall guy was relentless.

"It's a misuse of their role," he went on. "Maybe they'll stop giving grades...or refuse to reveal our class rank." He paused and smiled. "Or maybe they'll just give all of us straight A's."

"Straight A's for everybody," the Sigma Nu sweatshirt guy croaked from his perch on the ground. Everybody cheered.

I kept my head down and my thoughts to myself. The whole thing struck me as unfair, designed to set us up against one another. What about the guys who were already doing the fighting and dying? How fair was that?

* * *

I held my breath as the limo came to a stop in the fading fall light. My approach to the front door seemed to take forever, but just as I was prepared to knock, it opened and out stepped a beaming, gap-toothed black man in a shiny pink suit.

"You must be Bradley." His voice reminded me of the gravel in the parking lot. "And I'm guessin' you know who I am." I extended my hand, but Junior came in for a hug.

He sure seemed pleased to see me, which immediately helped me relax. As if we were old friends, Junior Walker and I drifted through the Field House and backstage to attend to the final preparations. The bleachers were pulled back and stacked, the basketball hoops cranked up into the ceiling, so all you could see was the sparkling gymnasium floor filling with eager college students and a few locals.

At 8 p.m. sharp the Field House lights dimmed, the spotlights came on, and I strode across the stage to the microphone. I'd rehearsed my introduction for several days, so I had it down pat. I mentioned Junior's hits, his unique sound, and his status as Motown royalty. Even referenced his hardscrabble Arkansas life where he was born Autry DeWalt Mixon, Junior.

Smiling his toothy smile, the saxophonist-singer, looking like a proud flamingo in his pink suit, led his "All Stars" and a couple foxy female backup singers, in a rousing version of "Shotgun." The crowd erupted and my relief was palpable. Maybe this social chairman thing was going to work out after all.

Our contract called for Junior Walker and the All Stars to perform for no more than two hours total in two separate sets, with a short break in between. But Junior was having so much fun that he didn't take a break until almost 9:30 when he giddily announced he had to take a leak. This cat was too much.

I probably should have been paying more attention to the technical details since we'd jerry-rigged the rented sound and light system into the Field House switch box. The Brainiac technician types on the Social Committee, the guys we cool frat boys branded as losers since they still lived in dorms, guaranteed their solution would hold up for the night.

But none of us had anticipated Mother Nature. Just as a very sweaty Junior Walker and his hard-working band returned to the stage for their second set, a furious thunderstorm erupted. Rain pelted the windows and hammered the roof, and no sooner had Junior stepped up to the microphone and sang: "*Money, who needs it/let me live my life free and easy...*" than the entire building went dark.

Even when the dim emergency lights came on, you still couldn't see a damn thing. My crack team of sound and light experts was clueless, the crowd hot and restless. Barely three weeks into my term as solo social chairman, and I'd left everybody in the dark.

Everybody except Junior.

"I seen worse," he consoled me. "But this baby can still make some noise!" he patted his saxophone. "I got just the thing for this nightclub setting."

Junior stood up and started playing a saxophone solo, a number I later learned was called "Cleo's Mood." The crowd hushed. The show was back, if not visible.

I was hollering at the technical team just as Jim Faust, an officious Bethany senior walked over to the wall panel. "Dr. Faustus" as we used to call him had almost single-handedly launched our student radio station my freshman year, wires and all. He was holding two of the longest, biggest, ugliest, industrial-strength yellow extension cords I'd ever seen. Faust connected them, then slinked them out the door to god knows where, and voila, the lights were on and the sound system worked. The concert was back on.

To mark the occasion, Junior Walker decided to debut what he predicted would be his next big hit record, "Come See About Junior." Suddenly, he was out on the floor, strutting his way through the crowd like a pied piper, saxophone gleaming in his strong hands. "Smiles have all turned to tears," he sang between sax riffs, "but tears won't wash away the fears."

Were those lines meant for me? Maybe. But, hell, a pied piper needs followers, so I caught up to him, placed my hands on his pink–suited hips, Locomotion-style, shimmying this way and that. Pretty much everyone in the audience joined in, forming a Congo line snaking through the Field House.

Moments later, back up on stage, Junior and his All Stars returned to the song they'd been playing when the lights went down—"I'm a Roadrunner." He shouted the last lines forcefully: *"I live the life I love. And I love the life I live."*

Had the unexpected storm and power outage been a sign of things to come? Both on the Bethany campus and beyond? Or just some minor cosmic joke? Junior sure as hell thought it was cool. Holding on to the hips of Autry DeWalt Mixon Junior as he pranced, swayed, and saxophoned his way across the Field House had connected me to something new and electric. Made me forget about the lousy summer, my aging parents, the absent Kirkpatrick…and the looming war in Vietnam.

Even if they all really had a hold on me.

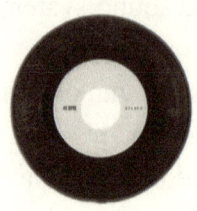

Track 19:

SOMEBODY TO LOVE

The throbbing in my head from my first ever, hard-liquor hangover compliments of Johnny Walker Red fused with a light piano plunk from Count Basie and a blistering riff from a Gibson ES-335 guitar by Jorma Kaukonen of the Jefferson Airplane. Fission or fusion? Whatever it was, it hurt.

I winced as I turned over. Hadn't the Count already performed? Weren't the Airplane about to land? On my aching head maybe? Or was that Junior Walker, not Johnny Walker? Smokey and the Miracles? Concerts and arrangements and payments and contract haggling crashed down on me in thunderous waves…I cradled my head in both arms and turned to the side. Something must've been wrong with my eyes because there was a pretty, blonde woman lying beside me in bed.

Where was I? What was Laura Hall doing here?

What the hell was *I* doing here?

In my haze, I replayed the frantic telephone call I'd received a few minutes earlier from Dean Darlene Richardson searching for Miss Hall who was indeed lying beside me at the Howard Johnson's Motor Lodge in Wheeling, West Virginia. Not exactly why Laura's parents had enrolled her at pious Bethany College.

I was up against a wall, literally and figuratively, this bright October morning. But before I could get out of bed and return Laura to Dean Richardson and fret about that afternoon's Jefferson Airplane concert, I just lay there, paralyzed by memory and music and the nagging fear of failing…

* * *

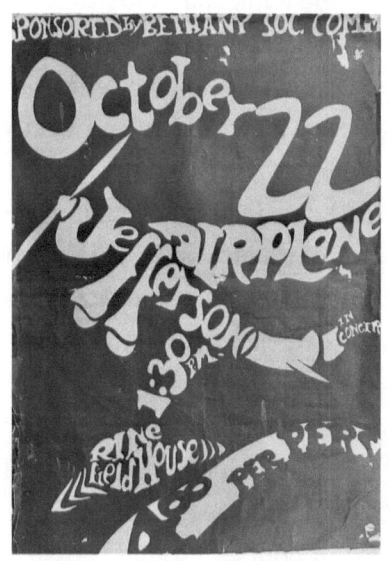

This crazy trip had started on a muddy spring day the previous April at Em's, the nearby watering hole a few miles outside of "dry" Bethany. After several watered-down 3.2 West Virginia beers, it dawned on me that the same song had been playing over and over on the jukebox, and that just about everybody else in the bar was lustily singing along, asking "don't you need somebody to love?"

The pretending-to-be-hip sophomore in me had to be cool, acting like I was into a song I didn't really know, while the co-chair of the college social committee part of me sized up a potential act to bring to campus. How had I missed this? Was I fast asleep in a Motown, R&B fog?

"Jefferson Airplane man," the frat type across the table from me was nodding to the song's rhythm. Name again? Marshall or Carson or something East Coast preppy. I nodded, pretending I knew what he was talking about.

"Don't you think the Airplane's bitchin'?" he shouted in my direction. I smiled and nodded, wondering what in the hell was a Jefferson Airplane.

Didn't matter. As a duly elected campus officer, I needed to pay attention to *this* song, the sound of which was different from what I'd ever heard, even the harder rockin' tunes by the Kinks and the Stones.

"Jefferson fucking Airplane," another drunk student shouted. I decided to take refuge in the men's room before I completely blew my cover. Luckily, my pit stop elicited one John Ballouz. The Bethany refrain about John was that all the women wanted to sleep with him and all the men wanted to be him. We'd recently become Beta Theta Pi fraternity brothers, and I still had the bruises and diarrhea to attest to his choreography of Hell Week. I figured my taking all of it with a smile had scored me some points. Now, John and I were pissing at adjacent urinals, John rambling on about some Zeta Tau Alpha fox he was intent on seducing, while I was reading the graffiti that boasted, "While You're Reading this, I'm pissing on your shoe."

Of course, I looked down.

"Don't you just dig the Airplane," I said to John, hoping he'd help me to get my musical bearings.

"What?" he grunted.

"The Jefferson Airplane, that group, uh, you know, umm, somebody to love?" I hoped I'd gotten it right.

A big grin crossed John's handsome, albeit intoxicated, face. "Fucking *Surrealistic Pillow* is the greatest album ever.

And goddamn Grace Slick, what I wouldn't do for her to sit on my face! White Rabbit man."

Unnerved by the X-rated image, I was more confused than ever. Grace Slick. *Surrealistic Pillow*. Jefferson Airplane. White rabbits? I felt like I was struggling to crack some Nazi World War II code. Exiting the men's room, I turned left instead of right, running square into the jukebox. There it was in black and white: "Somebody to Love" by Jefferson Airplane. Grace Slick must be the lead singer. But what the hell was a *Surrealistic Pillow*? And how had I missed this?

* * *

Next thing I knew it was summer 1967, and I was on the phone with my co-chair Kenny Miller just before Ron's wedding. Kenny had to run down my number from Bethany since my folks had moved back to Philly. While technically a graduate, Kenny was working at Bethany that summer and was planning to be back on campus that fall. Good news for me, of course, since Kenny's contacts and ballsy-ness delivered some of the best musical acts anywhere. No more Critters and third-rate Pittsburgh cover bands anymore.

"Brads," the voice on the other end of the line was friendly and warm, as always. "How's it going back east?"

"Okay. How's summer at Bethany."

"Terrific. Linda and I are having a great time." Kenny was newly married. No wonder he was good at being an adult.

"So, I've got some news," Kenny sounded genuinely excited. "In fact, I've got BIG news!"

Wow, were he and Kathy going to have a baby? "What's so BIG?" I asked.

"As big as an Airplane," Kenny offered, letting the words sink in. "As big as the Jefferson Airplane!"

Holy shit. Kenny rides again. I was speechless.

"Whaddya think?" he asked, not quite fishing for a complement.

"That's pretty damn amazing is what I think. Every college in the world must be working overtime to land them. How'd you do it?"

"Smartness and ubility," came his jocular response. I never understood that saying but he always used it, so I let it go.

"When's the Airplane landing at Bethany?" I asked, trying to be clever.

"Homecoming weekend."

"What about Count Basie?" I was starting to get anxious.

"The Count is Saturday night, off-campus in Wheeling with a bunch of drunken alumni. The Airplane are in Rine Field House on Sunday at 1:30 in the afternoon. Bethany will never be the same."

I let the news sink in, visions of Grace Slick, about whom I'd started fantasizing as soon as I saw the cover of *Surrealistic Pillow*. Kenny was still talking, but I'd stopped listening.

"That'll be a busy weekend for us, that's for sure," I said, coming back to reality.

Silence on the other end of the line.

"Kenny?" I asked, fearing an answer I didn't want to hear.

"That's my other news," his tone was fatherly. "I was in danger of being drafted, so I've enlisted in the Army Reserves. I'll be on active duty this fall. I won't be at Bethany."

Even with my brother's wedding looming that August, I decided then and there that this summer was a complete and utter disaster. My hands shook. Without Kenny, how in the hell was I going to deal with Count Basie and his big-ass orchestra, let alone the mind-blowing Jefferson Airplane?

* * *

Flash forward to that first six weeks of social chairing without Kenny and the Junior Walker concert. I was able to tap into a couple hard-working up-and-comers on the Social Committee to help with the grunt work. Meanwhile, I was spending most of my time on the phone arguing with agents for Dionne Warwick and the Airplane. They'd presumably looked at a map and were less than thrilled about their artists having to appear in the West Virginia sticks. They were looking for a way out. Dean Darlene Richardson, the college's advisor to the Social Committee, was on the calls, too, but I did most of the talking, and shouldered most of the abuse which usually came as a double dose of "we're the big shots" and "my client this and my client that" bullshit. But I had a signed contract in my hands, so the stars were going to have to perform in goddamn Bethany, West Virginia, at some point. At least that's what Bethany's part-time lawyer told me.

In Miss Warwick's case, this would be later rather than sooner—her agency exercised an option to move her scheduled November concert to January. And then to April. The Airplane's representative, some high and mighty New Yorker named Sammy, kept reminding me that the Airplane's psychedelic light show was as important as their music, so that I sure as hell better have it "pitch fucking black"—his words—in the Field House that Sunday afternoon.

Sammy delivered this message to me every other day for four weeks, so by the time Homecoming Weekend came around, I was a wreck, praying for clouds, rain, the return of the dust bowl, or divine intervention. Which was part of why I drank way too much Scotch at the Homecoming Dance, almost knocked over Count Basie's drink, and said "fuck" on the phone when I called my dad to tell him I'd met one of his big band idols.

* * *

Given my state of intoxication and agitation, I'd passed out in my three-piece suit on the motel bed with the lovely young Miss Hall sacked out beside me, her finest prom dress undisturbed. I don't even remember kissing her, which is why Dean Richardson's protestations were so annoying. It wasn't like I'd stolen Laura's virginity. I hadn't removed a single stitch of her clothing.

"Now hear this, Mr. Douglas Bradley," Dean Richardson scolded me. I flashed back to my mom using my full name. Never good news. How in the hell she found out where we were, I'll never know. "You had better get Miss Hall back to campus lickety-split. We will come up with an explanation for her parents, but, believe me, you will suffer the consequences. Do you understand me?"

All I understood was that my head was wedged somewhere between Count Basie's brass and percussion sections. I'd never had a headache remotely like this in my life. And at the same time, I realized I was looking outside where the sun had come up and the sky was a very bright blue.

Fuck me, I said to myself as I hung up the phone and nudged Laura's shoulder. *Suspended from school and sued by a big-deal talent agency, all on the same day.*

* * *

The drive back to Bethany went by too fast. Dan Reed and his date were our chauffeurs. He and Bruce Jones had agreed to help me to "darken" the field house, so we dropped our homecoming dates at Philips Hall and headed directly to meet Bruce who was already on the scene. I'd deal with Dean Darlene later. It was almost ten o'clock, the sun was shining, and I felt like Gary Cooper in *High Noon*. The Miller gang, a.k.a the Jefferson Airplane, would arrive in a matter of hours. I was a dead man.

The three of us worked non-stop, desperately taping dark brown wrapping paper over the Field House windows. No sooner would we finish with one section than we'd have to go back to where we'd started and re-tape, or add more paper. Sisyphus and his rock had nothing on us.

The Field House was adjacent to the football field, and since the coaching staff didn't want a bunch of concert goers hanging out on their turf, they convinced the campus higher ups, without even consulting with me, to open the doors to let the crowd in early. Even though we lowered the house lights, hoping somehow that would make it seem darker inside, the sun was streaming in through the papered windows. Just after one o'clock, a huge bus pulled up beside the Field House. Still in my three-piece suit from the night before, I headed over to welcome the Airplane and capitulate to Sammy's wrath.

Time froze as I watched an assembly of shaggy haired, wildly dressed hippies step off the bus in a cloud of what I later realized was marijuana smoke. I recognized Jack Cassidy from his headband, Marty Balin's youthful face, Paul Kantner and his glasses. Couldn't figure out which one was Spencer Dryden, the drummer, and which was Jorma Kaukonen.

Grace Slick was the last to emerge. I literally staggered when I saw her. Her dark brown hair dropped down forever, and her smile could have melted the Arctic ice cap. She was sleek and slender, wearing a peasant blouse, faded jeans, and moccasins. Erotic, sensual, perfect.

Kantner was the closest to me, so I walked over, introduced myself and shook his hand awkwardly. He looked me up and down and smiled.

"What time is the suit due back?" he teased me while the rest of the group laughed. For a minute I felt like confessing everything, throwing myself at the feet of the court of Jefferson Airplane and begging for mercy.

But before I could say anything, the band had strolled over toward the football field. They were lighting up—cigarettes I hoped—pointing animatedly to the end zone and making touchdown gestures. Grace Slick turned in my direction and headed toward me. My heart sailed over the goal post.

"This is fucking gorgeous. Let's do it out here!" Her voice was sweeter and softer than I expected, and she was the first female I ever heard say "fuck," so I was even more enthralled. But I couldn't say anything. What did she mean by doing it out here? Oh, yeah, the concert.

"Uh, well, um, we can't. I mean I can't, umm, you know, I mean, well, uh, I was told by your agent Sammy that we had to hold it inside and have it really dark so we could get the full effect of your light show."

Jack Cassidy exhaled a pungent cloud and shouted loud enough for everyone to hear.

"Fuck Sammy," he said. "I told you we should've fired that asshole." He came over to me and put his arm around my shoulder. "The goddamn guy messed with this kid's head, made him dress in a suit, and who knows what else. We should be playing this gig right here in the great outdoors. I can't stand that fucking guy."

* * *

Several hours later, watching the Airplane's bus pull away, I waved goodbye as if they were my family leaving home. I was all smiles. People kept coming up to me, kids who didn't even go to Bethany, telling me it was the greatest concert they'd ever seen. The Airplane even did a ten-minute version of "White Rabbit" that put everyone in a psychedelic trance.

My grin was as wide as a West Virginia quarry as I glanced down at an orange "Jefferson Airplane loves you" button Grace Slick had given me. At Kantner's urging, she'd kissed me on the cheek, which I could still feel glowing. At their collective insistence, I had taken a few puffs of what they called a joint in the men's locker room that was making my toes tingle.

This was without question the greatest homecoming in Bethany College history. I stood there smiling, humming the words to a song I'd remembered from the jukebox at Em's last spring. *"When the truth is found to be lies and all the joy within you dies... wouldn't you love somebody to love..."*

Momentarily, I'd found somebody to love, at least for one sunny Sunday afternoon. Rock star and all, the girl singing that song had kissed me. Who gave two damns about the Dean?

Track 20:

DOUBLE SHOT OF MY BABY'S LOVE

Here we go again. Another song playing in the back of my head. But it wasn't one of the tunes that moved me to tears or jumpstarted a reverie. Could trigger a smile. No this undulating rhythm was addictive, seductive, and grudgingly omnipresent. Simultaneously, I was listening to the music, responding, and playing it back. I'd become one with the calliope-like organ and the *dah de dah de dah de dah, de dah dah dah*!

Was I actually singing aloud?

Dah de dah de dah de dah, de dah dah dah!...

Now was I on the dance floor, sweating, swaying, acting oh so cool. Peanut shells and beer—and maybe even a defeated dancer or two—under my shoes. Intoxication beyond the watered-down 3.2 West Virginia beer or the college classes and grunt work in the cafeteria and fall rush and whatever else there was. No, at that moment I was cool, preening on the dance floor, actually able to dance, to move, to capture the beat, to instinctively know where the next step would be—left-right…front to back, reminding myself how great it was to shimmy and slide backwards, catch the eye of the girl behind you in case you got tired of the girl in front of you, the one you were dancing with.

And yet the felling, the music, the chaos was something beyond cool. Dangerous somehow, risky, *"up against the wall mother fucker"*-like. Shit, none of the other dancing boys on the floor of the Jolly Roger in Wellsburg, West Virginia, this particular night could do <u>that</u>. I knew that and felt it. Showed it. The song was on repeat, kept playing. Eventually the lyrics exploded: *"Double shot of my baby's love… Whoa oh oh oh"*

And then another, a real double shot, followed by something about wine and my baby's love. Where was my baby anyway? The song's gyrating organ was there beside me. No, it was actually following me and my steps. The drums and the guitar, too. Had somebody slipped me something? Had I taken a Double Shot of my Baby's Love?

I knew then, at that moment, if I were to give the directive, the order, that my entire generation would do what I said, follow as I'd command—up off the dance floor and onto the factories and the colleges. The streets and state houses…

And who was this? Janey Wells? Sharon Blake? All the coeds from West Liberty College morphed into this one girl, this tight, tiny ass wiggling in front of me. During that one moment when I was king, I was a dancing god. All the fair ladies at the ball were mine. The music would keep going as long as I held the rhythm, as long as we all kept on dancing…

And all the girls, every last one of them—the blondes, brunettes and redheads, Janey and Sharon and Eileen and

Mary Beth and Connie and Emily—all of them would want to dance with me, they all <u>were</u> dancing with me. Yeah it wasn't wine they had too much of, it was a double shot of…

Me?

Power?

The world outside the Jolly Roger didn't resemble the dance floor. The students looked different too…music played but there was no dancing. Even here at tiny, remote West Liberty College, there was anger, heated disagreements. Like at Bethany, all very cordial and polite, but the schism was there, the ground underneath us was shifting, not to the Swinging Medallions and double shot but to rebellion. To race. Sexuality. Now there were deans and presidents and administrators standing in front of us. We needed to talk back to them, needed to disobey them, needed to bring them down.

Lying there on that coed's dorm room floor...Janet? Jean? Bobbi? Was any music playing? Had everything about tonight been just a dream? Had I really got everyone at the Jolly Roger to chant *"Hey, hey, LBJ, how many more did you kill today?"* Did I shed tears for Dr. King? Picture myself standing up to my eventual Army superiors to defy an order?

"You're a terrific dancer," whoever she was purred, pulling down my pants and boxers. Was all that rebellious stuff years away? Whatever would happen, none of it would take place here on this little campus, or mine, or at the Jolly Roger.

What I came to understand that night, the last night of my college innocence, was the fast-approaching disintegration of my generation. Our Oedipal past and future, the World War II heroism of our fathers, the hopes and dreams of our aproned-adorned moms…

The plastic fantastic lover we all were moving toward.

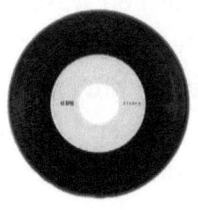

Track 21:

ABRAHAM, MARTIN, AND JOHN

Everybody, and I mean everybody, was listening to "Hey Jude" morning, noon, and night in the fall of 1968. Nothing but "Hey Jude" for weeks and weeks and weeks. I still loved the Beatles, another Kirkpatrick legacy—where in the hell was he these days anyway?—but couldn't we take a breath and listen to another song for once? "Hey Jude" was definitely not what I wanted as the anthem for my senior year. Yeah, there were plenty of sad songs that we had to make better, but it wasn't like the Beatles would be coming to campus. I'd booked Sam and Dave, the Fifth Dimension, and the Association that fall. How about some "Soul Man," "Aquarius/Let the Sunshine In," "Everything That Touches You"?

I was harboring my own musical secret, listening clandestinely to "Abraham, Martin, and John" by the old Doo-Wopper Dion DiMucci. He'd dropped the DiMucci part, and he sure sounded different. Quiet, lyrical, haunting. I'd bought a copy of the single after seeing Dion sing it on the *Smothers*

Brothers Show. It sure as hell wasn't the "Run Around Sue" Dion. And the Kennedys and MLK were dead and the world outside of Bethany was on fire and Vietnam was calling our names. That's how I felt when I listened to "Abraham, Martin, and John," and I didn't want anybody to know it.

Most of the conversations among my fraternity brothers that fall weren't about societal upheavals. The football, cross country, and soccer jocks all wanted to have winning seasons and the basketball players were just beginning workouts so most of the talk centered on whose coach was the biggest asshole and which players weren't pulling their weight. And, of course, who was getting laid.

I'd stopped playing intramural football and had long since abandoned my dream of basketball stardom. Besides, I was too damn busy. Exhausted really, as social chair and president of Beta Theta Pi along with Kalon, the Student Handbook, CLEW, the Interfraternity Council, and all the other organizations I belonged to. Not to mention classes and papers and exams. I didn't have time to reflect on missed opportunities—or consider the question of what would happen after graduation.

"Did you ever sign up?" came the question from my Beta roommate Dennis Fuchs, a bright, fun-loving Jewish kid from Long Island.

"Say what?"

"Brads, man, focus. Did you, or did you not, sign up to take the LSAT like you said you would?"

LSAT? LSAT? Oh, the Law School admission test. "Aye, aye, sir," I mock-saluted in Dennis' direction. "Mission accomplished!"

Dennis smiled. "Speaking of mission, we should go over to Frank's tonight to watch *Mission Impossible*."

"Why not here at the house with the other brothers?"

"Because Frank has grass, and even if you don't smoke, it's funny as hell hanging out with him and his stoned friends. Makes watching the show even crazier than it is. Fun!"

Fun was in short supply these days. I'd been running this "involved in everything" marathon since sophomore year, and it was time to quit. Law school would be more of the same, maybe worse.

Dennis ruffled through papers on his desk. "Where the hell did I put it," he shouted, throwing stuff all over.

"Put what?"

"That postcard we got from LSAT about when and where we're supposed to take the damn test."

"I got one too," I volunteered, "let me look."

Next thing you knew, the two of us were swearing and tossing folders and pens and packs of cigarettes across the room. We made such a racket that Rick Vincent, a barrel-chested New Yorker in the next room, came in to see what was going on.

"Whoa, brothers, take it easy."

"We can't find the fucking postcards about the law school test," I shouted in Rick's direction.

"You mean these," Rick pulled the door to our room closed and there on the back of the door, which we never closed, were the postcards thumbtacked in plain view.

"You two are going to be great fucking lawyers alright," Rick laughed as he strolled out of the room.

* * *

The world beyond the Bethany campus rarely intruded. Sure, we saw it on the news and knew that students on other campuses around the country were protesting, agitating against the war, for civil rights, for freedoms of all kinds. Yet Bethany students were going about their business as if that's what mattered—*their* business. Definitely the case with me and my overcrowded schedule. But not all of us. My old Alpha Sig friend Bill Jarman, who was heading our student government, had been in Chicago that summer on his way back from the National Student Association convention he'd attended in Kansas, and he said Chicago was like a war zone. At one point, he'd asked me to join him, but I was attending the Beta Theta Pi National Convention in Pennsylvania. Lucky for me.

"Brads, it was really scary." Bill looked frightened. "At one point we were marching and singing songs, the next cops were beating the crap out of everybody."

"I saw it on TV but I didn't believe what I was seeing. Were you in danger?"

"Anybody our age with long hair. I was lucky to get out of there alive." He paused, looked into my eyes. "And to think you might've joined me."

And to think, I considered again and again. Bill had taken over my old duties with Christian Living Emphasis Week (CLEW), and he and his Bethany CLEW colleagues chose "Social Involvement" as the theme for this fall's activities. They'd invited a guy named Beverly Asbury from Vanderbilt University to be this year's reverend-in-residence. His girly first name notwithstanding, Reverend Asbury was nothing like the conservative religious speakers we usually hosted for CLEW. Describing himself alternately as an "agnostic Christian" and a "post-Holocaust Christian," Asbury talked to us about civil rights and social injustice—he was a boyhood friend of the recently-assassinated Reverend Martin Luther King, Junior, the "Martin" of my then-favorite song. Reverend King's speeches and appeals to our better angels had resonated with me, only to come tumbling down that April when Bethany was playing host to Dionne Warwick.

During his visit, Reverend Asbury also raised serious questions about the Vietnam War—why we were there, who was the enemy, what were our objectives—sparking a backlash from a number of Bethany students, including many of my fraternity brothers. "That guy was a real jerk, they should get someone better," Bruce Trout was quoted in the campus newspaper, the *Bethany Tower,* while Dick Fitzsimmons sneered sarcastically, "I was glad to see that Mr. Asbury brought his secret service men with him."

Politics? Dissent? On the campus where I'd been a student for nearly four years? Whatever it was, I was captivated, jumping into contentious CLEW discussions, sharing opinions I didn't know I had. I was quoted in the *Tower* article saying, "this was the best CLEW ever…Asbury posed questions about Vietnam and race we couldn't agree on. That shows that Bethany students are becoming more involved."

At least for one week.

Then it was back to business as usual. Beverly Asbury returned to Vanderbilt, I went back to hosting the Fifth Dimension and Association, and Bill Jarman went back to the Alpha Sig house. I heard he'd caught hell for letting two kids from Cleveland who worked with the Student Mobilization Against the War crash in his room. A display table he'd put up with literature about the war got overturned and trashed. Later, he told me that over the Thanksgiving break, he'd visited the New York City offices of a student anti-war group to pick up buttons and bumper stickers.

"When I told them I was a Bethany College student," Bill confided in me later, "they said they'd heard Bethany was a 'hotbed of radicalism.'"

What was happening? Bethany, radical? What *was* radicalism anyway? Maybe that's where Kirkpatrick was heading years ago with his long hair and brooding attitude? I remember him telling us his boy Shelley had been expelled from Oxford for writing an anti-war poem…Would Bill Jarman get kicked out of Bethany? Everything seemed to be getting more and more confusing. Thank God I had music to keep me sane.

"I just looked around and they were gone," I sang to myself in the passenger seat of Dennis's Corvette Stingray as we drove to Washington and Jefferson College to take the LSAT on a dark Saturday in December. "Abraham, Martin, and John" was playing on the radio.

"What did you say?" Dennis asked.

"Just repeating some lines from that song."

"What a downer," Dennis remarked. "I wish they'd play 'Hey Jude.'"

Sonata:
POSTER NOTES

On a cold evening in January 1969, I was theoretically working on a paper about an obscure Robert Frost poem for my English senior seminar. But instead of concentrating on a close reading analysis of "Leaves Compared With Flowers," I was listening to a 16-minute version of an old blues song, "Spoonful" by the British hard rock group Cream, while writing my introductory remarks for my next, my last, concert—tomorrow's performance by the Brooklyn Bridge, whose syrupy ballad, "The Worst That Could Happen," currently topped the charts. I paused for a moment and thought about bringing some attention to that bittersweet occasion, but decided I didn't want to make a Brooklyn Bridge introduction longer than it absolutely had to be.

The poster for the show, taped on the wall of my room in the Beta Theta Pi House, hung alongside copies of the other 19 acts I'd hosted at Bethany in less than two years. That would be over soon, as would my reign as Beta president.

And then? No more music groups to welcome and introduce, no fraternity house to live and party in, no more BMOC. Could graduating from college in 1969, and losing my student draft deferment, be the worst that could happen?

Staring at the posters, I realized each of them, like the Frost poem I was avoiding, had a story to tell. Maybe my introductions to all those concerts were part of the story too? Doesn't every good story deserve a great intro? I lived for those moments, not because I was standing in front of a sold-out audience, but because I was using language and words, my current boring assignment notwithstanding.

And who deserved the credit for that passion? W. J. Kirkpatrick, wherever he might be. Hell, I probably wouldn't be an English major if it wasn't for him.

With "Spoonful" wrapping me in blues riffs, I leafed through my memories of a pick-up basketball game with the Miracles; being overcome by marijuana smoke from one of the aptly named Grass Roots; that peck on the cheek from Grace Slick; Junior Walker's locomotion line; the long ash at the end of Count Basie's cigarette. The anguish in the eyes of Miss Dionne Warwick…

* * *

Dionne Warwick

Thursday, April 4 was about as beautiful a spring day as you could get. Not just here in Bethany, West Virginia, but damn near everywhere. Bright sunshine, light breeze, balmy temps, sky bluer than blue, flowers bursting. "With the coming of spring, I am calm again," Bethany music prof George Hauptfueher quoted Gustav Mahler, and it was true. My Dionne Warwick anxiety was long gone—she'd canceled two previous dates for her Bethany appearance, but today was the day of her concert.

It helped that I had a budding new romance with Carrie Roberts, a spirited sophomore from New Jersey who shared my interests in music, movies, and books. Always smiling and relentlessly happy, long, tall Carrie seemed to glide blissfully across campus above the gossip and grousing. I was smitten. I'd also easily won re-election as Bethany's social chairman and had hand-picked Bob Thornton, a fellow Beta, to be my co-chair.

Spring brought an abundance of engaged Social Committee members who were volunteering to help out, so there was less heavy lifting for me. Life was good, especially a day as fabulous as this. Campus protests, Vietnam atrocities, the rioting and demonstrations going on across the country, none of it intruded on my perfect slice of West Virginia world.

Miss Warwick and her small ensemble—drums, piano, bass, and guitar—were flying into the Wheeling Airport late afternoon from D. C. on a private plane. Cliff Danielson, another Beta fraternity brother and the only guy I knew who was cleared to drive the Bethany College van, agreed to drive the combo to campus while a couple drama majors would join me, Miss Warwick, and her manager in somebody's parents' fancy car. I got a little tired of the drama types interrupting my conversation as they showed off their acting chops. I think I won Miss Warwick over when one of the chatty thespians asked about the best advice she'd ever received, and Miss Warwick acknowledged that Lena Horne had given her the most valuable advice of all.

"'Always be you,' Miss Horne told me, 'You cannot be anyone but you.'" She paused, and, thanks to my dad educating me on 1930s and '40s singers, I explained to the chatterboxes who Lena Horne was. Miss Warwick smiled her approval.

We arrived at Bethany's Rine Field House around 7 p.m. The concert wasn't supposed to start until eight, but the place was already packed. I was having a hard time believing this quiet, graceful lady was one of the finest rock and roll divas of all time. Ever since she'd blown audiences away in Paris in 1963, she'd been renowned for putting on a terrific concert. I guess once she got on stage, a switch flicked and she became…someone else?

I nailed my introduction and was rewarded with a big smile on her face and the small squeeze she gave my fingers when I handed her the microphone. Contractually, she was obliged to give us two 45-minute sets with an intermission, but on the ride from the airport, we'd agreed that she'd do one 90-minute set (encores notwithstanding) so that she and her ensemble could fly back east at a decent hour.

Dionne Warwick looked breathtakingly beautiful that night, her voice radiant and heavenly. She put so much of herself into her hits like "Anyone Who Had a Heart" and "Walk on By" and debuted "Do You Know the Way to San Jose" for us. By the time I was set to approach the microphone to bring Dionne out for one last round of applause, the evening had already become one of the best college concerts of that or any year.

And then our lives changed forever.

As I was making my way back to the stage, Dean of Students Sandercox cut me off. Charlie DeWeese, the Town of Bethany sheriff, a nondescript type whom I'd only ever observed handing out traffic tickets or ogling coeds, accompanied him. The tightness and pain I observed in the Dean's face let me know something had gone wrong, very wrong.

"Martin Luther King's been assassinated," the words jumped out of his mouth. "In Memphis just a few hours ago."

"Holy shit," was all I could say.

"We need to clear the Field House now," commanded Sheriff Charlie.

"But we can't...I mean we shouldn't," I was sputtering. "I promised Miss Warwick that she could sing one last song. Otherwise, it would look like some kind of emergency." I glanced at the Dean for some adult support.

"Mr. Bradley has a point," the Dean offered. "Let's finish the concert as we agreed, let the students find out on their own. We'll proceed as if nothing happened." And then I caught a glimpse of Dionne Warwick standing behind the sheriff, taking in our conversation.

"What's happened?" She was looking straight at me so I felt compelled to respond.

"Dr. King's been shot. He's dead."

I've never seen the life go out of a person so quickly. And then so swiftly return.

"I want to sing," she proclaimed. "I want to sing a tribute to Martin. I want to sing until I can't sing anymore."

The sheriff shook his head decisively. There were maybe a handful of non-Bethany students in the audience, but Sheriff DeWeese was convinced we'd have a riot on our hands any minute. He threw on the house lights and ordered the students to head to the nearest exit. What could have been one of the most poignant musical tributes ever was never to be.

We drove back to the airport in stunned silence and filed into the tiny terminal where the pilots awaited us. Miss Warwick and I stood near the end of the line when one of the pilots came over with a smile on his face.

"Jesus, you'd think you were at a funeral instead of a concert," he admonished us jocularly. "What the hell happened?"

One of my classmates told him the news.

"It's about time somebody shot that S.O.B."

I could not believe what he'd said. I wanted to strangle the guy, but Dionne's drummer lunged for him and…the next thing I knew they were gone. All of them. How Dionne Warwick let that pilot fly her plane back to D.C. is something I'll never understand.

I stayed up all night with a few of my fraternity brothers watching the news on the grainy TV in the Beta Theta Pi parlor. I hated that damn airline pilot, I hated James Earl Ray, the guy the police said killed Dr. King. I hated a lot about America that night. My dreams had turned to dust and blown away. If I'd had a car, I would've jumped in and driven far, far away.

* * *

The side of Cream's *Wheels of Fire* album ended, and I flipped the record to the last side which opened with "Train Time," a great old blues number. The blues? We'd had it that night for sure. Would Dionne have sung about hers if we'd given her the chance?

But the posters reminded me that every one of the concerts was special, beginning with the Miracles, then more Motown with the Contours and Velvelettes. The Fifth Dimension, Ian and Sylvia, the Grass Roots, the Association, Sam and Dave, the Lettermen, the American Breed. Had I really *listened* to all that music, learned from it?

Sonny & Brownie

I knew next to nothing about old-time country blues. Or folk music for that matter. How was it that my social committee co-chair Kenny had entrusted me with these two seemingly ancient black men? I was supporting them, literally, one holding tightly to my arm because of his debilitating limp, the other, blind, clinging to my elbow. I cursed my foul fortune until I heard Mr. Sonny Terry and Mr. Brownie McGhee perform.

And then I cursed myself for not appreciating how damn lucky I was.

We held their concert in the Old Main Auditorium rather than the cavernous Field House. Not much of a crowd and not much of an introduction by me, but Sonny and Brownie couldn't have cared less. From the joyous whoop Sonny emitted between raucous blasts on his harmonica—a "harp" as he informed me—to Brownie's raucous, bottleneck guitar, their songs conjured another world, a blues world…pain, injustice, and survival.

They didn't just talk it. They sang it. They'd lived it.

Small and white as the Bethany audience was that night, at one point we were all on our feet, responding to their call of "*I don't want, no cornbread, peas, black molasses*" with our own "*I don't want, no cornbread, peas, black molasses.*"

And then these two disabled black men came back with "*At suppertime, Lord, Lord, Lord, at suppertime…*"

Is this what country blues does? I'd learned something, but it would take me a while to figure out exactly what.

Josh White, Jr.

"My father was blacklisted," Josh White Jr. told a hushed Bethany audience in the fall of 1967. "He had to leave the country in search of work. He died too young." Then he paused, took a breath, and became bigger, stronger. "The American dream is not always obvious in the way it comes true," he mournfully added. "Sometimes it comes true through nightmares. And from the nightmares, dreams come true that serve to change the world."

Was this a concert or a lecture? A little of both, and a master class in survival. In between renditions of traditional folk tunes like "John Henry" and "Rock Island Line," Josh White, Jr. told us his dad had once been the toast of Greenwich Village's first integrated night club, Cafe-Society, in the 1940s and that he'd wrote his own songs. One of them, "Uncle Sam Says" about racism in the American military, caught the attention of President Roosevelt and his wife Eleanor, making Josh White Senior the first African American musician to perform at a presidential inauguration.

Like Sonny and Brownie's blues, Josh White, Jr.'s folk music rang with inspiration and urgency. Simply because his father had been outspoken about racism and inequality in America, he'd come under the scrutiny of the FBI, eventually leading to an appearance before the House Un-American Activities Committee. Hence the blacklisting.

You could've heard a pin drop that night. A couple weeks later I got a nice note from Charles Ramsey, Mr. White's "personal representative" at Yorktown Talent Associates in New York. In it, he thanked me and the Bethany students for making Josh White Jr., feel so comfortable...

But it was Josh White Jr., making us uncomfortable that warranted the real thanks.

* * *

I wasn't a drum solo fan, even though my brother had been a follower of Sandy Nelson, a big-deal drummer in the late '50s. As I listened to Ginger Baker pounding away on "Toad," the last track on *Wheels of Fire*, I thought about the night I'd heard the Count Basie Band's great drummer, Sonny Payne...

Count Basie and His Band

Kenny Miller had somehow brokered a relationship with the legendary William Morris Agency which represented Count Basie—and the Jefferson Airplane. For the Count and company, the challenge was orchestrating their October 21 performance off campus—at the Glessner Auditorium in Wheeling, West Virginia—where Bethany undergrads would party with older alumni. The motivation behind the change in venue was alcohol—attendees could imbibe in Wheeling but not on the Bethany campus. My fellow students were thrilled by the prospect of inebriation, even though most of them didn't know who Count Basie was. "Is he a real Count?" one asked. But top Bethany administrators weren't as delighted.

"You'd better keep a close eye on things, Mr. Bradley," Dean of Students Sandercox reminded me every time I saw him, which was often. "We will be emissaries to Bethany Alumni and to the greater Wheeling community. You are our chief ambassador. There can be no problems whatsoever. Is that clear?"

"There had better be no hanky panky in Wheeling," Dean of Women Darlene Richardson chimed in. As my go-to administrator for the social committee, she and I conversed daily. Miss Richardson was especially worried about motel parties and sexual hijinks. "We'll never have another homecoming off campus if the students drink too much and spend the evening off, *off*, campus if you get my drift."

"And?" I knew where this was going, but I wanted Dean Darlene to say it.

"And…I'll make sure that every angry Bethany parent has your phone number."

I had to hand it to Dean Richardson, she'd tripped me up with that line.

"You bet your boots," she continued. "I expect every Bethany student back on campus no later than 1 a.m. Sunday morning."

"But do you want your students driving back to campus drunk?" I asked sheepishly.

"Of course not," she said. "That's why they won't be drinking heavily. You and I will see to that at the Glessner Auditorium."

Couldn't we all just have a good time for once? With no extra responsibilities for me?

My other Count Basie distraction had to do with my dad. The Count was one of his all-time, big band heroes, and even though he wouldn't be there to see him, I owed it to my dad to make a good impression and ensure Count Basie and his orchestra were in fact treated like royalty. On those few occasions growing up when I wanted to have a shared moment with my father, I'd pretend to be interested in his Big

Band music even if I didn't quite get what it was that excited him or what exactly Count Basie's Kansas City stomp style was, or how much influence Basie had on the development of swing music.

Even though most Big Bands had gone the way of the dinosaurs, Count Basie and his orchestra were still busy with tours, recordings, television appearances, festivals, Vegas shows, and travel abroad. Now, I wouldn't just meet one of my dad's favorites—I'd skillfully introduce him to a packed auditorium.

Which wasn't quite what happened. By the time I came out from behind the curtain at the Glessner's 8,000 square foot ballroom, I was bombed. One of my fellow Beta Theta Pi brothers had filched a bottle of Johnny Walker Red from a distracted Bethany alum, and, well, it was my first time with Scotch, and let's just say the whiskey won. I was so out of it that I had to default to the "man who needs no introduction" fallback intro since I'd forgotten all the great lines I'd rehearsed.

Johnny Walker's revenge had me heaving my guts out in the men's room much of the evening, thereby missing a playlist that would have had my dad drooling. "Wiggle Woogie," "April in Paris," "Lady Be Good," "The Count Steps In," "Jumpin' at the Woodside." I could never, ever, admit to my dad that I'd missed hearing those classic songs live.

During a long intermission, I stumbled behind the curtain to apologize to the Count, and thank him. He was sitting at the piano, yachting cap slightly askew, a very long cigarette with an even longer ash hanging from it, and the largest glass of booze I'd ever seen. Was he plastered too? I wanted like hell to dab that long ash from his cigarette before he caught fire, but figured that would get me even deeper in dutch.

"Mr. Basie," I smiled and held out my hand. "Sir, it is an honor to meet you and a privilege to have you and your band entertain us tonight." He smiled, removed his cigarette, and took a big sip from the glass, then reached for my hand and gave it the slightest squeeze. His hand was cool, his fingers thin and long. It was the slightest touch.

"You're welcome son," he smiled up at me.

"My father is a huge fan," I blurted. "He sang with a couple big bands in the Army and he always said that yours was the purest sound, the best beat." The Count was still smiling, but he wasn't really listening. Maybe he was lost in an old radio reverie too? Whatever the case, he shook my hand once more, again soft and squishy, and lit another cigarette. Then he leaned over and pinged a couple chords on the piano he was sitting at.

"One O'clock Jump," I volunteered.

"Son, your daddy raised you well," was the blessing Count Basie gave me.

Even though it was nearing 11 p.m. and my dad was probably asleep at home, I had to let him know what happened. I found a pay phone in the auditorium and placed a collect call home.

"Pop, you wouldn't believe it!" I was shouting into the phone.

"Who's this?" I could tell he was teasing me.

"I just shook hands with fucking Count Basie."

Silence on the other end. Maybe he'd heard me say "fuck?" "Dad, did you hear me? I just shook hands with Count Basie!"

"And how was that?" he asked harmlessly.

"Well, it was a handshake. I guess no big deal...But it was the Count. *Your* Count Basie. One of your idols."

I paused, waited. And then I added, "He said you did a good job of raising me."

It seemed to take my dad forever to respond, but when he did, I could tell he was choking up. "Tell him that's the nicest thing anybody has ever said," my dad's voice fell off.

And then I heard the Count playing the piano, the band breaking into "Every Day I Have the Blues."

"Nobody loves me, nobody seems to care," a voice snaked toward me. "worries, trouble, you know I've had my share."

The soloist didn't sound like the famous Joe Williams. He sounded like my father.

* * *

"Sometimes the American Dream comes true through nightmares." I returned to that Josh White, Jr. line again as Cream's record full of "Negro Blues" came to an end. How could we escape our current nightmare? What would happen to America? Would the Vietnam War ever end? I was ready to give up, but I still had the Frost poem to analyze and the Brooklyn Bridge intro to finish and…

Maybe the musicians never gave up, their music never stopped. Josh White Jr. and his father never gave up…Was it the same for Dionne Warwick? Junior Walker? Grace Slick? Sam and Dave? They believed that things could, and would change, that music would help make that happen. Their songs—hell, even the Brooklyn Bridge's songs—all the music and all the musicians and all the concerts were part of who I was, was becoming…

Another look around the room, another glimpse at the posters. I lingered on Smokey and the Miracles, my first concert; the unique Jefferson Airplane poster, handmade by a Bethany art major. And Dionne Warwick's one because it broke my heart.

I glanced down at "Leaves Compared With Flowers," re-reading the lines

Leaves and bark, leaves and bark,
To lean against and hear in the dark.
Petals I may have once pursued.
Leaves are all my darker mood.

With echoes of *"that spoon, that spoon, that spoonful"* ringing in my ears, it finally hit me. I knew what I would write about for my English seminar paper—the fact that an old New England woodsman, one Robert Frost, simply had a bad case of the blues.

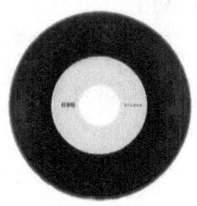

Track 22:

THE WORST THAT COULD HAPPEN

It was a cold day in January 1969 as I stood on stage in front of another SRO Bethany audience to introduce the Brooklyn Bridge. Their syrupy, sappy ballad, "The Worst That Could Happen," was the number one song, but I wouldn't have scheduled them for all the tea in China except their agents, not knowing the hit was coming, offered the group at bargain basement rates.

I knew the Brooklyn Bridge would perform "The Worst That Could Happen" at least twice this Sunday afternoon, and I was dreading every minute of it. Crazily enough, the Fifth Dimension had sung the same damn song here the previous November. That was the night I'd surprised a topless Florence LaRue in the men's locker room, flabbergasting me more than her...

The lead singer of the Brooklyn Bridge was Johnny Maestro, the former lead singer of the Crests, the popular 1950s group who recorded "16 Candles" when my brother was a teenager. I told Johnny Maestro the story about Ron turning 16 at the PAL dance in Philly in 1959 and having "16 Candles" dedicated to him as he and his date danced alone in the spotlight in America's teenage mecca. He made me repeat the story verbatim to other members of the group. Had that music moment really been *ten* years ago already? Meaning my brother was turning 26? Where in the hell did all that time go? I was having a hard time grasping the significance of all this, but I was certain it had nothing to do with "The Worst That Could Happen."

* * *

Part of my discombobulation had to do with a recent, undercover romance with fellow senior Dawn Tyndall. The other had to do with the elephant in the room—every room of every guy my age in Bethany or Pleasant Hills or Brooklyn or wherever.

Vietnam.

Like most guys with student deferments, I imagined the war would miraculously end before my graduation, but the closer I got to graduating, that fantasy evaporated. Maybe that's why I'd leaped into my liaison with Dawn. I'd harbored a concealed crush on her all through college, but she was off limits since she was pinned to Don Cocroft, an older fraternity brother of mine. Still, every time I saw her, it felt like the sun was in my eyes. Dawn always seemed to be bathed in white light, silhouetted like Sandra Dee in one of those *Gidget* movies, sparkles bouncing off her body. Four years on, she looked sexier and healthier and more beautiful than the day I'd met her in 1965, her sandy blond hair now streaked with sunny highlights, cut short but perfectly accenting her warm smile and lips, the finest, reddest, fullest lips I'd ever hoped to kiss. Everything about her was "A plus" as my brother would say. Out of my league. Still, lusting after Dawn beat worrying about Vietnam. Or listening to the Brooklyn Bridge.

Even though Don had graduated in 1968 and gone off to law school, he was still one of my fraternity brothers. If I made a move on Dawn, my fellow Beta brothers would have my hide. I tried to keep my distance, but Dawn was president of Alpha Xi Delta, our sister sorority. Every time groups of Alphas and Betas got together our senior year—which was early and often—it fell to me and Dawn to communicate, orchestrate, choreograph, and pretend to chaperone the proceedings.

Spending all this time together, we grew closer, too close, as in clandestine kisses and embraces. Jesus, where was this headed?

"Where is this headed?" I asked her one perfect fall night as we necked in the dark alongside a garage behind the Beta house. She was driving me crazy in her orange blouse and short skirt and come-hither smile.

"What do you mean?" she asked.

"Is this headed anywhere?" Long pause. "Are you going to tell Don?"

"Tell Don what?"

"About us?"

"What about us?"

"Jesus, Dawn," I nearly shouted. "This, THIS!" I pointed at her and back at me.

"And?" she seemed to be enjoying this. I pulled her out of the shadows. I was done playing 20 questions.

"We're sneaking around like this all the time as if we're doing something wrong…" She frowned at the word *wrong*. "As if we were trying to hide something and I don't see why. I mean, I see why but I don't want to see why…" I was confusing myself.

She reached over and grabbed both my hands, holding them tightly in hers.

"Can't we just enjoy this for what it is?" She smiled coyly and moved in closer. I pulled her into my arms and gave her a long, passionate kiss. She kissed back, stronger than she ever had. Voices exited the Beta house, so we quickly drew apart.

"Are you going to tell Don?" I whispered desperately as a handful of Alpha Xis and Betas approached us.

"Tell him what?" She turned away.

It went on like that for weeks. I was head over the heels in lust, torturing myself with guilt about wanting to steal my fraternity brother's girlfriend. If Don were in Vietnam, I cross-examined myself, I sure as hell would've felt even worse. But this was still the ultimate betrayal, wasn't it, even if Don was only in law school in Delaware?

And why wasn't Dawn wracked by guilt like I was?

I couldn't stop thinking about Don and my treachery and just how far I would try to go with Dawn, so I slowed things down. How in the hell was I supposed to know Dawn didn't want me to slow down? I didn't ask and she didn't say, so I ended up spending hours upon hours dialing her home in New Jersey over Thanksgiving and Christmas vacations, leaving vacant messages with her father—just where in the hell was her mother anyway?—imploring Dawn to call me back.

She never did.

Most likely, she was with Don, busy not telling him about me. By the time we returned to Bethany after winter break, Dawn had a new companion, one she trotted around with in broad daylight no less. How could I have made such a major miscalculation? All Dawn Tyndall really wanted was someone to spend her senior year with, out in the open. It could have been me, but now it was Bill Travis, a senior from another fraternity who obviously didn't share my hesitancies about making Dawn as happy as she deserved.

* * *

Dawn was in the audience for the Brooklyn Bridge, arm in arm with Bill. Fuck me. I spotted a guy my age in uniform...not anybody I knew but someone I couldn't take my eyes off. What was a guy in an Army uniform doing at a Bethany concert? He reminded me of the photos we'd seen of Stewart Tweedy who'd graduated from Bethany a year before I arrived on campus. Lt. Tweedy, we were told by our Dean of Students at the convocation honoring him in 1966, married a nice Bethany girl and enlisted in the U. S. Army right after graduation...

And was killed on a search and destroy mission in Vietnam on December 18, 1965.

I wasn't sure if we were supposed to be depressed or scared, but I remembered Stewart Tweedy's face blending with that of the soldier in the audience.

Or was I just imaging things? Was I projecting my own Vietnam catastrophe, the worst that could happen, onto me?

There was another face in the back of the Field House that Sunday that looked like someone else I knew a long time ago, someone who hadn't aged very well, hair long and unkempt, glasses too big for his face. Sure looked a lot like Kirkpatrick.

Nah, couldn't be…

Turned out it wasn't him, but that night my world was filling with ghosts.

Track 23:

YOU MADE ME SO VERY HAPPY

Listening to Blood, Sweat & Tears sing their cheerful ballad for about the tenth time during a very long, very strange, very drunk summer evening, I asked myself why wasn't I so very happy? How many guys in America, how many people in the entire world for that matter, would give anything to be in my shoes? I'd graduated from college with honors and only a tiny bit of debt and been named the school's Most Outstanding Senior. I'd done well on the LSAT—hell, I even took the GREs in English—and been accepted to a handful of a pretty good law schools, deciding on Boston University with my Beta brother Dennis Fuchs. If that didn't work out, I could always follow-up with corporate giant Proctor & Gamble about the brand manager job prospect they were dangling in front of me.

Best of all, earlier tonight, while I was still sober at Teddy Wilhelm's wedding reception, two eye-catching women had found me desirable. Light-brown haired Deborah was smart and matched me one-liner for one-liner; platinum blonde Karen was sexy and sultry. Earth to Doug Bradley. What's wrong with this picture?

Ah yes, Vietnam. I'd spent most of the summer trying to pull a rabbit out of a hat, or at least a deferment and/or a get-out-of-jail card out of thin air. I was going around and round in hyper-concentric circles, making myself dizzy and nauseous and petrified.

Focus on the here and now. Like Kirkpatrick advised us in high school, *"Carpe diem."* Advice I never followed. Wasn't until I read the metaphysical poets in college that I realized they were using *carpe diem* as an excuse to get into some girl's pants. I had to stop looking back to my glory days at college and ahead to my potential undoing in Vietnam. "Seize the day, dammit," I shouted at the record player. At the very least tether yourself to one of those two lovely young women.

If I wasn't happy, David Clayton Thomas, lead singer of Blood, Sweat & Tears, sure sounded like he was. Not just on this song but all over the album, even on "And When I Die." Now "Spinning Wheel" was doing a number on my head. I was going up and down and round and round. I'd let the spinnin' wheel spin and my troubles were sure enough a cryin' sin. Right on the fucking mark. What goes up must come down. Yes indeed, down, down, down…

* * *

I'd gotten a phone call from Dennis a few weeks earlier. "Brads, man, how's it going?" A happy lilt accompanied his Long Island accent.

"Not bad," I lied. "How's by you?"

"Up and down," Dennis seemed cool, aloof. A pause. "Hey, I've got some good news and bad news. Which do you want first?"

"The bad news," I said without hesitation.

"Okay, so…" Dennis hesitated. "Looks like we won't be roommates." He proceeded to explain that having been reclassified by Uncle Sam as 1-A upon graduation and knowing he'd be drafted, he'd leveraged family connections to enlist in the Army Reserves. He'd spend six months on active duty beginning late that August, followed by six years of weekend warrior games. I'd stopped listening.

"Brads, you still there? Brads?"

"I'm here. I'm guessing I won't 'see you in September' then?" I tried singing those last lines to make light of Dennis's news. But I couldn't talk. I was devastated beyond words. Among other things, Dennis's father had offered to cover our Boston apartment rent. No Dennis, no rent subsidy. No rent subsidy, no law school, with or without the draft.

"Afraid not."

"Jesus…" I exhaled so hard and so long that it probably reached Hempstead Long Island. "What's the good news?"

"I got us tickets to Woodstock."

"Wood what?"

"Woodstock. You know, the New York peace, love, and music festival in August. All of the great bands will be there. Three days of non-stop music. I figured we could head there after Teddy's wedding, pick up Casey at that camp she's working at, maybe even get to Bethel early…That's where the concert is and…"

Dennis sure was fired up. Maybe that had something to do

with the fact he'd just busted my balls about Boston? Or because he was still seeing Casey, a cute, cool Bethany junior.

"So, whadya think?" he asked. Had he already asked me that?

"About what?"

"Jesus, Brads, aren't you paying attention? Woodstock."

I didn't know what I thought. I let the silence on the line consume us. I was not going to law school. I was going to get drafted and sent to Vietnam where I'd die.

"Brads, I'm sorry man. I really am," came Dennis's voice from some place in my hand. Was I holding him or the phone? "Everything's gonna work out. You'll see."

* * *

I didn't see. Couldn't. After his phone call, I spent weeks contemplating military (enlisting) and non-military (Canada, jail) options, talking to anyone and everyone who'd listen—friends, family (other than my parents), clergy, counselors, strangers, you name it—about what I should do. I even took a subway into a ramshackle part of Philly to visit the offices of the Central Committee for Conscientious Objectors (CCCO). The name struck me as something more aligned with the Soviet Politburo. None of the liberal, well-intentioned folks there could make the biggest decision of my life.

So, I so sat and waited and worried. *Carpe diem,* my ass.

* * *

Back to here and now. "What goes up, must come down" the record kept repeating. Or was it "You Make Me So Very Happy"? Who cared? The drive from Philly to Dennis's house and then the long ride from Long Island to Buffalo in his Sting Ray XKE seemed like a million years ago. And while Teddy's wedding reception was exceptional and the booze was flowing and the joints were rolling and the women were willing, all I knew was that my life as I'd lived it was over. Nothing could make me happy. Not sex or pot or music or Woodstock, which turned out to be just like law school—another exercise in futility. Monsoon-like rains and miles of mud had something to do with that, a precursor to Vietnam I feared.

"I got mad and I closed the door."

End of song. End of college. End of summer.

End of me.

Part Three:
HARMONY

"Music is the mysterious key of memory, unlocking the hoarded treasures of the heart. Tones, at times, in music, will bring back forgotten things."

Lord Edward Bulwer Lytton

Track 24:

LEAVING ON A JET PLANE

Packing my bags and flying off to Nassau in the Bahamas without any advance planning wasn't the only reckless thing I did in January 1970, that long winter of my uneasy discontent. But it was up there, alongside transporting marijuana *into* the Bahamas via Trans World Airlines and being robbed at knifepoint by a reggae local who'd befriended me. What the hell was I thinking? Nassau was the place where I could *score* dope.

But I wasn't thinking, not sensibly. I'd spent the seven months following graduation working in a dead-end factory job in a state of apprehension, stoned most of the time thanks to my hippie co-workers. I'd dropped out of law school—why even bother if I'd only be there for one lousy semester?—and passed my Army entrance physical in October, counting the days until the draft board sent my "Uncle Sam wants you" greetings. But President Tricky Dick canceled November, and then December, draft calls, meaning guys like me who were already classified as grade A prime beef by the Army were, for the moment, off the hook. I had something to be thankful for at Thanksgiving.

Not for long. My number, namely my June 7th birthday, did come up in the infamous December 1, 1969, draft lottery at numero 85. Back on the hook. With maybe two months before I'd actually be a soldier, I decided to bolt the USA for the sunny climes of the beautiful Bahamas. Peter, Paul, and Mary may have been singing sadly of "leaving on a jet plane" on the radio, but I was all smiles. My bags were packed, and I was ready to go.

The snow and cold of Philly were rapidly replaced by the sounds of steel drums, lilting Bahamian voices, and soft sea breezes. As soon as I stepped off the plane, I felt lighter, freer. Everything was a shade of blue, chocolate, or glimmering white. Maybe this wasn't such a crazy idea?

My hotel room was straight out of *Casablanca*, complete with ceiling fan and bamboo curtains. I tossed my bag on the bed, which made a funny, squeaking sound, and unpacked my contraband. Adopting a "what are they gonna do, send me to Vietnam?" attitude, I lit up.

Bad idea. In a strange place, hundreds of miles away from home, stressed up the whazoo by the draft and the war and THE DECISION, paranoia struck deep. Probably didn't help that I was reading *Midnight Cowboy* by James Leo Herlihy, another major buzz kill. I fell into a troubling sleep and woke up in a cold sweat. Somebody was outside my door. I was sure it was General Westmoreland with my orders to Vietnam. Or Joe Buck with his hand reaching for my zipper.

Turned out to be Robert from housekeeping.

"What da wybe is?" he asked in a voice that was the perfect blend of creole and cockney.

"Huh?" I was coming out of my fog. Robert had a slender build and looked like he'd spent too many days in the same brown and orange uniform. He had a big, bright smile, shimmering eyes, and the darkest, waviest conked hair I'd ever seen. Ah, and that voice.

"What da wybe is?" he repeated. "You o-keh manh?"

I nodded. He glanced at the roach in the ashtray next to the bed and gave me a wink. "T'ings is good wid you, no?"

I nodded back. Next thing I knew Robert and I were sharing a joint as he gave me a crash course in the local lingo and customs. He neglected to tell me just how poor he was which I discovered a few nights later when he pulled a knife on me and demanded cash. I was so stoned all I could remember was how the tip of the blade of his knife picked up the light from the bar across the alley. Robert apologized for robbing me and was nice enough to not take all my money. Never did see him again at the hotel.

I spent the sunny beach days hanging with a bunch of frat boys from New Jersey or New York or wherever, vigorously enjoying their winter break. My Bethany BMOC experience had taught me how to get along with loud, clowning guys like this. Plus, they were playing touch football and had lots of booze. Best of all, they were pursuing the cutest girls on the beach, so I ignored their fortunate son politics and bad manners. Our so-called camaraderie was diurnal, a fifty-cent word I'd learned in college. They never invited me to hang out with them at night while they frequented the clubs and the bars. Maybe I was too old? Not macho enough? Just as well. Thanks to Robert and my hotel bill,

I was near broke. I started to worry about having to return home to my draft status.

"Leaving on a Jet Plane" took on a new feel.

I headed down to the beach to enjoy another sunny morning, only to discover the frat boys had decamped. The party was over. And then I saw her. Or did she see me? I'd noticed her one day when the boys subjected her to numerous catcalls, trying to lure her and her friends into their web. She was short and cute and built and had this gleaming jet-black hair and bright pink bikini top and…

And she was heading in my direction with a taller, less alluring, friend. Probably wondering where the frat party had gone.

"Hi," she smiled a bright smile. "I'm Gina. And this is Joy. Don't I know you?"

"I don't think so," I mumbled from free fall. Get a grip. "I'm Doug. I was with those guys that were here the last few days."

"Oh," she wrinkled her nose. "No offense, but I didn't like those guys."

"To tell you the truth, I didn't either."

Gina paused, looking me up and down. I should have bought a better bathing suit. "Well, that's good." Another pause and an even better smile. Was I staring at her pink bikini top or at her eyes? Both?

"If you're not doing anything, why don't you come hang out with us?" she pointed down the beach toward a couple of towels and a beat up, tie-dyed umbrella. I sensed Joy wavering, but Gina was doing the talking and I wasn't about to blow my chance.

"Cool. Sure. Let me grab my things." I retrieved my hotel towel, *Midnight Cowboy*, and the journal I'd been keeping since my arrival. Gina seemed intrigued by my cache.

"Is that any good?" she asked. "I saw the movie and thought I might like the book."

"It's pretty depressing," I deadpanned. "The movie's way better, thanks to Dustin Hoffman."

She smiled. Joy was heading back toward their hippie umbrella. "What are you writing?" Gina pointed at my notebook.

"What else but the great American novel?" I laughed. She smiled. "Of course, that's already been written."

"And what might that be?"

"*The Great Gatsby*."

Gina gave me a slight, knowing smile and took off her sunglasses to get a good look at me. Little did I know that my comment had struck gold. Gina, I'd learn later, adored F. Scott Fitzgerald. But what I did know was that Gina's raven hair, nicely rounded face, big brown eyes, and small frame, all inside that pink bikini set against the deep blue sky and white sand had brought me to my knees, literally. I joked to her that I'd tripped, but I was hooked. Line and sinker.

Thirty-six hours later, Gina and I were snuggled on the beach in blankets, talking nonstop about poetry and language and ideas and tomorrows and the next time we'd see one another. She was headed back to her junior year of college in Buffalo, and I was heading…where was I heading? On a jet plane. To fucking Vietnam.

Since that first day on the beach, Gina and I had been inseparable. She'd landed a waitress job at the only Chinese restaurant in the Bahamas, but when she wasn't working, we were together, simpatico romantics who believed in the power of words to accomplish almost anything, including foreplay.

Our last evening together, Gina brought a bottle of rum from the restaurant, some leftover pot stickers and sweet and sour chicken, two beat-up blankets, an old signal flashlight, a tiny cassette tape player, and a copy of *Stanyan Street & Other Sorrows* by her favorite poet Rod McKuen. Turns out the tape also featured Rod the God, reciting what I thought was the worst poetry I'd ever heard, complete with waves, seagulls, and an encyclopedia of annoying sound effects.

But I was in love with the girl of my dreams. I could put up with some sappy poetry. I'd forgotten about the Army and Vietnam. Gina seemed as adrift as I was, not wanting to return to the all-girl Catholic college in the same town she'd spent her entire life. All she was sure of was that she wanted to get the hell out of Buffalo.

"Promise me something." She paused the tape deck and held my hand as we looked up at the stars.

"Anything." I meant it. I squeezed back, hoping this would be the beginning of something special.

"Promise me you won't go to Vietnam if they send you there."

Damn! The last thing I wanted was to spend one of my last nights of freedom thinking or talking about Vietnam. But if this was going to be the night when we were going to make love, I could play along.

"I promise."

Her dark hair blowing in the ocean breeze, Gina raised herself on one elbow and pressed her other hand into my chest as tears welled in her eyes. "Damnit Doug, promise!"

"Can we not talk about this now? Please?" I had tears in my eyes too and that seemed to make a difference.

"I'm sorry," she sniffled. "I think I'm falling in love with you, and I just can't bear the thought of you going to Vietnam and getting killed."

"Nobody's getting killed," I replied with more confidence. "Besides, I'm not falling in love with you. I *am* in love with you."

We kissed and petted and snuggled under the bright Bahamian stars. Eventually, the battery on the cassette deck wore out, so I didn't have to listen to any more Rod McKuen. Holding Gina tighter, repeating lines from Peter, Paul, and Mary, I asked her to wait for me, all the while worrying if, or when, I'd be back again. The music, and my heart and the Bahamas night, were telling me that I'd finally met the girl who would wait for me when I went off to war.

★ ★ ★

We both left on jet planes, Gina's flight departing Nassau the day before mine. My "Greetings, this is Uncle Sam" letter had arrived while I was gone, devastating my parents, especially my dad. In a few weeks, I was to report to the Army Induction Center in Pittsburgh, where I'd registered for Selective Service in 1965 on my 18th birthday. It was still winter, I'd smoked all my dope, and I was out of money.

But I was in love. Gina was my true north star and would guide me safely the rest of the way.

Or so I hoped.

Track 25:

RAINY NIGHT IN GEORGIA

Between Nassau and nowhere, between Rod McKuen and ruin, between taking tokes and swearing oaths, I daydreamed my way to my March 2, 1970, induction day. But not without a few wakeups along the way.

One came via a phone call. My mother seemed thrilled to hear another voice in their apartment since I wasn't talking much. I had my poor parents walking on eggshells because of my pending death sentence.

"Doug, honey, wake up, telephone!" My mom's long nails were scratching on my bedroom door. I was in some sort of alcohol or marijuana-induced trance. Maybe both.

"Who is it?"

"I didn't ask."

"Tell them to call back." Long pause. I could feel my mother standing her ground, Everything about the apartment screamed of my mother's habitual housekeeping. Lysol clean, well-lit, always smelling of something delicious. I'd started to pack away some of my college awards and belongings, but my mom wanted them to stay where they were so everything would be the same when I came back from the Army.

If I came back...

"No. You need to get out of bed, open the door, walk in the kitchen, and answer the darn telephone."

Obviously, little Lucy had had it with my Sad Sack stoner routine.

"Hello?" I exhaled into the phone.

"Dube, hey Dube, it's me, Cliff." Who in the hell was using my old high school nickname? And what's his again? Oh yeah, Cliff...Cliff...Tom Clifton? What the hell does he want?

"How's it going Cliff?" I feigned wakedness.

"Great, good, thanks. How about you?"

Jesus, now I'd have to give my death march explanation again. "I'm getting drafted. Report to Uncle Sam in a few weeks."

Silence and then I thought I heard him sob.

"Jesus, Dube...man, I'm so sorry." Another pause. Now I'd have to cheer him up.

"Yeah, well, maybe I'll get lucky and not have to go you-know-where. But how about *you*? How are you? And where are you?"

"Believe it or not I'm right here in Philly," his voice lifted. "Going to Med School at Temple. Got your number from Bethany...You have any time to get together before you leave?"

"I've got nothing but time," I deadpanned. "Give me your address and I'll come down and pay you a visit."

"I could come your way," he volunteered. "But, sure, yeah, let's get together."

If you'd forced me to guess which of my old Thomas Jefferson High School classmates would come to my rescue, Tom Clifton would not have been on the list. But rescue me he did, via his friendship, genuine concern for my wellbeing, and letting me crash at his apartment when I was too drunk to drive home…

Less than three weeks from my March reporting date, Cliff presented me with the ultimate gift—a reunion with Dawn, my very own Dawn Tyndall from Bethany College. He was dating a nursing student who said she had a friend who might want to go on a blind date and, well, much to everyone's surprise, Dawn was back in my arms again. Even with the newly kindled romance with Gina, this old heart of mine skipped a few Dawn Tyndall beats. Maybe, just maybe, this was meant to be? Maybe she and I would finally consummate a relationship five years in the offing.

My brother likewise roused me with a wake-up or two. He was happily teaching chemistry at a nearby high school while his wife Carol merrily flew the friendly skies with United Airlines. In order to enhance his teacher's salary, Ron had signed on to coach high school wrestling.

"What do you know about wrestling?" I asked him incredulously.

"Don't you remember what huge Bruno Sanmartino fans we were?" he grinned.

"That was TV wrestling. Theater," I shot back, recalling the many Saturday nights we watched role-playing wrestling on TV in Pittsburgh. "None of those guys were really wrestling."

"I'm learning," he said. "Get down on the floor, and I'll show you some moves."

Basketball was our usual extracurricular, but I humored Ron and let him toss me around a few times. Made me miss our games of one-on-one b-ball even more. At least music was always playing in their apartment. Ron remained an R&B guy at heart, enjoying Eddie Holman's "Hey There Lonely Girl," "Didn't I Blow Your Mind This Time" by Philly's own Delfonics, and Clarence Carter's "Take it Off Him and Put it On Me." A musical sentiment I wish I could make come true.

There were other stirrings over the four, or was it five, weeks? I'd lost count. The potheads from my old assembly line job getting me high; the older workers getting me drunk; the long, lonely nights with Cliff; the phone calls with Gina; the trip to see her at the end of February where we talked endlessly about draft avoidance and Canada. These weren't so much political discussions as preservation strategies. My preservation.

There were a couple of dates with Dawn, one at my brother's apartment when he and Carol were gone. I expected to finally sleep with her that night but got too wasted to make the right moves. The evening ended with me listening to "Bridge Over Troubled Water" and crying in the living room, Cliff's arm around my shoulder, the girls long gone.

The best moments were the quieter ones with my parent's dog, Monty, given to them by an old Pittsburgh neighbor who'd moved to a place where they didn't allow pets. Major animal lovers since the old Philly days of Jeep the dog and Smokey the cat, my folks were thrilled. A miniature French poodle who had a buck tooth that made him look goofy, Monty had an honest-to-goodness personality. In the car, Monty would lean across from the passenger seat, rest his front paws on your armrest, and stick his nose out the window, a habit he must've picked up from his original owners. I'd never seen a dog do that, but in that position, Monty looked like he had the world on a canine string. Most days after I'd take him for a long walk, talking aloud to him as if he was a real person, I'd give Monty a ride in the car so he could enjoy the view.

"Rainy Night in Georgia" rose to the top of my personal hit parade. I knew Brook Benton's old hits, but this song was raw and real. Made me tear up. Monty right there in front of me with his fur flying in the breeze, while "Rainy Night in Georgia" cemented our bond. Me and my dog. Jesus, no wonder I was getting drafted.

March 2 drew closer and closer. Not even a quick flight to Buffalo for some love and happiness with Gina could slow down father time. More half nelson demos from Ron and more doomed looks from my folks. "Rainy Night in Georgia" just kept on playing…

And then I was on the midnight bus from Pittsburgh to Philly where I would arrive at 0700 hours for my Monday, March 2 appointment with Uncle Sam. Only to be flown back to Philly later that same day and bussed to nearby Fort Dix, New Jersey, for Basic Training. My introduction to U. S. Army A-1 efficiency.

My second week in Basic, I got a letter from my mom.

"Sorry to have to tell you this," she wrote, "but Monty died. He was such a sweet dog. Missed you terribly. He looked for you in your bedroom every day."

It was raining that day at Fort Dix. Felt like it was rainin' all over the world.

Track 26:
FIRE AND RAIN

Basic Training mornings started with a fellow recruit nicknamed "Baby Fat Bob" singing "Fire and Rain" whether the sun was up yet or not, whether we were awake or asleep. No matter how shitty I felt about being in the Army, I loved waking to the lilt in his voice. Even the guys who cussed him out and tossed their pillows at him loved it. Baby Fat Bob didn't just sing "Fire and Rain," he inhabited every note and syllable in a way that would have made James Taylor envious. That song helped us survive the gloomy days of late winter and early spring.

Most days I wanted to just keep listening, without opening my eyes and realizing I was on a floor in an Army barracks with 49 other doomed souls. No, let me go back to the dream about that Bahamas beach cuddling with Gina… But I was here, Fort Dix, New Jersey, for eight excruciating weeks, property of Uncle Sam, facing an endless string of calisthenics and bad food and brow beating and soldiering.

And after these eight weeks?

The only smart thing I'd done since the start of basic was to take the tedious Army aptitude tests seriously. When I handed mine in to the young Spec. 4 who was proctoring, he'd glanced at my answer sheet, raised his eyebrows, and gave me a big thumbs up. I was following advice I'd received from Vincent, a soldier I'd sat next to on a flight to Buffalo to see Gina in February. Given my pending enlistment, the last thing I wanted to do was spend precious time on a plane beside some gung-ho Army type. But since he and I were both flying standby, we wound up seated together.

After a long bout of silence, I noticed he was reading a copy of *Slaughterhouse Five* so I figured he couldn't be all that bad.

"Great book," I mumbled.

"More than great," he volunteered with a smile. "Far fucking out."

Okay, maybe I was wrong? Over the next 90 minutes, Vincent schooled me on basic training "Do's and Don'ts." A crash course in survival.

"By the end of the first couple days of Basic, you're going to be totally frazzed and really pissed," Vincent explained matter-of factly. His cropped brown hair and sallow complexion blended into his olive drab Army uniform. I'd guessed he was younger than me since he said he'd joined the Army out of high school. But there was something in his eyes and voice that made him seem much older.

"Then they lay a battery of aptitude tests on you," he continued. "DO NOT BLOW THESE OFF!" He raised his voice and pinned my wrist to the arm rest. I nearly jumped out of my seat. "When you get there, be focused. Be serious. STAY

THE FUCK AWAKE! Take those damn tests as seriously as if your life depends on it. 'Cause it just might."

Long pause. Could Vincent feel my fear? What would Vonnegut's Billy Pilgrim do at a time like this? Time travel far, far away…

Vincent kept talking. "Those tests are critical to your getting a good MOS."

"Emmo est? What's that?" I asked, trying to follow.

"MOS is your military job. It stands for military occupational specialty. Mine is 25C40, radio operator. Those tests that you don't want to take and find completely annoying can go a long way toward determining what Uncle Sam is going to do with you."

He stared into my eyes so deep that I thought he could see into my frightened soul.

"Even if you're, like, drafted?" I could hardly get my question out, figuring my ass was grass by rolling the draft dice.

"Hell, yes, even if you're drafted." My spirits lifted.

"I was drafted," he continued, "but the Army sent me to radio school. Did a tour in 'Nam but stayed out of harm's way. Not everybody that's drafted becomes cannon fodder." He paused. "Of course, where the Army's concerned there are no fucking guarantees."

* * *

Stuck inside of Basic with the freedom blues again, I thought back on that conversation and wondered if Vincent was having some fun with me, an early bit of Basic Training hazing? Maybe the aptitude tests were just a way for the Army to cover its ass if anyone ever wondered why a certain GI was doing a particular job? Forget it. Right now, just getting the hell through Basic Training was all that mattered.

Which meant a daily badgering from belligerent drill sergeants who knew my college boy status, taunting me to sign up for OCS, Officer Candidate School, lest my "sorry ass" be made "11 Bravo," a.k.a. a hopeless grunt. I'd be "KIA" in Vietnam before Jody could steal my girl. For them every college student was an anti-war, anti-Army, anti-everything privileged hippie. I never said a word in opposition, figuring that eventually they'd pick on somebody else. But it sure was taking them a long time.

Writing and music were sources of comfort. I wrote letters whenever I could, mostly to Gina, but also to Dawn. But it was music that connected and lifted and consoled us in the platoon. When permitted, somebody always had a radio blasting or a cassette playing or Baby Fat Bob would burst into song. All of us—regardless of background—would join in, holding onto a lyric or a melody to get us through the long days and all-too-short nights, and keep our minds off whatever awaited us.

For fun, we'd sometimes wage "battle of the bands" contests, pitting Motown soul against the Beatles rock and roll. Wagering cigarettes or photos of our girlfriends. Usually I'd find myself in both camps and would have a hard time deciding if "My Girl" was better than "Yesterday," or if "Help" bested "Dancing in the Streets." All those songs took me back to high school and Kirkpatrick, wondering how many of my TJ classmates were in the Army, in Vietnam, already dead. Why hadn't Kirkpatrick and the music saved us?

There were other songs that, given the present circumstances, could tear us up—"He Ain't Heavy" by the Hollies, "Bridge Over Troubled Water," and my old friend "Rainy Night in Georgia." And Baby Fat Bob modifying "Fire and Rain" to fit our situation, changing *Susanne* in the second line to "Uncle Sam" and mixing in "hours of time on the firing line." His lyrics could remind us we were in Basic Training, sure, but somehow his voice offered hope that maybe we'd get through it, through all that fire and rain in our lives. That we might, just might, get past it all…

To what?

Our bodies were aching and our time was at hand. Our sweet dreams were in pieces on the ground. And those flying machines would eventually drop us off in the jungles of Vietnam.

That's probably why I never knew Bob's last name, or anyone else's in my Basic Training platoon, all those polyglot recruits from New York, Philly, Trenton, and McKeesport. Didn't learn the real name of the guy they called "Pops" who was all of 23 years old, and our platoon's only other college grad. Or the name of the kid the drill sergeants called "Hippie," a granny-glasses goofball who became our platoon leader, even though everybody, drill sergeants in particular, picked on him unmercifully as if "hippie" was the dirtiest word in the English language.

Truth be told, my greatest fear was that if I remembered their names, one day I'd visit Arlington National Cemetery and try to find them…unless I was buried there myself. I didn't want to think about how many guys in my platoon wouldn't come back to get married, have kids, and live long and happy lives.

So, I contented myself with music, embracing Motown, the Beatles, and all the rest. Waking and sleeping to the sound of Baby Fat Bob's sonorous voice caressing the only song he ever sang.

Track 27:

YELLOW SUBMARINE

There weren't many times we recruits had the slightest notion about what was going on, or going down. Buck privates were so far down the chain of command we had to stand on stilts to reach a toilet seat. Our job was to obey orders, to do whatever our superiors told us to do morning, noon, and night. "All power to the people" wasn't part of our Army lexicon.

But there was one unexpected evening when music and mud and mayhem came together, and, for a few brief minutes, all of us felt alive.

Following several days of drenching rain, Fort Dix looked like I imagined a village in Vietnam after a torrential monsoon. Dark, deep, oozing, brown mud; lots and lots of it. As a result of the deluge, the training schedule was off kilter, annoying the clock-punching powers that be. For us, that meant double trouble. When we'd completed the 15K foot march to and from Poorman's Range, the brass decided we had to turn around and go out again *that same night* to complete a required Night Infiltration and get back on schedule. The only good news—instead of our being forced-marched both ways, we'd be transported back to the barracks in cattle cars to ensure our arrival at a reasonable hour. Get everything back on schedule.

Watching the vehicles pull up, it became obvious why those Army cargo trailers were called "cattle cars." Suited more to beast than man…long, clunky, with chains even, bus doors added to the right side of the trailer, back doors sealed. Bench seats and an extra fifth wheel. We were the cattle being hauled to…wherever the hell they hauled human cattle. I didn't want to think about where real cattle went.

After crawling through the mud for hours, we boys of Company D were more earth than human. A cattle car filled with Pigpens from *Peanuts*, but our filth was wet, muddy. Beyond tired. Beyond frustrated. Beyond hope.

The GI driving the trailer was as pissed off as we were, hauling ass, screeching tires, taking turns at breakneck speeds. We careened from one side of the car to the other, guys tossed on top of each other in mucky piles, screaming, cursing. I thought for sure a fight would break out and was hanging on for dear life to Hippie who was holding on to one of the speeding trailer's poles that ran from floor to ceiling. Doubt cattle could do that.

We all knew that once we got back to the barracks, as late as it was, we'd be ordered to formation, made to clean our weapons and hand them back in BEFORE we could go to bed. It would be two o'clock in the fucking morning by then, with 0500 hours revile awaiting us. In that one muddy moment, we'd had it with the United States Army and basic training and drill sergeants and cattle cars and orders and all the rest.

And then Pops and Baby Fat Bob broke into "Yellow Submarine."

"In the town, where I was born," Pops began, his voice sounding pure and clear. He sure had some pipes. Sounded kinda grown up.

Baby Fat's voice was sweeter and fuller than Pop's when he sang about the man who sailed the sea.

Suddenly, it got quiet on the cattle car. We were still careening around corners and banging into one another, but everyone was listening to the two of them as their voices grew louder. When they finally got to the chorus, Pops banged the butt of his M-16 on the floor of the cattle car for emphasis. Such a great accent, the sound a perfect *thump/clang*. Spontaneously, we all banged our M-16s on the floor to emphasize every syllable of yell-oh-sub-ma-rine.

In that brief moment, 50 of us came alive, transported to some other time, some place better than a cattle car in Fort Dix, New Jersey, a place where bands played, people sang songs, and everyone had fun. In our reverie, we'd lost track of how fast the cattle car was going, so when we arrived back at company headquarters, the cattle car was still reverberating with the banging of M16s to a chorus of voices belting out "Yellow Submarine." After one last full-throated chorus, Hippie opened the side door where someone was knocking to encounter a very pissed-off Master Sgt. Willie Brown and First Lt. Cory Watkins looking him in the face. Hippie didn't shout "ten-hut" or anything. He just smiled and said, "Come right in, gentlemen."

That only made Brown and Watkins madder. They ordered us to stop singing, which we did. But we kept on banging our M-16s on the floor of the cattle car. It sounded like a round of heavy artillery. So loud it was hard to hear what the two lifers were saying, but I picked up on our being "insubordinate," guilty of "gross disciplinary infractions," and something about all of us getting Article 15s.

Brown and Watkins spent the rest of their time calling us names, like "jerk-off" and "scum bag." It reminded me of the parents in *Bye, Bye Birdie* complaining about their kids being "disobedient, disrespectful oafs. " We knew something would have to give and that somebody, us, would have to pay a price. But, in that one sonorous moment, we had the Army by the balls. We'd fucked up their tight ass schedule and done something they hadn't expected.

And we still had our goddamn M-16s.

An equally pissed-off, sleepy base commander showed up to dictate our three-fold punishment:

<u>One</u>: After we got our sorry assess off the cattle car, we would stand in formation, at attention, in complete silence, for as long as he wanted.

<u>Two:</u> We would surrender our weapons <u>without</u> cleaning them and do pushups until the cattle cars came home.

<u>Last</u>: We'd reclaim our weapons, clean them, and turn them back in by 0400 hours.

Meaning, of course, we'd get all of about an hour of sleep before packing up and heading out for the company's 10K march to the bivouac site for our "final" field training exercise.

To top it off, at our upcoming graduation ceremony that Saturday, as the rest of the Basic Training battalion was presented with their Army insignia and mementos by their Drill Sergeants, we'd be served Article 15s, Army parlance for a non-judicial, misdemeanor type offense that didn't require a jury but could burn your ass and hurt your career, nonetheless. All in front of our friends and family.

But all that was still a few days away. Even though we were beyond exhaustion and would be despised, belittled, and threatened until the moment we said goodbye to Fort Dix, nobody, not even the all-powerful and all-knowing U. S. Army could take that night away from us. They couldn't silence our voices, or take the song out of our hearts.

In a strange way, "Yellow Submarine" accomplished what the military had been trying to do for the entire eight weeks of Basic Training—it had brought us together as a unit. I mean, hell, "all our friends had been aboard," singing with one, loud, collective, unified voice.

Track 28:

DAWN

The euphoria of a ten-day leave right out of basic training—"that never fucking happens," one of my astounded Fort Dix drill instructors told me—was tempered by the fact that none of the guys I'd spent my first eight weeks of Army life with had similar luck. Most were heading directly to eight weeks of Advanced Individual Training in infantry at Fort Polk, Louisiana, and, after a 30-day leave, the jungles of Vietnam. No wonder I hadn't learned any of their names…

On top of that, Nixon and his national security advisor Henry Kissinger decided to invade Cambodia just as we were graduating from Basic. Talk about pouring gasoline on a fire. The news distracted the Fort Dix brass enough so they forgot to give us our Article 15s. The whole damn country was erupting from coast to coast, and even with my ten-day leave, I sure as hell wasn't eager to display my clean-shaven head in public.

But damnit, I needed to celebrate my good luck. Thanks to that helpful advice from Vincent, the GI who sat next to me on the plane ride to Buffalo in February, my primo MOS was 71Q20, Army information specialist. My first posting would be the U. S. Army Hometown News Center in Kansas City, Missouri. No more "Bridge Over Troubled Water" for me, I was singing along to Chicago's "Make Me Smile."

Then again, between here, May 2, and there, May 12, the country had some antiwar upheavals to resolve, and I had some major romance issues to resolve. The feeling I'd experienced that night with Gina on the beach in Nassau hadn't dissipated. Even with all the Cambodia chaos, I felt like my survival depended on the love of a steadfast female, a committed relationship I could hold on to, something permanent and lasting to tether me to here and now. So, priority number one was flying back to Buffalo to show Gina Carpelli that I was dead serious. I had to make sure that she was *the* girl I'd leave behind.

But as with everything else in the world, there was a major wrinkle, namely Dawn Tyndall. She'd seemed genuinely happy to see me before I went in the Army, and I had to find out once and for all if my feelings were anything more than leftover flickerings of a college flame. Both she and Gina had written me quasi love letters during Basic. Was my heart stuck in the past with Dawn or moving on to a future with Gina? Or did I just want to be in love with someone, anyone?

Geographically, Dawn was closer, so I decided to see her first. It was a couple days after the Kent State killings, and massive protests were underway nationwide. I prayed like hell the Army would leave me alone until I arrived in Kansas City, fearing I'd be called into active duty and ordered to report to a nearby college campus and point my rifle at college students who looked like me. I added an extra "Hail Mary" to my prayers to confirm that the feelings I'd harbored for Dawn for so many years would finally be rewarded. There had to be a reason why she'd ended up in Philly and became best friends with my buddy Cliff's girlfriend. Maybe we were meant to live happily ever after? Or at least consummate our five-year platonic relationship?

I sat at attention waiting for Dawn at a bar in a trendy new spot in downtown Philadelphia, curiously named the Knave of Hearts. The place made we wonder if I might encounter Alice and the White Rabbit…Where was Grace Slick when I needed her? I was self-consciousness as hell about my Basic Training look, as if I were displaying a sign that said, "Doug Bradley supports President Nixon and U. S. aggression in Vietnam."

Instead of nursing my Yingling beer, I guzzled it down and ordered another. My palms were sweaty, my heart racing. Suddenly, there she was. Were my eyes playing tricks or was it the way the light shone by the door? Dawn was aglow in blinding blond light, Sandra Dee-esque as usual. Her trim, athletic body filled every inch of her bright blue top and short white skirt.

Dawn's pace quickened. When she got close to me, she nuzzled my ear and whispered, "I'm so proud of you." I almost fell off the barstool. Was it really going to happen? Finally, after all these years?

"You look terrific," I smiled my Knave of Hearts smile. She pulled her barstool close to mine and smiled warmly, the restaurant light glistening on her lips. Her words felt like kisses. Wait a minute, what had just come out of her mouth? I needed to pay fucking attention.

"What you're doing is really brave. And incredibly patriotic." Dawn seemed to be pledging her allegiance to everyone seated around us. "You're not like the draft dodgers and hippie protesters." Did she mean it? Dawn continued talking, lecturing, still spectacularly spotlighted, but her mouth seemed less beautiful, her demeanor less warm. I studied her, trying to figure out what I was going to say, wondering just how in the hell she'd gotten that way. How could we disagree on just about everything—the war, Nixon, protests, Cambodia, law and order? And how in all those days and weeks and years, in all that time together in college, in all those conversations, those embraces, those stolen moments and secrecy, why had we *never* talked about what really mattered?

As I went back and forth in my head about what I could and should do—order another drink, change the subject, go to the bathroom—I thought I heard Dawn say something complimentary about Henry Kissinger.

"He's a goddamn war criminal," I nearly shouted. Dawn shrank back as if I'd taken a swing at her. "He lied about the Paris peace talks, expanded the lousy war, and is bombing the shit out of Southeast Asia!" Did I need to worry about insubordination on a ten-day leave? "And Henry Fucking Kissinger could give a flying fuck about lowly GIs like me."

I hadn't dropped that many F-bombs during my entire four years at Bethany College. But that was then and this was…this was now. This was war. And Dawn, oh so beautiful and so tempting, was my adversary. I'd decided it was people like her who were sending guys like me to Vietnam. I couldn't pretend she was something she wasn't just because I wanted to sleep with her. It was about time I took a stand.

"Right on, brother," nodded a bar patron seated nearby. When I looked his way, I noticed he was talking to the guy next to him and not to me. Things went quiet between me and Dawn. Neither of us moved.

Next thing I knew we were back to idle chatter, comparing notes about our favorite Bethany professors, who dated whom in college, the weather. All very polite, avoiding the mastodon in the room. We kissed goodnight and hugged. Dawn looked me straight in the eyes, as if she didn't know who in the hell I was.

"I'll write you every day in Kansas City," she lied, adding as an afterthought "and we'll spend a few nights together when you come home," almost as if everything that had just passed between us was mere talk and didn't mean anything. As if nothing had changed, as if it was okay to sleep with someone whose ideas you disliked.

Things had changed. For one time in my life I'd actually stood up for something I believed in. In the process, I was turning my back on making love with a girl I was once crazy about because I didn't agree with her politics. My principles had trumped sex.

Jesus, what was I thinking?

Dawn liked Nixon, disapproved of student protesters, and supported the war. She was uninformed and dead wrong, bigoted and narrow-minded. But I didn't say that to her face. I just left her standing there.

When I turned over the engine in my dad's little red Volkswagen to drive home, "Dawn" by the Four Seasons was blasting on WIP radio. I laughed out loud, put the VW in gear, turned up the radio, shifted to second, then third, and sang along, making up my own lyrics to suit my mood.

"Dawn, go away back where you belong. Girl we can't change the ideas you have wrong...I want you to think,

think, what Dick Nixon would say. Think, think, I disagree with all you say. Now think what the future would be with a draftee like me..."

"Me-ee-ee!" I screamed into the warm Philadelphia night.

America was ablaze. I still had my orders and my Army buzz cut and who knew what the fuck was going to happen next. I bought an airplane ticket for Buffalo to be welcomed by Gina's open arms. If nothing else, she and I agreed about Henry Kissinger.

Track 29:

KANSAS CITY

It was weirder than weird. Riding in the cab on the way from the airport to the Army Hometown News Center in Kansas City, Missouri, I had to pinch myself to make sure it was all really happening. A fairly painless eight weeks of basic training with some pretty decent guys and three weekend furloughs. A tremendous Army MOS—71Q20, information specialist. And a ten-day leave that allowed me to remove any and all obstacles to being head over heels for Gina, who likewise confessed her love for me and planned to come to Kansas City as soon as she graduated from college later this month.

I was pinching myself so hard I almost said "ouch." Or maybe I did because my cab driver turned around and asked if I was okay.

"More than okay," I smiled, the Army insignia on my extremely well-pressed uniform (thanks to my mom) almost blinding him.

"Where you from son?"

"Philadelphia."

"Ooh, wee, 'Trane country," he whistled.

His mouth seemed too large for his face. A beat-up Kansas City A's hat came down over his ears. He seemed at ease driving fast while turning around and talking. I didn't know what to make of the "train" reference, so since the old hit song "Kansas City" by Wilbert Harrison was a favorite of me and my brother, I thought I'd show off my vintage rock and roll chops.

"Can we stop at Twelfth Street and Vine?" I asked jokingly, "I hear they got some crazy little women there.'"

This time when the cab driver turned around, he wasn't smiling. "Son, you do NOT want to go anywhere near Twelfth and Vine. No way. Any day."

I must have crossed some kind of line, because the cabdriver and I were done talking for the rest of my ride to the Troost Avenue Offices of the Army's Hometown News Center.

"The mission of the AHTNC is to improve, supervise, and control the flow of informational material to hometown news media," my new commanding officer Colonel Richard Stewart explained as if he'd given this speech a thousand times. He had a crew cut like Montgomery Cliff's in *From Here to Eternity* and a solid build and square jaw like Vic Morrow in TV's *Combat*. "It is designed to receive, evaluate, and edit all hometown news and feature stories in order to obtain the maximum hometown interest and to ensure that each release is appropriate as to style and content. It receives hometown news from all Army units worldwide and handles the time-consuming details required for each hometown news story, e.g., writing, duplication, media selection, addressing, and mailing."

Did this guy just say "e. g." I marveled? He must be reading from a script. I sat off to the side of his desk, blinded by the light bouncing off his glass table. I was surprised to notice that much of his crossed leg was bare, his blue sock at parade rest down by his spit-shined shoes, leaving an expanse of bare leg between there and his calf.

"The work of the AHTNC is based on the assumptions that hometown news material fills a real need to inform the people back home of the accomplishments of a local soldier, and that timely, newsworthy, well written releases will be printed by the hometown newspapers."

"Yes, sir," I replied a little too enthusiastically, hoping he was finished.

"Unfortunately," the Colonel continued, "the closest Army base is Fort Leavenworth, Kansas, more than 40 miles away, meaning you soldiers won't have access to a PX and the other base amenities."

Colonel Stewart droned on, socks dropping further, bare leg dangling. It dawned on me that what he'd said meant I'd be spared what nearly all my fellow Fort Dix soldiers, and millions of others, would have to do—guard duty, formations, KP, marching, and all the rest.

"Do you read me Private Bradley," the colonel's question interrupted my mini-reverie.

"I'm sorry, sir, I missed that last part. Lots of activity out there," I pointed toward the large open space beyond the colonel's office and waiting area which had printing presses humming and typewriters clacking and a roomful of workers, not all of them in uniform. Most of them female.

"To repeat. Major Flanagan and Sgt. Olson will see to it that you have some place to bivouac for the next few days and help you secure permanent housing. They'll make an advance on your monthly stipend for room and board so you won't go hungry." His lip curled in a little smile.

"Thank you, sir."

He stood, and I jumped up quickly and saluted.

"At ease, Private Bradley," he said, his voice dropping. "We expect more from college educated draftees like yourself since we only get you for two years. But maybe you'll re-enlist? Make the most of your time here young soldier. Dismissed."

I turned to see a tall, young, good-looking officer I figured was Major Flanagan waiting for me.

"Bradley, one more thing," the Colonel's raspy voiced came from behind me. "No fraternization whatsoever with the civilian workers, especially the young women."

* * *

That was the first of many orders I'd disobey while assigned to the Army Hometown News Center. Eventually, I'd take fraternization to another level with a couple of the attractive women at the Center, walling my dalliances off from me and Gina. The Army was already giving me a crash course in situational ethics. Kansas City did indeed have some crazy little women there.

My Army enlistment notwithstanding, that summer of 1970 was everything the summer of 1969 wasn't. I was living the life I thought guys like me were supposed to enjoy after college—a hip apartment with two other cool guys, a swimming pool, parties, cute women, unlimited alcohol and marijuana, music, conjugal visits from my girlfriend, books, and enough flexibility to continue my education.

And then the rug was yanked out from under me and everything wasn't so goddamn rosy after all…

I awoke on Monday, July 27, with an aching headache, evidence of the previous weekend's drinking and smoking. Add to it a huge dose of Catholic guilt. My roommate Rico, a fun loving, first-generation Italian kid from the Chicago suburbs who was one of my AHTNC comrades-in-news, had a surprise visit from his hometown girlfriend that weekend. She'd brought along a friend and, well, I was up to my old fraternization tricks.

For some reason what I'd done was bothering me more this morning than the morning before when I'd awakened with this lovely young stranger lying beside me. In my not so relaxing sleep, all I could see was Gina's face, tears streaming down her cheeks, mascara running, telling me how much I'd let her down and what a liar and a phony I was. And she was right. As I brushed my teeth, put on my Army khakis, and prepared to drive to the News Center with my roommates, I made a vow to "straighten up and fly right" as one of my dad's favorites, Nat King Cole, used to say.

Relieved at deciding to return to my former altar boy status, I felt a twinge somewhere deep inside when I saw my good friend and fellow draftee George Moriarty standing by my desk. His face was ashen, his eyes hollow. "Sgt. Olson wants to see us right away," he said with his conspicuous Massachusetts accent. Why did I feel like I was being sent to the gallows?

"At ease, privates," Sgt. Olson's broad back and square shoulders were turned to us. When he turned around, his thin blonde hair and regulation Army eyeglasses shimmered a little in the early morning light. Or was that an ever so slight tear I'd detected?

"I'm afraid I've got some bad news," his voice was flat, almost non-human. "The Levy turned up your names this weekend. You're both going to Vietnam."

I thought George was going to pass out. The poor guy had a wife and a baby and he was getting sent to fucking Vietnam? Then it hit me. So was I! And what in the hell was the goddamn Levy anyway? Sgt. Olson was still talking about orders and AWOL and a bunch of other stuff I didn't hear.

"Your 30-day leave will commence on 5 October," he added stoically. "At the end of the 30 days, you must report to the Army Terminal in Oakland for processing en route to Vietnam. It's all in your orders. If you don't show up, they'll find you, believe me. Any questions?"

I was stunned beyond words and could barely hold back my own tears. "Kansas City" song lyrics were flying around me. Forget Twelfth Street and Vine. I was going to Vietnam...

We walked out of Sgt. Olson's office and sat down at our desks in silence.

Everybody in the building could tell from the looks on our faces what had happened. One of the Army lifer assholes we worked with, who'd recently returned from a year in Germany, smiled at us and sang, "Ain't no time to wonder why, whoopee, we're all gonna die." Instead of punching his lights out, I puked on my desk.

* * *

My last two months at the Hometown News Center were like one long going away party. Most of the time I was high or drunk or both. Gina came and went. I flew to Buffalo over

Labor Day weekend. Pledge of fidelity forgotten, I kept fooling around with Shaina, one of the girls in the office. George moved in with us when his wife returned to the D.C. suburbs with their little girl, Tara, whom I adored. Somebody was always pouring a drink or rolling a joint. Music played constantly. We'd burst out laughing when "Ohio" by CSNY or Edwin Starr's "War" came on. What did they know about the Army and Vietnam anyway? The Temptations' "Ball of Confusion" fit my mood better, and I cranked it up whenever it came on the radio.

Every time we talked, Gina implored me to go to Canada—she claimed to have contacts in the "underground railroad" in the Buffalo area that could get me out of the USA and put me up in Toronto. We'd had these conversations before, always theoretical. Now it was real—my ass was being sent to Vietnam. As much as I appreciated Gina's concern and her principled stance against the war, I was too numb to agree, disagree, or take any action. My life was over, so why not party as if there was no tomorrow?

On my way to the airport for my flight home to Philly on October 5, I thought I spotted my first cabdriver at the curb, the one who'd dropped me off at the News Center in May. Was that only five months ago? I peered into his cab, hoping to make eye contact and say hi. Wilbert Harrison's voice came back in my head and I remembered the lecture I got about Twelfth Street and Vine.

"Boy, what the fuck you lookin' at?" the cabdriver snarled at me.

Next Stop, Vietnam…

Track 30:

WALK ON BY

Those thirty days of leave were about the worst of my life. Every time I said hello or goodbye to someone I was ready to cry. It was worst with Gina and my mom since they could sense my helplessness and fear. I was a scared little boy, and I was being sent off to war.

And they couldn't protect me.

I scheduled my leave so I'd have a week at home, then two weeks in Buffalo, and another week back home, with Gina flying down for those last few days before D-day. I never thought to run the schedule by anyone since it was my leave and my life, but maybe I should have. Or maybe I should have eloped with Gina so I'd have a devoted wife waiting for me back home. Then again, if something happened to me in Vietnam, who'd want to marry an Army widow? We never talked about things that way, but the hint of tragedy was always around. It made Gina's political protestations seem irrelevant.

With Ron and my dad working, my days at home were lonely except for the breaks in my mom's housework. She'd knock on my bedroom door and peek her greying haired head in as the Isaac Hayes version of "Walk on By" was blasting on my stereo.

"Whatcha doin?" was her usual entry line. Then she'd put her hands up to her ears to demonstrate she couldn't hear because the music was too loud. I'd smile, turn down the volume, and watch as she puttered around my room, pretending to be busy. Not admitting she just wanted to make sure I was still here.

For some reason, my dad took me and Ron to see a boxing match the first week of my leave. He'd boxed some when he was young, and we'd religiously watched the Wednesday and Friday night fights on TV, so I guess he thought this was somehow meaningful. It wasn't, but I didn't have the heart to tell him. Ron seemed unimpressed too, maybe because the fights between his wife and my parents were never ending.

It snowed heavily in Buffalo while I was there so I decided if Gina and I were going to stay together that we sure as hell wouldn't live there. We spent most of our time listening to Laura Nyro and screwing. Her parents seemed unmoved by my plight, and her friends thought I was a sucker for going to Vietnam.

"Man, you can't be serious about going to V-et-nam," her stoner comrades intoned through a purple haze. I'd take a hit off the joint they were passing and grin.

"Who said anything about V-et-nam," I'd hum, "I'm on my way to Am-ster-dam."

Back home for my last week of freedom, I was shocked to enter my folks' apartment to hear Isaac Hayes' voice booming from my bedroom. My dad was at work, so it had to be my mom. When I opened my bedroom door, that resonant, deep voice was breathing fire into the words "walk on by," as my mom dusted my Bethany awards hanging on the wall, tears streaming down her cheeks. As soon as she saw me, she straightened up and stopped crying.

"You're always playing this song, so I wanted to listen… and think about you," she said innocently, the pink curlers in her hair bobbing up and down. She looked so tiny and frail that I had to hug her, but she held back. "I don't want to get dirt all over you."

She shook dust from her rag. "Would you like some lunch?"

Mom was right about one thing. I played the hell out of *Hot Buttered Soul*. I'd liked Dionne Warwick's "Walk on By" and Glenn Campbell's "By the Time I Get To Phoenix," but they became something different with Isaac Hayes. Not just soulful, but rich, poignant story songs, experiences I could touch and feel. Maybe my mom heard it too, even if she had no idea who Isaac Hayes was.

The Sunday before I was leaving for Oakland, my mom decided to host a Thanksgiving-style dinner for me since I would be spending my November Thanksgiving in godforsaken Vietnam. She'd invited her favorite sisters, Kay and Helen, and their husbands. Ron and Carol passed. Smart move.

The eight of us dined on turkey and all the trimmings in front of the TV in the living room of my parents' tiny, two-bedroom apartment, watching the Oakland Raiders and Kansas City Chiefs wage pigskin war. Between first and second helpings, as I passed the gravy boat to Aunt Kay, my dad and Aunt Helen leapt from their chairs and ran toward the TV. A skirmish had broken out between opposing linemen.

Aunt Helen hollered something that sounded like a racial epithet, and my dad seconded her emotions.

I exchanged a pained expression with Gina whose body visibly tightened. She was embarrassed for me, and I was angry with my family. On the 28th day of a 30-day, pre-Vietnam leave, I was pissed off about everything—my parents, boxing, aunts and uncles, racism, genocide, Nixon, Vietnam, Cambodia, Kent State, the draft—everything. But there wasn't anything I could do about it except eat more of my mother's home cooking.

"Touchdown!" Aunt Helen shrieked. I shook my head, swallowed my rage, and left to look for Gina who, according to Aunt Kay, "was missing all the excitement." Gina wasn't in my bedroom which was serving as her guest bedroom. I'd been told to sleep on the sofa in the living room, my parents making sure there would be no hanky panky. And here I was going off to war. Yet another reason to be pissed.

I moved down the narrow hallway to my parents' bedroom. Even though they always had the heat in their apartment turned up too high, my folks usually kept the large bedroom windows open. The pitch-black room was cool, almost cold, like a cave hidden away among the nearby Pocono Mountains. I thought I heard something when I entered the room, but I was so exhausted that I collapsed on my parents' firm, king-sized bed. It was then I detected the sound of another person's breathing. The rhythm of the barely audible sighs told me that it was Gina. We just lay there, not wanting to talk about what had just happened, or what was going to happen in less than 48 hours.

"Do you remember how much you liked those first Laura Nyro songs I played for you?" she asked quietly. "So different from the stuff you were listening to. *Eli and The Thirteenth Confession* and *New York Tendaberry*. 'Wedding Bell Blues,' 'And When I Die,' 'Stoned Soul Picnic.' You were crazy about her."

Gina was right about that. Laura Nyro's music was like nothing I'd heard before—bright, distinctive, innovative, and oh so very New York, filled with blue-eyed soul. The piano, the tempo, and that voice, loud and shrill and sort of piercing. And sweet Jesus, those lyrics. I tried to remember a few lines, but all I could hear was "Walk on By."

As Gina reminisced, I realized she had a Laura Nyro-like way about her. Mystical. Bohemian. Was that enough to save me? Enough for me to hold on to for 365 days? Were we really in love, or was all this…all this crazy headstrong stuff only because of Vietnam?

We lay there, Gina breathing in the cool night air and breathing out her anxiety.

Just then, a crack of light from the hallway signaled the opening of the bedroom door. Someone else had entered the room. Neither of us moved. I wasn't alarmed because I figured it was my mom or dad…and when he laid down on the bed, moving Gina between us, it seemed inexplicably natural.

"It broke my poor mother's heart when I went into the service," my father recalled softly, almost privately. Gina and I listened to his whispered memories. "She was never the same after I went off to war, and I think that's why I hesitated, knowing that might happen…"

"Did I ever tell you what an unheroic fellow your father was?" he continued confessionally. "It was late 1943, almost 1944, 1944 before I joined the Army. 1944!" Gina and I jumped when he shouted the date. "Did I enlist? Did I run down to my local recruiting station and sign up to stop Hitler and Hirohito? No. I waited to get drafted. It's the end of 1943, and the world was going to hell, and I didn't have the guts to sign up and go fight."

None of us moved. We were floating through space and time on a bed in a bedroom in an apartment in a city somewhere between Pearl Harbor and Saigon.

"They had to come and get me," my dad admitted. "Sure, I wanted to beat the Japs and the Nazis. But I was scared to death. I didn't want to die. I didn't want to have to kill someone. I didn't want to go. I didn't want to leave my mother alone and heartbroken…And now," he paused, nearly choking on his words. "Now, all these years later, my youngest son has to do the same damn thing…only this time it's worse. It's me who can't save him, protect him…and it's my fault because I stopped paying attention…"

Was Gina still listening? My father's dead mother? Laura Nyro?

"I stopped paying attention to what was going on," my dad's voice grew a little stronger, "spending too much time watching *Gunsmoke* and *Bonanza*. Turning off the TV when the war reports came on. And here I thought we weren't supposed to have to fight wars anymore."

He stopped, drawing in a breath that took in me and Gina and the darkness.

* * *

I'm not sure how long the three of us stayed in the bedroom. Sometimes I wonder if that conversation really happened. But I realized that night how much my father loved me and how helpless he felt about my going to Vietnam. I sensed that more strongly two nights later when he fell to the floor, weeping and out of breath, at the Philly airport as we ran to the gate for my plane to San Francisco and beyond. He was alright, but as I steadied him and dried his tears, it struck me that my mom was the strong one, stronger than either of us. Hell, she was probably making my bed right then, singing along to Isaac Hayes.

Track 31:

THE TEARS OF A CLOWN

George and I spent one night together in a nondescript Oakland motel near Travis Air Force base and the U. S. Army depot, listening to the radio and singing songs from the *Sweet Baby James* album, George's favorite, acapella. No sooner did we report for duty the following morning, November 4, 1970, than George was called out of this huge formation. I wasn't. I doubted we'd ever see each other again.

Summoned to large formations twice daily for the next several days, I wanted, and waited for, the invitation to step up and take a seat on a plane to Vietnam. It wasn't like I hoped my name would be called, but I sure as hell didn't want to be stuck doing all the Army bullshit they made GIs in limbo do—clean barracks and latrines, pull KP and guard duty, pick up litter on the base—mindless stuff that almost made you want to go to Vietnam. Lucky for me, I was able to avoid a lot of this scut work thanks to a conversation among fellow detainees I'd overheard in the barracks the morning George departed.

"This fucking sucks," a chorus of beleaguered GI voices bounced off bunk beds and knapsacks. A radio somewhere was blasting "War." What is it good for? Less than damn nothing.

"Chill out man," said a short guy in wire rim glasses. He was sitting on the edge of his bunk smoking a Camel. "There are lots of ways to get out of this bullshit duty."

"Such as?" asked the guy across from him. His stiff crew-cut resembled an aircraft carrier.

"Giving blood, for one."

My ears perked up. I was set to ask a follow up, but one of the soul brothers beat me to it.

"How's that, my man?" asked the GI who had a pick in his Afro since there wasn't anyone around to order him to take it out.

"Simple," wire-rims responded, his eyebrows bobbing up and down above his frames. "At the morning formation, you tell the drill sergeants you want to give blood. They'll send you to the infirmary where you'll wait around until they poke you. They'll give you a note saying that you gave blood and you can't do any other duty for 24 hours."

A couple guys whistled their approval.

"And then what?" the guy with the Afro hairdo insisted.

"Then you go back and do it again. It's not like they keep a daily list or anything. You just volunteer, fall out of formation, go over to the infirmary, lay back and let them drain that good stuff out of you. Shit, man, giving blood is a very hero thing to do."

He smiled and the room erupted in laughter. I joined in, knowing that now I'd have to do "absolutely nothin'" while stuck in Vietnam limbo.

* * *

Embracing my blood-giving, freeloader status, afterwards I'd head off to the tiny base library, carrying the copy of James Joyce's *Ulysses* my folks gave me just before I left. How they knew I wanted to read *Ulysses* I'll never know. Had my old English prof at Bethany, John Taylor, turned me on to Joyce? Or was it Kirkpatrick? He'd had us read parts of *Portrait of the Artist*, so maybe that was it. Where in the fuck was Kirkpatrick anyway? Nowhere near Vietnam that's for sure.

I buried my nose in *Ulysses* every chance I got, as if there was a secret clue in it I needed to find, something that might save my ass in Vietnam. The Army library didn't have a copy of Homer's *Odyssey*, but there was an encyclopedia, so while I was reading sections of *Ulysses*, I'd check the Encyclopedia's section on Odysseus and try to figure out who represented whom in Joyce's remake of Greek mythology. Bloom being Ulysses and Stephen Dedalus being Telemachus were easy. But what about Buck Mulligan? Blazes Boylan? If I decoded the mystery, would it help me survive Vietnam and return to my family like the homesick Ulysses?

As I was exiting the early morning formation on November 10, I ran into wire rims, looking like forty miles of bad road.

"Bradley, isn't it?" He was looking directly at the name on my fatigues. "Where you headed?"

"To give blood," I smiled.

"No, you ain't," he cut me off. "They had some bad needles or something there and a bunch of guys got sick yesterday. Hell, I turned three shades of yellow and spent last night in the infirmary puking my guts out. They're shutting the blood draw down for today."

"Then I guess I'll hide out in the library," I waved the note that had yesterday's duty restrictions on it.

"That'd be another no," he looked at me strangely. "Weren't you even paying any fucking attention? They called your name this morning, man. You're going to Vietnam."

* * *

Part of me was glad to be getting out of Oakland, the Army tedium, and the not knowing. The other eighty-seven percent was scared shitless. All of us FNGs, Fucking New Guys—the Army loved acronyms—were jumpy and some guys were talking non-stop to cover their anxiety. I kept my head down and my mouth shut, rubbing *Ulysses* to release the genie. By the time we were seated on the commercial jet and told our stops would be Alaska, Japan, and, finally, Vietnam, and that it would take 15-16 hours to get there, all I could do was mumble "fuck" under my breath. The guy next to me nodded, but the three guys across the aisle gave me a weird look.

"You got a problem with going to Vietnam?" the pudgy guy in the middle snarled in my direction. The other two nodded. They looked like a three-headed hydra.

"Nope."

"Are you scared?"

I held my breath and pondered my response. If I said "yes" they'd probably call me a pussy. "No," I said softly, but affirmatively.

The fat guy in the middle stuck his elbows in the ribs of the other two, looking incredulous. "Did you hear that?" he laughed. "This guy ain't afraid of Vietnam." They sneered as my nemesis pointed a finger in my direction. "Son, you'd best be afraid because it is the scariest fucking place you'll ever see."

For the next few hours, even when I got up to go to the bathroom, the know-it-all and his sidekicks regaled me with horror stories. Fierce fighters in black pajamas with AK 47s, lurid tales of torture, snakes, tunnels, and prostitutes with razors in their vaginas. The nearer we got to Vietnam, the happier the three musketeers, all of them returning for their second tours, were to go on and on about the heat and the smell, a wet hotness that could knock you down, and the overwhelming odors of fuel, fires, and the foul-smelling food the Vietnamese cooked. Nothing I could do to stop the barrage. After every anecdote one of them would look over at me and say belligerently, "You're scared now, ain't ya?"

I was scared. Shitless. No George, no Kansas City, no Gina, no life buoy. One of the blonde SAS stewardesses must've noticed my unease, because she stopped at my seat, placed her hand on my shoulder, and asked if I was okay. I nodded. The hydra had finally fallen asleep, so I asked her a question.

"Is it really that hot? And smelly?"

She looked at me with pity. "Our airline food is about as good as it gets," she sounded sorrowful. "And it'll be the best you'll taste for the next year."

Jesus, now all my senses would be subjected to a Vietnam assault. As we drew closer and closer to Vietnam, it seemed like everybody was talking about the heat and the odors and the noise and…

They were right, sort of. When the doors opened and we walked off the plane, I stepped back from the overpowering heat. My nose picked up a scent that was beyond foul. But what nobody had prepared me for was the sound of Vietnam…it was the sound of music. Rock and roll. Our music. A cassette deck was cranked up somewhere on the tarmac, blasting Smokey's "The Tears of a Clown." Took me back to Bethany and pick-up basketball and better times. To slow dancing to the Miracles at TJ dances.

Smokey's voice came clear as a bell, reminding me that there weren't many things sadder than…than *this*, I sang to myself. Damn straight! Did either of us have any idea our worlds would collide three years after Bethany on a tarmac in Southeast Asia?

One thing was for certain: I was a card-carrying clown, part of the U. S. Army's never-ending, greatest show on earth.

Track 32:
KNOCK THREE TIMES

Where was that knocking coming from? Was there really a knocking? Somebody talking about knocking? In my dream state, I was snuggling with Gina on the beach in Nassau, the sun warming our bodies, the ocean shimmering like a diamond. Our hands were moving and our bodies were willing and…and then this voice from nowhere took me back to Dawn Tyndall behind the Beta House near that garage, and I was so very much wanting to…Jesus, here came that same voice again, and the knocking…

"Tony Orlando and Dawn coming to you from the studios of AFVN radio in Saigon," the voice sounded strangely familiar. *"This is your good buddy Les Howard, and we're in the middle of three hours of the best music this side of San Francisco…"*

Whoa, hold on, wait a fucking minute. I was wide awake now, on a cot in a hooch in goddamn Vietnam…but that voice, that smooth, cheery voice, wasn't that…?

"Brads, time to get moving," my hooch mate Roger Belmore from Atlanta, Georgia, cajoled in his slick southern drawl. Was I really here? With him, in Vietnam?

But what about the voice?

"That voice," I said aloud, "Who is that guy?"

"Les Howard," said Roger. "One of the AFVN jocks. Why?"

"I know that voice," I stammered. And then it hit me. WVBC. **W**est **V**irginia **B**ethany **C**ollege. Les Jacoby. An almost fraternity brother of mine. We were DJs together at the student radio station in 1965-66. The Bradley-Miller Groove Spectacular era. And now here he was, here I was, here we were, in 1970. In messed up and fucked-up Vietnam.

"Brads, you okay? Brads?"

I snapped out of it. "Did that guy I knew in college just play 'Knock Three Times' by Tony whosit and Dawn?"

"I think so."

"Jesus, he used to have taste," I muttered and got out of bed.

* * *

Every last thing about Vietnam was like that—an echo, a phantom, a dream blistering in the heat, the perspiration, the pot, the noise, the smells, the music, and the "nobody wants to be the last GI killed in Vietnam" insolence. Les Jacoby and Bethany College were light years away and then again right here, alongside Tony Orlando and Dawn and bad Top 40 music being played by American Forces Radio DJs. I was 23 and had only been in country for a little more than a month, but I felt like I'd been here forever.

Hunkered back here in the rear, not a person, including many of the younger officers, seemed to really give much of a shit about the war. They cared about getting a promotion and/or getting the hell outta this place. Everybody had a nickname—*Shirt* for a guy who preferred not to wear one; *One stroke* for Roger because of a less than stellar showing at a Saigon whorehouse. Mine, early on, was *Freak*, bestowed by a departing first lieutenant because I liked to get stoned. Rank did have its privileges. But no sooner had he departed then I was "Brads," "DB," or just plain Bradley. One of my hooch comrades called me Omar in deference to the renowned World War II five-star General with whom I shared a last name. The real Omar didn't keep me out of going to Vietnam.

Crazily, I got stationed again with George Moriarty, now my teammate at United States Army Republic of Vietnam (USARV) headquarters, in a relatively safe, rear echelon public information office with desks and typewriters and air conditioning during work hours, and cute Vietnamese girls wandering about. Was this really a war? Were guys like me actually fighting and dying while I pretended to love my job but would spend most of my time bad mouthing the Army and getting high and listening to music, good music, not Tony Orlando AFVN crap.

Had someone intervened? Did George have some clout I didn't know about? Or did I just roll a winner on the Vietnam dice while other guys rolled snake eyes? Probably the latter. Pure luck that Uncle Sam needed to replace two information specialists in the IO office who'd gone home—that's the way the Vietnam deployment two-step worked.

So, I got to spend my days in the air-conditioned jungle instead of out in the field doing interviews. We had a huge staff of writers, editors, photographers, and combat correspondents who did their Army work about as well as expected. Nearly everyone, except for most of the lifers, was a college grad. The place felt a lot like a graduate seminar. Colonel Brock, our small, bald, sunny dispositioned commanding officer, had gone to grad school in public relations at the University of Wisconsin. He treated us like professionals and never questioned our allegiances.

Our office produced a weekly newspaper, *The Army Reporter,* a slick, glossy quarterly magazine appropriately named *Uptight*; scores of hometown news releases; and an abundance of command information newsletters. My days were spent editing articles for, and laying out, *The Army Reporter*, writing an occasional newsletter for Colonel Brock or one of the generals, and, when called upon, preparing the "Morning News Roundup" (there was an "Evening News Roundup" too) for the thousands of soldiers based on Long Binh Post. Rounding up only the good news, of course. How we Americans were winning the war as well as the hearts and minds of the Vietnamese. Not how Charlie was kicking our ass or the Army was falling apart or guys were disobeying orders or LBJ (Long Binh Jail) was filled to overflowing. Nope, we were here to lift everybody's spirts—the journalistic equivalent of what Les Howard and his fellow DJs were doing on AFVN. Boosting fucking morale. I did it with an upbeat headline; Les with "Knock Three Times."

Of the countless Army writing jobs, the Roundup provided the most room for creativity, if not whimsy. After we'd grabbed relevant news copy from the three giant teletype machines in our office, slapped them on two sides of a sheet of paper, and run off hundreds of those suckers, we'd hop in the colonel's special limo with his own private driver, Mr. Trung, and deliver copies to the brass first, and then to the mess halls and main offices. In that way, the brass, lifers, enlistees, and draftees could consume their daily morning or evening news with their meal, just like back in the USA.

The execution of the Morning News Roundup was nocturnal and solitary. You had to be a hermit, to savor the quiet, the isolation of being the only person in the office late at night. We had such a guy—a long, lanky kid from New Jersey named Tim Merriman. He loved doing the Morning News Roundup and didn't want to surrender it to anyone. That meant we never hung out with him much. After supper, when we were ready to get stoned or watch a movie or listen to music or write letters home, Merriman would shuffle off to the IO office to do his thing.

But when he'd get sick or was on guard duty or R&R, somebody had to step up. George had a little bit of Merriman in him, but all of us pulled the Roundup night shift at some point. I wasn't crazy about it—I needed the company of my comrades to keep me from remembering I was in Vietnam. The one thing I enjoyed about the Morning News Roundup was the competition over who could find the best "kicker." Some enterprising GI before Merriman had started the tradition of finding the weirdest, funniest, quirkiest story to place as the *last* story in the Roundup. Turns out that was usually the first thing most of the GIs turned to, and I gotta say I never felt better than when I saw a bunch of guys smiling and laughing about a tidbit I'd inserted at the bottom of a Morning News Roundup.

Merriman was, hands down, the undisputed master of the perfect kicker and always found the zaniest, most obscure articles. His all-time best had to do with the time it rained frogs in Kuala Lumpur. Couldn't top that. But we all tried.

One night when I was bored and homesick with the coming on of Christmas, I decided to fabricate a kicker to steal some of Merriman's glamour. Channeling my best Charles Dickens a la *A Christmas Carol*, I concocted a story about a British guy named Miles "Scrooge" Malcolm who was going to force his London employees to work late on Christmas Eve. One of the workers told him he'd be sorry if he did that. In my imaginary article, Miles the Scrooge dismissed this threat, but at the end admitted to hearing the sound of reindeer hooves on top of the building and a shout of "Ho, ho, ho."

Crazy, yes, but who the hell cared? Everybody who read that Doug Bradley-invented anecdote in the Morning News Roundup got a kick out of it, letting off steam with therapeutic belly laughs. So I was told by the guys when I got back to my hooch to get some sleep. You always got to go to bed after you'd delivered the Morning News Roundup since you'd been up all damn night.

There was that damn knocking again. Les Howard? Tony Orlando? Dawn, his and mine? Nope, my hooch mate, Roger with an urgent look on his face as he shook me out of my sleep. "Brads, wake up man." He was shaking my shoulders with his hairy arms, his droopy brown mustache looking like a dead caterpillar. "Brads, you gotta wake up!"

"Jesus, fuck, what do you want?"

"General Weyand wants to see you."

"General who?"

"*The* General Weyand, the commander of all of Long Binh Post. He wants you in his office A-SAP, and he wants you to bring the teletype copy with the Miles Malcolm Christmas story."

"Say what?" I heard what Roger said, but I was hoping against hope I'd heard him wrong.

"He wants to see the original teletype story about Miles Scrooge Malcolm you posted in this morning's Roundup."

"Holy fuck," I turned over and buried my head in my pillow. "I'm screwed."

I didn't have time to confess to Roger. I dressed quickly, exited the hooch, and found Mr. Trung waiting to drive me to the office. He and I usually explained pleasantries in French, but I felt like a man who needed a blindfold and a cigarette more than a ride.

"*Ca va?*" Mr. Trung smiled, glancing in his rear-view mirror.

"*Je suis foutou,*" I mumbled, lowering my head to avoid his questioning look.

I ducked into the IO teletype room. The three big teletype machines were clanking away, bringing the news of the world into our little chunk of paradise. I rooted through the discarded teletype paper collecting in three large bins, as if my made-up story might magically materialize. I was freaking out. What in the hell was I going to tell General Weyand? What would he do to me when he discovered my hoax? Would I be the first GI in the history of the Army to be court martialed for making soldiers laugh? Would they send me to the DMZ on account of my phony kicker? Was this really the end for me?

I heard a knock on the door. Then another. Were two knocks in that stupid song good or bad? Where was Les Howard or Les Jacoby or whatever his name was when I needed him?

Soon, Master Sergeant Williams, Colonel Brock, and Lt. Johnston burst into the room. I looked up from the discarded paper bin I was rummaging through, ready to explain myself, confess my sin even, when Colonel Brock dove into the bin next to me.

"Nice digging Specialist Bradley," he sounded upbeat.

"Yes sir, I'll keep at it."

"Here it is," Lt. Johnson was waving a story in front of him. I was completely bewildered.

"Give it here," Colonel Brock demanded, then proceeded to read the AP release aloud *"Congress today passed the Cooper-Church Amendment to the U. S. Defense Appropriations Bill,"* his voice sounded like a teletype. Williams and Johnson were nodding their heads. I still had no idea what was going on. *"The bill forbids the use of any U. S. ground forces in Laos or Cambodia.* This is what General Weyand wants to see. Good work Bradley."

And they ran out of the office. I figured General Weyand now had bigger fish to fry than my silly Christmas story prank. Congress was handing him and the rest of the Army a huge lump of coal in their stockings. "Twice on the old pipe and the answer was…no!"

* * *

Later that night at the hooch, as I was giving a dramatic rendering of the Scrooge kicker saga to my IO brothers, I turned serious.

"Colonel Mustard, in the teletype room, with the lead pipe."

"Say what?" someone hollered from the rear of the group.

"I said, 'Colonel Mustard, in the teletype room, with the lead pipe.' Just like the game 'Clue,' I'm here to reveal the culprit. It was one of you fucking guys with the lead pipe in the teletype room."

I saw looks of bewilderment, astonishment, and a few smug smiles on the faces of my fellow GIs.

"Dude, what the fuck are you talking about?" came the commanding voice of Steve Downs, one of the hooch's senior inhabitants.

"I'm saying I got played. I succumbed to the IO hooch hazing. And I lost. You guys set me up and scared the living shit out of me."

A volley of "fuck yous, eat shit, and *dinky dau*," rained down on my head like frogs in Kuala Lumpur. Maybe I was wrong? Or maybe I was right? Hell, at least I said the lead pipe was the weapon, a shout out to "Knock Three Times."

Even after the close call, or practical joke, or whatever it was, I kept on making up kickers for the Roundup, including several about Punxsutawney Phil, the famous Pennsylvania groundhog who predicted the weather. "Where have you gone Punxsey Phil," I had the citizens of Punxsutawney mimicking Simon and Garfunkel's "Mrs. Robinson." "Our nation turns its frozen eyes to you, woo hoo hoo."

Hell, if anyone did ever rat us out to the brass, or the brass got pissed, what were they going to do? Send us to Vietnam?

Track 33:

THE PUSHER

We homesick GIs rang in 1971 sitting on the roof of our hooch watching flares along the perimeter, taking in a spectacular aerial light show courtesy of several hovering helicopter gunships. Lots of "oohs" and "aahs" as if we were kids back home on the Fourth of July. Pretty damn surreal sight for a war zone. Still, any notions of a New Year elicited alarms about the Oriental, lunar version. During the Tet new year in 1968, pencil pushing Long Binh GIs with jobs like mine had to fight off the Viet Cong tooth and nail.

Not something any of us were eager to do, least of all dovish me.

The next night, January 1, 1971, a bunch of us gathered at our makeshift bar in the hooch to share New Year's Resolutions when Rick Roberts and Bill Ward shouted for us to pipe down and pay attention to whatever was being broadcast on AFVN radio. What we heard was an acerbic voice that sounded like it was laced with equal parts marijuana, No

Doz, and barbed wire. "*Vietnam, in just 30 seconds your radio experience will change forever,*" the radio voice warned. "*Turn your radios to 69 Megahertz on your FM dial. If you don't, we are going to re-up you for another tour of Vietnam.*"

We followed that order too, found the frequency...and our jaws dropped. A steady stream of whacked-out, druggie, psychedelic music burst forth—"Double Cross" by Bloodrock, "Soul Experience" by Iron Butterfly, "My Flash on You" by Love—punctuated by the most stoned-out voice we'd ever heard from a DJ who identified himself as Dave Rabbit. This wasn't Uncle Sam's AFVN. In between the James Gang's "Funk #49" and "The Pusher" by Steppenwolf, Dave Rabbit emerged as a surrogate sound pusher, trashing the brass and the war while extoling the virtues of getting high and staying there. Who was this guy and what the hell was he doing on Armed Forces Radio?

Turns out Dave Rabbit wasn't "on" AFVN, just right next to it on the radio dial. But that was close enough. For the next few nights, we tuned in to "Radio First Termer," the name he gave his radio show. Brother Rabbit kept cranking out "hard acid rock music to blow your mind with" and bad mouthing the brass. Almost daring them to come and find him.

Rabbit informed us Radio First Termer was being broadcast from a whore house in nearby Saigon. He and his sidekicks—a fellow he called Pete Sadler and a woman named Nguyen who sounded more like she was from Detroit than Danang—put on off-color skits and told bawdy jokes. The trio would also supply regular "news reports" they uncovered in restrooms. "We have just gotten word," they told us one night, "that a new Korean massage house is open in the Saigon area...available are steam bath, back massage, hand jobs, and blow jobs."

Radio First Termer dispensed helpful hints for local listeners: "If you're at the Magic Finger Lounge tonight," he advised as John Kay of Steppenwolf sang about visiting damnation, "stay away from the Korean at the door, he's pushing some bad H."

God damn.

What in the hell was going on? Nobody knew for sure, but we were digging it. Mind-altering music at the center. Acid rock courtesy of Cactus and Vanilla Fudge. And of course, the 17-minute version of Iron Butterfly's incomprehensible opus, "In-A-Gadda-Da-Vida."

"This is one long motherfucker," signaled Rabbit's raspy, stoner voice, "so I think I'll go down the hall and take a shit, smoke a joint or two…"

We were hooked. For 21 days we tuned in. And then as unexpectedly as it had appeared, Radio First Termer vanished. January 21, 1971, was the last broadcast. Not a damn sound at 69 Megahertz on our FM dial. We all figured Dave Rabbit and his pals had been busted and were singing the court martial blues in Long Binh Jail.

But oh, what a liberating 63 hours it was.

"That was far fucking out," Rick Roberts marveled the night Radio First Termer went silent. "Music's damn near all we have left, and Brother Rabbit gave it to us right between the ears." Heads nodded all around. "Beats the hell out of Vietnamese and Korean cover bands and AFVN. That's the real shit. Here's to Radio First Termer!"

Everyone raised a glass of something. Dave Rabbit had given us our say. For three wild weeks he had the brass on their heels, telling them and Nixon and the rest of the powers-that-be to get fucked. A GI Revolution in A minor…

After that, it was back to AFVN. But the DJs and their selections started to change a little…maybe because of Dave Rabbit? And thanks to the guys from the hooch who went to Taiwan on R&R, we could get our hands on popular albums for a measly dollar, so we had a steady supply of recent, decent tunes—Jefferson Airplane's *Volunteers*, Cat Stevens' *Tea for the Tillerman*, Traffic's *John Barleycorn Must Die*. But no Dave Rabbit to provide raunchy play-by-play.

Over time, with the war winding down and most guys lighting up and nobody giving much of a fuck since the U. S. was getting ready to head home, the music melded into one long "short timer" symphony. "Dragging the Line" signaling the invasion of Laos; "Riders on the Storm" counterpointing the rigged South Vietnamese elections; "What's Going On" punctuating the release of the *Pentagon Papers*. "Me and Bobby McGee" reminding us that freedom was just another word for having nothin' left to lose…

We wrote our stories, obeyed orders, and counted the days.

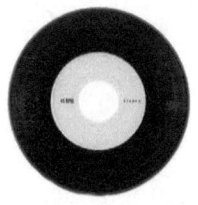

Track 34:

WILD HORSES

Among the enigmas we debated in Vietnam was whether the old rule of threes meant good news or bad. The Catholics among us—former altar boys like me who knew the Latin translation *"omne trium perfectum"*—figured it was kinda good since it represented the Holy Trinity. Others countered that with Hendrix, Joplin, and Morrison dying within a year of each other at the same age, things coming in threes heralded catastrophe. We could've kept on arguing, but I was distracted by my own soul-shaking set of three titanic jolts.

It began with an early February rocket-propelled, grenade attack here at safe and secure Long Binh. That was the Viet Cong response to Nixon's decision to have the South Vietnamese Army, ARVN for short, invade Laos. Having witnessed the Cambodian debacle and its upheaval in the USA, we irony-loving reluctant pencil pushers figured the latest "incursion," code name *Lam Son 719*, would likewise backfire.

So why not have a little fun with it?
QUESTION: What is Lam Son 719?
ANSWER:

a. Name for a new NVA rifle
b. A super-lubricant prophylactic
c. A little town in Bethlehem
d. The place where Apollo 14 landed
e. Jane Fonda's nickname
f. False

We tossed around jokes in the IO office and back at the hooch as we followed the Lam Son news. There was simply no way the ARVN could stand up to the NVA, so why even bother? And why the fuck now? For us, laughter trumped bewilderment and skepticism. We would've kept making jokes about it until the water buffalo came home if one of the guys in our office, Spec. 4 Steve Warner, hadn't volunteered to cover the campaign.

"Jesus, Warner, what in the fuck are you thinking?" a group of us asked him one night over beers at the hooch's makeshift bar.

"Whaddya mean?" His regulation Army glasses gave him a professorial look, but his face was all innocence and sincerity.

We looked at each other and shook our heads.

"A. It's dangerous," offered Rick Roberts, his bushy brown hair sliding down in front of his eyes.

"B. It's really dangerous," added Roger Belmore, his droopy mustache bathed in Budweiser suds.

"C. It's stupid and dangerous," Mike Goldberg, shirtless as always, tossed in for good measure. Steve kept a wry smile on his face as if he was in on some secret the rest of us weren't. He removed his glasses and his brown eyes sparkled in the dim hooch light.

"Seriously," Kevin, our TDY comic, piped up, "the ARVN will be sitting ducks. They'll get their butts kicked and yours, my friend, in the process," he paused and smiled. "We'd like your cute little ass to stay here with us in good old Long Binh."

Steve let out a sigh. For a minute we thought he might change his mind.

"No can-do GI," he smiled, aping the broken English spoken by our mamasans. "This is a war gentleman," he went on. "And it just might be the closest we'll ever get to observing actual combat."

What did he mean *we*? For some reason, I'd kept my mouth shut during the exchange, something I usually didn't do. Especially late at night over beers. Maybe it had something to do with my not knowing Steve very well. Or not having the least bit of appreciation for the ugly side of this war, namely the fighting and dying. Or because of my overriding anger with the powers that be in Washington, D.C.

"What do you think, Brads?" a question with my name attached came out of nowhere, merging with the strains of a twangy country and western song playing somewhere in the hooch. "Wild horses couldn't drag me away." From what? From here? The question came again—"What do you think Brads?"—and I realized it was coming from Steve.

"A man's gotta do what a man's gotta do," I tried mimicking my best John Wayne.

"That's your best advice?" He put his glasses back on and looked intently at me.

It would have taken way too long to explain all that I was thinking, so I didn't. "And that's the way it is," I chuckled, this time trying to imitate Walter Cronkite.

Everybody laughed but Steve.

We got the Lam Son news a few weeks later. Spec. 4 Steve Warner stepped on a land mine while accompanying troops into Laos on Valentine's Day. He was the first guy in our office killed in Vietnam. Wild horses couldn't have kept him away from covering the war. His death took the wind out of our sails, scaring the shit out of those of us who still had to go into the field to cover stories.

But we never talked about our fear, nor shed a public tear, for Steve. We felt silently fortunate, I guess, that it was him and not us.

* * *

Jolt number two arrived a few weeks later in the form of nurse Jenny. With the short blonde hair.

Still harboring my long-distance love for Gina via letters and memories—she was completing her senior year and preparing to exit Buffalo as soon as possible—I looked down on my fellow GIs who pursued their earthly delights in Saigon whorehouses. To me, it seemed hurtful to the young Vietnamese women whom I presumed were forced into prostitution. And somehow it seemed deceitful, too, not just to our wives or girlfriends back home, but to ourselves...

So, while I admired the bevy of Vietnamese beauties who worked on the base, I kept my distance. Then one day I stopped by the snack shop in our HQ building and encountered a cute, friendly, flirty "round eye" as we referred to American girls, at the lunch counter. At the time, I was adorned by a large cast on my right leg, compliments of torn ligaments in my ankle from, of all things, a pickup basketball game. I sure as hell wasn't going to broadcast that inglorious war wound to anyone.

"You're butting in, buster, it's my turn," she elbowed her way in front of me in a way that was more welcome than standoff. "I gotta get back to work."

"Me too sister," I said, grabbing her by the shoulders and sliding her behind me. "How about showing some respect for the disabled."

"I do that every day," she pointed convincingly to the Red Cross insignia on her blue nurse's uniform. "Besides, you look pretty healthy to me. Except for…what dumb thing did you do anyway?"

I broke into a big grin. "It wasn't that dumb," I deadpanned. "Plus, it's my business not yours, unless you're going to administer first aid."

"You wish."

"Maybe I do."

"And who might that I be?"

"Spec. 4 Doug Bradley, drill sergeant." My response was louder than I wanted it to be, but I was enjoying this too much.

"Well, specialist Bradley, nurse Jenny Kovacks at your service. But if you'll excuse me, I need to go out and save a few more lives. So, step aside, if you don't mind." Her sandy blonde hair accentuated the blue of her Red Cross uniform. It was hard to tell her proportions but her skirt was as short as the Red Cross would allow. And there was an alluring sparkle in her deep blue eyes.

"Just this once," I grabbed her by the shoulders again and moved her ahead of me in the line.

I saw Nurse Jenny in line at the snack shop a couple more times over the next week or so and each time the banter was funnier and flirtier. Something was happening here, and I knew very well what it was. But I convinced myself it was nothing like what my fellow soldiers were doing in Saigon. This was an independent, all-American girl, and we were just having a little fun.

A few nights later Jenny and I shared a passionate night in her hooch on the other side of Long Binh post. We were stoned out of our minds, and I remember her putting up a sheet between her part of the tiny hooch so her roommate couldn't see Jenny climbing on top of me because of my cast and taking control… and of hearing a song I thought I knew, some guy echoing my own emotions telling Jenny she was a graceless lady who knew who I was. No way I was going to let this seductive Red Cross nurse slide through these hands. Roger that. I was actually in bed in Vietnam with a cute nurse from Cleveland. Or was all of this, including Steve Warner's death, a dream?

"That was special," Jenny whispered to me as she took a sip from the bottle of Mateus wine on her nightstand. "Here." She handed the bottle to me.

I took a long sip. Intoxicating like everything else that evening. But that song?

"Who's that singing?"

"Graham Nash, I think," she mumbled. "It's a tape one of my girlfriends has. The song's called 'Wild Horses.' Like it?"

"It doesn't sound like Graham Nash," I tried to soft peddle my disagreement, but knowing Nash from the Hollies and CSNY, I knew it wasn't him.

"Okay smarty pants, who is it then?"

"Not sure… let me see… hell, maybe you're right…"

Jenny leapt off me and the bed, pulled the cassette tape out of the player, and handed it to me. Her body silhouetted in the candlelight—Jesus, there were candles?—and for a moment I was breathless. What a beautiful figure. And how lucky was I?

It was hard to make out the writing on the cassette in the dim light, plus the words didn't make sense. *Burrito Deluxe*.

"Burrito Deluxe," I said aloud. "Who the fuck?"

"Oh yeah, the Flying Burrito Brothers," Jenny volunteered. "My friend Cassie loves them. Kind of a haunting song, isn't it?"

Later that week, Jenny went up north to help with the post Lam Son carnage, and I was sent, sans leg cast, to the USS Ranger, an aircraft carrier in the Gulf of Tonkin, to write a story about the Navy, all the while thrilled by the realization I'd be able to have amazing sex with Jenny for the rest of my days in Vietnam. But wasn't I cheating on Gina? Committing the same sins as the whorehouse patrons? Not really, I rationalized. I wasn't paying for sex or demeaning an Asian woman or falling in love, or… hell, I was a righteous GI a long way from home in a war zone helping a fellow countryman, woman, to make it through the night. Whatever my doubts, the pot and the sex and the female company were all too tantalizing.

There was a shitload of mail waiting for me when I got back from my brief off-shore experience on April Fool's Day. Several from my mom and Gina, a couple from some young coeds from West Chester State Teachers College who'd "adopted" me as their charity case/pen pal. And one from my new part-time lover Jenny telling me she and her Red Cross compatriot had been busted for pot and sent back stateside. "Write me please, because I feel like I could fall for a guy like you," she closed. My heart sank. My libido too. Gram Parsons was singing in my head.

* * *

The third jolt took the form of a letter bearing a most familiar name—W.J. Kirkpatrick!

Just how the Bradley-Kirkpatrick correspondence had kicked back in was as unexpected as Warner being killed and Jenny being deported. On one of the few occasions I ever read the *New York Times* magazine in Vietnam, I stumbled on an article about a poet who'd been at Ohio U. and was a friend of Kirkpatrick. Eager to know if my old mentor was still alive, I wrote the poet and, voila, he forwarded my address to Kirkpatrick.

So here we were, back to where we'd almost started, as if it were again the summer of 1964 when I was hurting and he was prospering at Ohio University.

"What the hell are you doing in 'Nam?" that first letter opened. Then he went on about his world. He loved his tenure-track teaching gig at Carnegie Mellon University, his students, a film class he was teaching, Percy Bysshe Shelley, the Beatles, going to movies and…he despised almost everything about his three years at Thomas Jefferson.

Except for me and Will Beale.

"You and Beale meant the most to me," he wrote, mentioning how Will had shown up in his life one night, only to disappear again forever.

"He's married now," Kirkpatrick added parenthetically. *"So, I guess Mrs. Beale's worst fears are ended."*

Just what were Mrs. Beale's worst fears? I was afraid to ask. Here I was 9,000 miles from home in a perilous war zone with one of my fellow soldiers dead and the NVA and Viet Cong everywhere, and I was fixated on some old high school drama. Why should I give a damn?

But with everything that was going on in Vietnam and America, plus all the departures in the IO office and the Army falling apart and the war going to hell, I immersed myself in that back-and-forth with Kirkpatrick. Totally submerged in it since Gina and I, following a disastrous R&R in Hawaii where nothing went right, including the sex, were struggling to figure out how whatever it was we'd had before evaporated in the Polynesian sun. I doubted Kirkpatrick would be much help with that. Still, I wrote him back and he wrote me back and we kept on going in the way we always communicated best—words, distance, letters—interspersed with his analyses of music and movies and books and feelings and anxieties and...very little about Thomas Jefferson High School. Just enough to keep my head spinning. I didn't tell a soul, not even George or Gina, about his letters.

"Send my love to your parents," he closed one of the first letters. *"I appreciate them very much. They trusted me and never questioned my relationship with you."*

Which was what exactly, I wondered aloud.

"My love is strong for you," he wrote in another. *"I almost feel a bit queer, sort of like if you were here, I'd hug you, hold on to you, and want to hold on to you all night. But that's my problem."*

No, now that you're told me, it's my problem too, I realized.

"After grad school, three suicide attempts, a lot of sex both hetero and homo variety, some drugs, and two trips to

England, I'm sort of adrift," he penned. "When you knew me, I was falling in love with everyone I met. But a few Mrs. Connie Beales along the way blew my mind for me and left me as I am."

"Have you heard 'Wild Horses' by the Rolling Stones?" he asked. "Best thing they've ever done. The entire album, Sticky Fingers, is genius. You remember my obsession with the Beatles? They're dead and gone—Lennon is the only one who has his shit together—so the Stones are my new favorite, thanks to that album. Can you get new music over there? Albums and tapes? If you can, get a copy of Sticky Fingers and listen to 'Wild Horses' and you'll see what I mean. Listen to the lyrics. Jagger talks about dreaming a sin and a lie, faith being broken, time running out. The song is about us, you and me, back at TJ...and me now and...who knows what else? We can listen to it together when you're home."

Thanks to Jenny, jolt number two, I knew that song alright. It, like the ghost of Steve Warner, jolt number one, had been haunting my Vietnam days and nights. Add to that jolt number three in the form of Kirkpatrick...Goddamn, not even wild horses could drag me away...

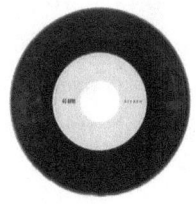

Track 35:

WE GOTTA GET OUT OF THIS PLACE

Between Steve Warner's death and DEROS, between R&R and FUBAR, between Dave Rabbit and heroin habits, the war in Vietnam kept on churning. From the sky we were decimating the Vietnam countryside while on the ground the fiercest battle was more between us and the brass, the lifers who wanted us to look and act and fight in a certain way, even as we all knew the enemy was biding its time, waiting for us to get the hell out of that place.

Our numbers in the IO office had dwindled considerably. By late summer George and I were senior guys in the office, more or less responsible for the nightly goings on. When AFVN announced that it would be celebrating the upcoming labor day weekend by playing the greatest rock and roll hits of all time, we decided to tune in. As was our usual fashion, we made a game of it.

"Friends, Romans and in-countrymen, this is what you've tuned in for," the enthusiastic Army DJ's voice blanketed the American enclave. "In just 10 minutes, 600 ticks of the clock, we'll kick off AFVN's end-of-summer rock 'n' roll music marathon! 72 hours of non-stop oldies. Vintage tunes from the '50s and '60s just like you remember them. The songs you grew up with, music for good times, good friends, and that very, very special someone who's back in the world, still waiting for you.

"So, sit back, listen up, and sing along with the music that's the soundtrack of your life…"

BAM!

"Five bucks says the first song they play is by the King," challenged Spec. 5 John Paul Jones from Fayetteville, North Carolina. Jones liked to act in charge. He patted the five spot he'd just smacked down on the hooch makeshift bar, his silver dog tags adorning his neck.

Specialist Jones was one of the more vocal guys in the hooch, and one of our few Southerners. He leaned back on his bar stool, took a long swallow of his can of Carling Black Label beer, and smiled broadly. "Back home they always start and end shows like this with Elvis. This ain't gonna be no different."

"Bullshit," snorted Rick Smith from Billings, Montana. He was one of our latest newcomers and seemed to be enjoying the IO comradery and the pot, not necessarily in that order.

"You're in Vietnam, man—V-ET-NAAM. It's 19-fuckin'-71," he was teasing and taunting John Paul. "Out here we got us a brand-new king, brother. Hendrix! They've got to start it with Jimi. 'Purple Haze,' man, 'Purple Haze' without any fuckin' doubt." Rick laid five Washingtons next to Jones's Lincoln.

"Easy money" Spec. 4 Peter Milton, a tall drink of water from Hoboken, New Jersey, stepped up to the bar and added a bill to the growing pile. "That AFVN jock is a New York city kid and those guys just love the Doo-Wop oldies." Milton paused as he savored the sound of smooth harmonies and lush vocals in his head. "The Five Satins. 'In the Still of the Night.' Genuine East Coast R&B."

"Them's fightin' words, Yankee." drawled my Atlanta, Georgia, cubicle mate. He shook his head. "And anyhow, five bucks ain't shit. Let's make this meaningful." Georgia's best reached into the breast pocket of his fatigues and placed the holy grail of Vietnam currency—his ration card—on the bar.

"A case of beer—good beer—none of this Carling Black Label shit." He glared at the can of beer on the bar in front of him. "A case of Budweiser, the King of Beers, and a carton of smokes, says it's Creedence."

Several heads in the rapidly growing crowd nodded in agreement. Now the stakes were considerably higher since ration cards allowed each of us to purchase requisite amounts of smokes, beer, and hard liquor for the month.

"'Proud Mary,' 'Run Through the Jungle,' 'Fortunate Son,'" he continued. "I don't know which one it'll be and I don't much give a damn, but no way it ain't CCR."

"Just a teeny-weeny minute, my fellow brothers-in-arms," interjected Spec. 5 Tom Newville of Newton, Massachusetts. Newville was small and sinewy. Always full of electricity and seemingly on permanent TDY in our office from some godforsaken place up country. He winked as he placed his own ration card on top of Roger's.

"It will be the Beatles, lads," he intoned in a Cockney accent. "Guaranteed. 'Hey Jude' or 'A Little Help from my Friends.' Our old pals John, Paul, George, and Ringo."

Shouts of "Right on," "GI number one," and "There it

is," ran up against an equal volley of "Numbah ten," "Eat shit," and "Dinky dau." I wasn't sure where the crowd had come from—had some of the comptroller guys from upstairs joined the party?—but there were a couple dozen of America's finest waving their ration cars and shouting the names of their favorite artists and songs.

Eventually, Ben Fritz, a mustachioed maverick from the Midwest, jumped on the bar and pushed down the air with his arms, as if trying to physically quiet the Southeast Asian cacophony.

"What we have here is a failure to communicate," he smiled, proud of his *Cool Hand Luke* reference. "We all know who's the true troubadour of rock n' roll, the greatest poet of modern times, and damn straight the only one who understands what a shit show this really is. Boys and girls, the one, the only, Bob Dylan. 'Like a Rolling Stone.'"

"Y'all forgettin' about the brothers," disputed Spec. 4 Arthur Howard, our hooch's only non-white member. There were numerous black GIs on Long Binh and in Vietnam, but Arthur was the only one granted access to our college-grad fraternity. "They start it off with a Minnesota cracker and there's gonna be trouble in cell block number nine." Peals of laughter. "Motown, man. 'Nowhere to Run' because there sure as hell ain't nowhere to run between here and the DMZ."

"'Chain of Fools,'" shouted a voice from the back of the hooch. Ben Fritz started making a list on the small chalkboard above the bar where our weekly "to do" list was inscribed.

"'Satisfaction'—Right on!"

"'Light My Fire'—There it is!"

"Sloop John B" elicited howls of derision "too pop, too

California." Edwin Starr's 'War' meets a similar fate: "too political, too obvious."

"'Ring of Fire.'"

"Something by Smokey."

"'For What It's Worth.'"

Ration cards were spilling over the sides of the bar. I was having fun watching my Vietnam brothers, especially the new guys, getting into this. George hadn't volunteered a song either—probably for fear if he mentioned his singing sweetheart Joni Mitchell he'd get laughed out of the hooch.

"Listen up, everyone!" Tom Newville jumped on a box and waved his arms for attention. "We gotta have some order here. We need to do this right."

Calling out for a show of hands, Newville calculated some quick odds. The Beatles and CCR at 4-1 had gained the upper hand, but the dopers were hanging tough with Hendrix and the Doors. Dylan and Elvis partisans also refused to give up the fight.

Almost midnight in Southeast Asia. But it was more like we were all back in our hometowns with our buddies, waiting for our music to play and comfort us. Was there a sound anywhere else in Vietnam at that moment except for the crackling of the AFVN radio waves?

And then…a bass guitar laid down a hard line. In a matter of mini seconds, as the bass riff started to repeat, I knew I had the same look of recognition spread across my face as everybody else in the hooch. How the fuck did we miss this? Jaws agape, mouths wide open, our GI faces were draped in 'are you kidding me?' grins as the Animals' lead singer Eric Burdon growled:

"In this dirty old part of the city

Where the sun refused to shine"

By the time he and the rest of the Animals hit the chorus, our whole dumbfounded bunch was singing along, punctuating with gusto the lyrics of that old hit song that expressed what every soldier in Vietnam was always thinking: "We Gotta Get Out of This Place!"

The record played and we sang. LOUD!

When the song was over, nobody said a word, embarrassed no doubt by the fact none of us had gotten it right. Arguing about our rock and roll music, we'd all forgotten just where in the hell we were. Shit, we even left our ration cards on the bar.

Track 36:

RIVER

I got used to the ups and downs and sideway tilts of Vietnam, or maybe just grew numb to them. Music, movies, books, my fellow GIs, and opium-laced pot helped. The smoke cast me under an intoxicating Southeast Asian spell of liquid sky, nuoc mom, and pica poles. All the way to my DEROS day. For once I loved an Army acronym: **D**ate **E**ligible for **R**eturn from **O**ver**S**eas.

Besides music, letters had been my main medicine. As the days ticked down, they were a safe place to show off my non-Army propaganda writing chops to Gina—and Jenny, who now was writing me regularly from Cleveland. Not to mention the twice-weekly letters from Kirkpatrick. I'd read many of the books he'd enthusiastically recommended—from *Sons and Lovers* by D. H. Lawrence to Arthur Janov's *The Primal Scream*—and compiled a list of the films he screened for his Carnegie Mellon students. Once again, I was a student in his classroom, expecting, hoping, that my old teacher possessed the answer to every question, the solution to every problem. I knew better, but if he didn't, who did?

And then my own personal, gift-wrapped, DEROS day arrived.

I nestled in my "Freedom Bird" headed for San Francisco and the rest of my life. Nobody around to hassle me like the guys on the flight over to Vietnam. Nobody to give me a fucking order, to tell me to get a haircut or trim my mustache or…suddenly, the plane was lifting off the shimmering Tan Son Nhut tarmac, and we departing GIs burst into a chorus of "We Gotta Get Out of This Place!" Everyone smiled as if the weight of the world had been lifted from their shoulders. Little did we know we'd be carrying the weight of that godforsaken war the rest of our lives.

I sang along, not as lustily as I might have. Looking out the window, I imagined watching big chunks of my past 365 days being discarded, tossed into the air like so much excess baggage. *Out* with Miss Mai, our cute Vietnamese receptionist; *adios* Col. Brock, by far my best commanding officer; *farewell* IO hooch mates and Vietnamese mamasans; *good-bye* one-week leave in Australia where I dropped acid and partied with hippies; *sayonara* bogus South Vietnamese elections; *later* for the Red Alerts when the VC wanted to remind us they were still around; *ciao* sanitized stories about South Vietnamese Army recruits and kickers of the Morning News Roundup; *bye-bye* names, faces, ranks, and serial numbers. Not one damn thing about Vietnam remained on that plane except me, my discharge papers, my journal, my letters, and my cassette player and headphones.

I popped the Joni Mitchell tape George had given me before he'd left Vietnam in the player and put on my headphones. And I listened to that album all the way back home...

"It's comin' on Christmas/They're cutting down trees..."

Was it that close to Christmas? To winter? Foreign concepts, but every line, every lyric, every element of every song on that album spun its web. From "All I Want" through "The Last Time I Saw Richard," I was mesmerized by Joni's insights and feelings. And that haunting voice. Her honest pain, as if I was eavesdropping on her private life. Could she help me to figure out mine? I'd listened to a lot of music during my 365 days in Vietnam, but I'd never *listened* this closely, concentrated so hard on what someone was singing. Just to me.

* * *

I owed George for the gift of Joni Mitchell. He knew all her songs and sang along to them, which was something guys didn't do in Vietnam. Janis Joplin, Grace Slick, Aretha, the Motown girl groups, maybe even Carole King on a special occasion could be tolerated. But *not* ethereal voices like Joni Mitchell or Judy Collins or Joan Baez. Why I wasn't sure, but that was the code we masculine Army guys lived by. It hadn't kept George from joining Joni in sing-alongs when nobody else was around.

Except me.

His favorite Joni album during our time in Vietnam was *Ladies of the Canyon*. I never told George, but I hadn't gotten into that piercing, undulating, agonizing voice at first. A higher-pitched Laura Nyro. But as George sang along to "Morning Morgantown" and "Big Yellow Taxi" and "The Circle Game," something sunk in.

Over time, George and I were able to win over a few of our fellow GIs. He'd explain to us how she'd written "Woodstock" for Crosby, Stills, Nash, and Young, and that they were part of the backup chorus for "The Circle Game" and, well, Joni was probably sleeping with some or all of them which made her way cool. So, late in the evening, when most of the hooch was turning off lights to the Doors or the Moody Blues or CCR, George and I would listen to "For Free" or "Willy" and go to bed with Joni Mitchell.

★ ★ ★

Back on the long plane ride home, Koss headphones clamped to my head, *Blue* filling my ears and my soul. Yes, it was "comin' on Christmas," and I couldn't stop listening to "River," wondering what awaited me in Richard Nixon's America...

And then a feeling seized me hard, one I didn't expect to have—my relief at being out of Vietnam and Uncle Sam's Army was already fading...and maybe, just maybe, I would miss my year at war, miss working at the IO office, miss living in the hooch with George and our fellow Information Office brothers, talking, laughing, complaining...getting high and listening to Joni Mitchell. Was that really possible? Wasn't life back home in America the reward for enduring 365 days in Vietnam? The pot of gold at the end of the monsoon rainbow?

Or, as Joni sang, was that just a dream some of us had?

Panicking, I grabbed onto the hope that Kirkpatrick could help me peel this onion. He'd mentioned that he'd been back and forth to merry old England twice, so maybe he could relate to my coming back to the USA after being away and finding everything different, changed. But the more I thought about our months of recent correspondence, the more I realized his letters offered more mysteries than solutions, more lectures than lessons. Just like high school.

At least I still had Gina to hold on to, literally. I'd be getting back on a plane tomorrow to fly back to Hawaii, where she'd decided to relocate after our July rendezvous there. Should I, could I, hold on to Kirkpatrick too?

And why would I want to?

Part Four:
TIMBRE

"Music is the literature of the heart; it commences where speech ends."

Alphonse de Lamartine

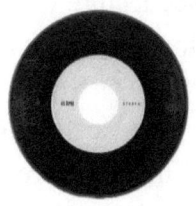

Track 37:

IT'S TOO LATE

My first order of post-Vietnam business was a return to Hawaii to see if Gina and I were destined to live happily ever after. This was so unlike the chain-of-command orders I'd been following in Uncle Sam's Army for the past 20 months, but it sure had an air of live-or-die necessity. The *idea* of Gina that I'd held on to had kept me going during my 365 days at war, and now that we'd worked through what had gone wrong on R&R in Hawaii through letters, it was time to start living with the idyllic life we envisioned. I'd been lucky enough to survive Vietnam, all the while with Gina—give or take my fling with Jenny—as my true soul and inspiration.

Or was that just a Righteous Brothers romance revolving in my head?

I'd written Kirkpatrick for relationship advice, hoping he might know something about what it was like to make a person into an ideal, someone who didn't actually exist in the world the way they did in your head. All he'd given me was another D. H. Lawrence lecture on how guys can love one another the way they loved women. And vice versa. Thanks but no thanks.

Gina had fallen in love with Hawaii during our rocky R&R visit in July and moved there lock, stock, and barrel late in the summer. Now it was November, I was a civilian again, and the rest of my life was about to begin. Everything depended on whether I was really, genuinely, in love with Gina, so I had to fly to Hawaii to find out if she'd become who I'd envisioned she would or…I didn't even know what I had, what I wanted to know. Jesus, this all seemed too deep, almost metaphysical. Were any other returning soldiers wracking their brains like this? They were probably just fucking their brains out and forgetting about Vietnam.

The first face I saw when I exited my Freedom Bird and walked through the airport doors at Travis Air Force Base belonged to a beautiful, young Vietnamese woman. A thought flashed that I'd been fooled and had never really left Vietnam. She must have been meeting someone, maybe one of the other DEROS-ing GIs on the plane, but it took my breath away. Why didn't my girlfriend meet me at the airport like this?

Then I remembered Gina was in Hawaii—where my plane had stopped on the way to California—and I was still sort of in the Army…

Next thing I knew I was trying to navigate my way through the Honolulu heat and smog and traffic. Finally, I was standing on the steps of Gina's apartment at 413 Ala Moana Boulevard. A deep breath, and then a peek through the tiny window wedged in the green front door…

And my entire body sank.

There was a naked man splayed across the living room sofa!

"What the…?" My heart stopped. Then its pounding filled my ears. I dropped my bag and sat down on the sidewalk. I checked and double-checked the address. Maybe this was the wrong apartment? Maybe I was like the guy in the song "Silhouettes" by the Rays…I was on the wrong block?

I got up and peeked in again as if I were Burt Lancaster sizing up the enemy through a submarine periscope in *Run Silent, Run Deep*. No torpedoes, just that goddamn naked guy. I searched the room for a signal, a sign. There it was—Gina's Laura Nyro albums nestled in front of the tiny stereo. This was her place all right. Jesus fucking Christ, my new life was over before it started. Hadn't she pledged her everlasting love? Hadn't we just made plans to be together in Hawaii 'til death do us part? Or had I been hallucinating all that?

Back down on the sidewalk, I realized I was talking to myself out loud. I didn't give a shit. Should I just leave? Go straight home to Philadelphia? Look up the only other person I knew in Hawaii, Brian Matshushima, whom I'd met on guard duty in Long Binh? Get a room at some shady motel and off myself?

Or maybe knock down the goddamn door and kick the living shit out of that no good, sleeping Jody who'd stolen my girl.

Just then I heard Carole King's less than melodious but oh-so-honest voice: "*It's too late, baby, now it's too late/ Though we really did try to make it…*"

Where the hell was it coming from? Inside me? We played *Tapestry* a lot in Vietnam, that song in particular. We figured we'd be the ones saying that we couldn't stay together and asking our wives and girlfriends if they could feel it too. Definitely not having them say it to us. For sure not courtesy of some butt-naked guy on the sofa in your girlfriend's living room.

It sure was too late baby...

Carole King was still singing somewhere, and I knew I had to do something. So, I walked back up the small steps to Gina's apartment and knocked on the door. Probably banged on it a little too hard because I could see Jody jump like he'd been shot. His hair was blonde and much longer than my regulation GI cut. He grabbed a pair of boxers and walked toward the door.

What the hell was I going to say? And do? I wasn't prepared for this but it was too late.

"Fuck it," I muttered. "I'm outta here..." And just then the door opened and I heard a voice behind me.

"Hey, are you Doug?" I stopped and turned around to see a huge smile. "Man, Gina is expecting you! Aloha, brother!"

"And you are?"

"Oops, sorry, man, I'm Pat," he held out his hand, his blonde hair glistening in the Hawaii sun. I let it hang there, my fists still clenched. "Gina is sort of my landlady. She's letting me crash here since the Navy gave me the boot," he paused and then smiled broadly. "She's out making herself beautiful for you my man!"

My new friend Pat, clothes or no clothes, liked to talk. Turns out, the native Floridian had been kicked out of the Navy for selling weed and been befriended by Gina who traded a place on her sofa in exchange for pot while he figured out what to do next. A typical lost puppy rescue move on Gina's part. I could tell from talking to the kid that he wasn't her type—a roommate, not a lover. But my heart was still beating fast, wondering what was going to happen, or not happen, with Gina.

A few joints and several beers later, and we two Vietnam vets were giggling our fool heads off about my regulation Army haircut, Gina's new obsession with monkey pod furniture, and Carole King and *Tapestry*. Pat was more of a Janis Joplin fan and couldn't grasp how a bunch of Vietnam GIs would listen to "fucking Carole King."

"It's an age thing. You're too young to get what she's saying," I offered. Pat looked totally perplexed, but I wasn't going to waste my time explaining the vagaries of love and pain and rock and roll. He was digging my Vietnam stories, and I was enjoying playing the experienced soldier. The pot helped. Pat shouted "far out" and "right on" and slapped me five after every one of my anecdotes. The two of us were so wasted that we didn't even register when Gina entered the apartment.

When I finally saw her, she looked puzzled, hurt. Pat jumped off the sofa, went over, and gave her a big hug.

"Hey little lady, your special delivery has arrived safe and sound!" He gestured in my direction. Gina stood there. I rose, stumbled, fell back on the sofa, laughed, and then stood up again.

"Specialist 5 Bradley at your service," I sputtered. "Or rather willing to provide you service, or to be of service…" Pat was chuckling, but Gina was having none of it. She was tinier than I remembered, her hair much darker, her body beautifully tanned.

She was wearing a light blue, one-piece dress that accentuated her legs and her curves. But she was holding back. I stepped closer toward her. She took a step back. I took a breath and started singing "kiss me and smile for me/tell me that you waited for me."

"Oh Doug," she sighed and jumped into my arms. My brief acapella recitation had taken us back to that beach in Nassau where we'd fallen in love. Pat applauded, and, for those few moments, I was home.

By the time Gina and I cuddled in her bed together, the moment for lovemaking wasn't quite right. We listened to a little Laura Nyro and then the entire *Tapestry* album two times through. She liked everything about it—King's voice and piano and playfulness and seriousness. I reminded her about the more soulful versions of "Natural Woman" by Aretha and "Will You Still Love Me Tomorrow" by the Shirelles. That latter song struck a note, and the second time through Gina asked me that same question.

"Are you going to love me tomorrow?" she asked. For a moment I thought she was repeating the song lyrics, but when I looked at her, I saw she was serious. Her teeth were white in the dark, but I could see some lines on her face and pockmarks where her old acne had been.

"So, Doug Bradley, are you going to love me tomorrow?" she repeated, rising on one elbow.

"I'll love you tomorrow, I love you today, I loved you yesterday, and I'll love you in as many time zones and latitudes and longitudes as you want." I smiled.

"Be serious. Answer my question."

"Honestly, given this past year, how the hell do I know?" I was not enjoying getting grilled by my girlfriend during my first real day of civilian freedom. "And why would you ask me that when I just got here, welcomed by a naked guy in your apartment no less."

She looked hurt and I was pissed. Where had my anger come from? "It's Too Late" was playing again and something happened as we listened.

I asked Gina what was wrong. And she asked me what was wrong. And then we both asked one another what we were feeling, and the next thing I knew it was way past midnight, and I was no longer stoned. I told her about my dalliance with Jenny, the Red Cross nurse at Long Binh, and Gina told me about hers with another Doug who'd helped her out when she first got to Honolulu. She was still seeing him, off and on. Our confessions hung in the tropical Honolulu night.

By the time we eventually had sex, our bodies sensed we weren't in love anymore, if we ever had been. Maybe we both knew it was too late. In the dark, unable to sleep, I realized that for the past 365 days, I'd been in love with the idea of Gina, not the real her. Maybe whatever it was we once had was still alive somewhere back on that beach in Nassau?

It was time to get back home, show my parents I was okay, listen to old records with my brother. Grow my hair…

Call Kirkpatrick.

Track 38:
1-2-3

Were there any two lives more different than mine and my brother's in 1970-71? While I was grappling with the draft, Canada, war, and everything else exploding at the time, Ron was navigating marriage, high school chemistry teaching and coaching, and soon-to-be parenthood. There wasn't a language that could bridge that chasm, so maybe that explains why Ron never wrote me a letter, not one, the entire 365 days I spent overseas.

Not that I held that against him, as uplifting as it would've been to read his words, to hear his voice in my head, lifting me "higher and higher" as only he, and Jackie Wilson, could.

Thinking back on that need for uplift, I was reminded of a boost Ron gave me when I was a freshman in college. Not about how to study or navigate higher ed. But about how you needed to be able to dance if you wanted to have any luck dating in college. Maybe the first, and only, piece of advice he ever gave me because, well, because he wasn't just four-plus years older, he was the absolute best at baseball and basketball, the most adept with girls, best dressed, best dancer, highest falsetto…you name it and he was expert at it. Ron was so busy being cool—and keeping his distance from our father—that he didn't even share his expertise with me, his little brother, never ever took the time to show me the ropes.

But on that Thanksgiving weekend in 1965, my older brother took mercy on me, his baby brother, and, in a very real way, saved my adolescent life…

It was just the three of us that holiday—Ron; our tiny, Albanian-Italian mother Lucy; and me, one of the few stretches when we were living life minus our father, John Steele "Jack" Bradley. Poor pop had been unceremoniously dumped by General Foods, Inc. after selling Maxwell House, Sanka, and Yuban coffees for them for nearly ten years. In desperation, Jack Bradley returned to his Philadelphia roots to try and find a job, any job, at the ripe old age of 46.

Looking back from a distance of nearly 60 years, I've come to think that maybe we were lighter that way, or I should say my mother and brother seemed more carefree minus dad's bad moods and bleak outlook. His recent unemployment added extra fuel to that fire, so my father's absence that late fall evening was definitely invigorating us, literally lifting us off our feet.

Which might explain why Ron and I were dancing in the living room. Well, more like he was dancing and I was trying to dance. No younger brother ever wants to admit his social deficiencies to his cooler, older brother. But from the way I was flailing my arms and tripping over my feet, it was pretty obvious, even to my mother, that I couldn't dance to save my life.

Which was exactly the point at the time. My life as a college freshman needed saving, and dancing was going to be my salvation, my surest way to connect with the many college coeds I longed to get next to.

Maybe it was the absence of our father, the weight of him and his neediness and his negativity that gave us an extra lift? Whatever it was, I confessed to my brother just how uptight I was about dancing, as in fast, up-tempo dancing, with college girls. After a mere three months as a Bethany College freshman, I'd realized you had to be able to dance if you wanted to get anywhere and, unlike high school, you couldn't just walk up to somebody you didn't know and ask them to slow dance. Besides, the bands and the DJs never played any slow songs anyway. No, if I was going to fraternize with the opposite sex, I had to "get off my cloud" and shake my booty on the dance floor.

But I was as disconnected from my backside as e.e. cummings was from capitalization. Even this fatherless respite at home for Thanksgiving break hadn't done anything to build my confidence. Rather, I was dreading going back to college and being a complete and utter wallflower. I even admitted that to my mother and brother during our last meal before I had to return to campus.

My brother to the rescue. Somehow still in college himself—I'd lost track of how many times he'd started and stopped—he seemed to be living in a separate universe. But no matter what was going on in his life, the boy sure could dance!

So that cold November night in 1965, I confessed my lyrical liability to my mother and brother, expecting sympathy from the former and derision from the latter. Surprisingly, my usually supportive mother laughed and told me to stop whining while Ron went into the living room, grabbed a stack of 45s, and placed them on my parents' big ass Hi-Fi. He turned the volume way, way up.

And he was up too, jumping, shaking, and shimmying, all of it in time to Len Barry's hit song "1-2-3."

"It's easy/it's so easy," sings Barry, former lead singer of the Dovells, "like takin' candy from a baby."

There were a lot of instrumental parts to the song, and I can still see my brother, almost floating in midair, turning, twisting, and returning to earth on the downbeat, shaking his money maker with delight and smiling like Alice's Cheshire cat. How the hell did he do that?

We danced, in my case I tried to dance, to that song for the rest of the night until my ride back to college showed up. By the time I said goodbye to my mother and brother, I could at least move in sync and even jump up and down and turn around in tune to the music. Of course, if anybody played a song different than "1-2-3" I was screwed.

Luckily, beer, and lots of it, can do wonders for your senses, so the following Saturday night when I was back at college, my buddies and I were at the Jolly Roger in nearby Wellsburg, West Virginia, admiring the many good-looking women who were dancing with one another to every song. Eventually, I jumped—literally jumped—into the middle of sophomore girls during the band's covering my song, "1-2-3." Totally uninhibited, I was back in my parents' living room dancing with my brother, feeling the music and the beat. Next thing I knew, Karen Barnes, the cutest of the sophomores, was hanging on my arm and my fellow freshman were giving me the thumbs up. They told me later that

I even did the "Shotgun" to Junior Walker's number one hit, even though I've never done the shotgun in my life before or since.

But for that night, and many nights after, I was one with the music, comfortable with my body and just letting go. All thanks to my brother playing Arthur Murray that previous Sunday night.

* * *

But now here we were, just the two of us, trying to reconnect in late November 1971 after my 365 days in Vietnam compliments of Uncle Sam. Ron didn't know what to ask me about my year at war, and if he would've asked me, I'm not sure what I would have told him.

So, not able to talk meaningfully, and with no Len Barry songs around to lighten our load, we reverted to our usual brotherly dynamic—a spirited game of one-on-one basketball. He and I had faced off on b-ball courts all across Pennsylvania for years, and it wasn't until I was 18 that I finally beat him—I still remember where and when—but this day's b-ball was different from any of our previous encounters. Sweating, banging, fouling, falling, making, and missing, this was one of the few times we didn't talk the entire time except to say what the score was. We played to 11, each basket worth only one point. You had to win by two, and no make-it take it for us. No three-point baskets either. Ron easily won the first. I bulldozed my way to the second in overtime, 13-11. We were tied at nine in the rubber game until we both collapsed. We had physically abused one another in complete silence for nearly two hours. I kept thinking this type of physicality would've ended that damn Vietnam war in no time.

Drained and exhausted, we both dropped to the ground. The look Ron gave me made me realize that my brother now knew what my year in Vietnam was like. The way I shot and faked and rebounded and cussed and fouled had communicated my year at war. Basketball was the only language we could draw on.

"Jesus, Dube. Talk about a goddamn raw deal," Ron murmured to the night air as we left the basketball court.

I suppose he knew, too, that I didn't do that much dancing in Vietnam.

Track 39:

WITHOUT YOU

Where was the music coming from? Some sad sack moaning about not forgetting this evening, a face, a leaving, and a line about guessing "that's the way the story goes." God, I hated this song. But was it all true? Had this sad, schmaltzy ballad by Harry Nilsson crept its way into Kirkpatrick's bedroom.

Wait? Whose bedroom?

This wasn't your customary dread of waking up in a strange bed in a strange place with someone you didn't want to be with and wondering how in the hell you'd gotten there. This moment was worse. I was lying in bed beside William J. Kirkpatrick, my former high school English and Creative Writing teacher and mentor, in his Pittsburgh apartment on a cold February morning in 1972. Richard Nixon was in China and I was back from Vietnam, but east wasn't meeting west as much as my life was heading…south? Maybe forever?

I looked at Kirkpatrick, still wearing his large, black-rimmed glasses but sound asleep, finally, after an all-night drunken crying spell over being slighted at a party by one of his Carnegie Melon colleagues whom Kirkpatrick apparently had a crush on. I'd stayed behind in his apartment while he was being jilted, comforted him when he came back, and we'd both finally fallen asleep. My stopover here was part of my post-Vietnam Magical Mystery "Thank You" tour whereby I decided to visit, and thank, everyone who'd kept up a meaningful correspondence with me during my year in Vietnam. Kirkpatrick and Pittsburgh were a whistle-stop between the coed pen pals in West Chester, PA, Jenny in Cleveland, my summer of '69 flame Deborah in Hamburg, New York, and multiple trips to George and his wife Patti in D. C.

And a long, last goodbye to Gina on the steps of her parents' home in snowy Buffalo.

As I lay there in the cold morning light, I knew Kirkpatrick was more than a minor character in this Doug Bradley play cycle. The past eight months of letters had proven that, in spades. I was still holding on to them…to him. Why? Maybe because they held the answers to my high school past or the keys to my post-Vietnam future?

Lines from the letters haunted me, as if they were writ large on the bedroom walls. Everywhere I turned, there they were…

Above the bed –
12 April 1971
"I don't think about TJ much. It was a time. I figure almost three wasted years. I regret spending that TIME OF MY TIME as a high school teacher in a Puritan community. Relationships were stunted and grotesque."

Next to his nightstand—
20 April 1971

"I am a bit inhibited about being completely open via the mails, since I wouldn't want to risk writing a letter that would ever fall into hands other than your own.

Therefore, no comment on 'male sex,' D. H. Lawrence notwithstanding."

Beside the bookcase—
19 May 1971

"I don't know what to write you since we are not about to fall in love or even to see much of one another."

Atop the doorway—
7 July 1971

"I want to know if you have freckles on your mind and heart. Do you have them on your cock? You should look and see. Examining your cock can explain a lot about life. But not a lot about sex. Or happiness."

By his dresser—
16 August 1971

"Thanks to your encouragement, I had dinner last night with Will and June Beale in their apartment. It was a lovely evening and June was delightful. All my feeling for him has finally disappeared. That part of my life is over…but I was hurt, no, devastated, when I pulled down a copy of *The Painted Bird* that I'd given him and he'd used a razor to cut out the pages in the book I'd written on when I gave it to him…"

On the ceiling—
2 September 1971

"You're afraid I might be a fag? Afraid for whom? You? You've lost your sense of humor and are as paranoiac as ever, in spite of your claims of bliss and peace. You have focused your own discontent with yourself onto me…You were a sad young person when I knew you. Virtually friendless in high school, you turned to me for attention and love. And I gave it to you.

Upon his sad face—
22 October 1971
"If you don't write again, I'll understand. But I look forward to seeing you, not as the freckle-faced hard-on I knew at 16 (he/you was), but meeting a new friend who forgives me."
ENOUGH!

What was happening. What had happened? Why was I here? Even with the high school past we shared and the Vietnam letters, nothing presaged this quasi-conjugal conundrum. I'd stayed awake all night, fearful Kirkpatrick might do himself bodily harm. Nothing had transpired between us. Or would. But the very fact I was in the same bed with a man I'd once upon a time idolized but now knew was an unhappy and despairing homosexual was as bizarre as Vietnam.

Fucked up is what it was. Earth to Doug Bradley, how do you get yourself out of here without further breaking Kirkpatrick's heart? And if you manage that, where the hell do you go? My own heart had been aching, my life a fucking mess thanks to Vietnam and Gina and shame and too much marijuana.

"No, I can't forget tomorrow/When I think of all my sorrows." Jesus, can't someone please put Harry Nilsson out of his misery? And me too while they're at it? Maybe this was the end of the road, the final stop. I no longer had a desire to pursue law school, but where was the road less taken? Three months back in Nixon's America had convinced me I hated the U.S. more than ever, would never forgive my country for Vietnam, and that I was, in some strange way, responsible.

Kirkpatrick stirred. Holy shit, he's going to wake up, and then what? Do I make a run for it? Bolt out the door with my shirt and pants in my arms, as if I was leaving some salacious tryst? What if he asked me about what he'd confessed last night?

Or about what in the hell I was going to do with the rest of my life? For a moment, Vietnam didn't seem all that bad...

"Dube..." Kirkpatrick called me by my high school nickname. "Jesus," he looked around the bedroom for what?

"Dube..." he started retching, then shook his head back and forth three times.

"What the hell?"

My sentiments exactly. I handed him a wastebasket for his upchucking. I didn't have the time or the inclination to go into detail about last night and his drunkenness and hysterical crying and threats of suicide. No Army training manual or *Baltimore Catechism* had prepared me for this. Besides, any more talk would likely lead to both of us being back on the midnight special, the proverbial last train to Clarksville.

I had to get my own shit together pronto, and I was already in *di di mau* mode, "scram" in Vietnam parlance. But the poor guy looked so sad and lost lying there in his white t-shirt and boxer shorts. Maybe I could help him clean up and organize the place before I left. Bradley, man, what are you thinking? Get out! Now.

Too late. I was already bending over to pick up the books lying on the floor next to Kirkpatrick's bed. *Slaughterhouse Five* and *Absalom Absalom* deserved better treatment. I felt a hand on my shoulder. I kept my head down, not wanting to see Kirkpatrick's big blue eyes in his big ass glasses full of those alligator tears again. I didn't want to see his face period.

When I finally looked up, Kirkpatrick was trying to smile, patting me on the shoulder as if I was 17 again and had just said something very smart in class. "Good old Duber, what are we going to do about you?" He kept on trying to smile but his face wasn't cooperating.

"What do you mean *me*?" I asked incredulously.

"Well, dear boy, here you are stuck in some sad sack's apartment trying to make your escape and you have no idea where you're going or what you're going to do next or…"

I recoiled as I heard my own thoughts echoing in Kirkpatrick's words. He was right. I wanted to bolt. I had no idea what I was going to do, where I was going to go, how I was going to move on from Vietnam.

"We're a pair alright," I tried to laugh.

"I'm sorry, Dube, I really am." Coming from a guy who'd experienced some major deep despair in the wee hours of this morning, Kirkpatrick looked like he meant it.

"And now it's only fair that I should let you know, what you should know" surged from the apartment across the hall. I'd briefly glimpsed the young woman who lived there—an Asian grad student majoring in computer science according to Kirkpatrick. She had the worst musical taste imaginable. She must be suffering from some kind of setback—a departed boyfriend maybe—because she'd been listening to "Without You" by Harry Nilsson over and over and over again.

Was her story that much different than mine? BMOC and premier college social chairman derailed by the draft. A rebel without a cause in a divided America? Or just some lost and lonely English major, trying to find meaning in Harry Nilsson and Kurt Vonnegut and William Faulkner?

In Kirkpatrick even?

Was that why I was here in this Pittsburgh apartment? Not to say thanks or to get reacquainted but to find answers, discover clues, recover my sense of direction...

Next thing I knew I was standing in front of the Asian grad student's door, peppering it with knuckle knocks.

"S'cuze me?" she opened the door only slightly, revealing the look I'd seen day after day for 365 days in Vietnam. Maybe not Vietnamese—how could she be—but the long, straight, black hair and the dark eyes and the flat face...the small nose...and then I found myself searching her face for what Phuong, a "Saigon tea" girl I'd had a minor crush on, had once pointed out to me during one of our many conversations in the Imperial Bar—"look for the small webs of skin over the corners of Asian eyes."

"S'cuze me sir, can I hep you?" How long had I been standing there?

"Oh, hi, yes, I'm sorry," I smiled through my new beard and post-Vietnam haze, "I just wanted to apologize for making so much noise last night. I hope it didn't bother you."

"Without You" was still playing, but she opened the door and little more and let out a slight smile. Wow, she was pretty.

"Kickpatic, he okay?" she asked earnestly.

"Oh, yeah, he's fine." Awkward pause. "I'm his friend Doug. We both wanted to say we're sorry."

"Is okay Duck," she smiled and closed the door.

"This idleness will get you nowhere," Kirkpatrick announced when I reentered his apartment. "I am not in favor of it!"

He was dressed and raring to go—black jeans, penny loafers, and a bulky black mohair sweater. A major transformation. Had last night been some kind of a life-altering catharsis for him? Did he think we were boyfriends since I'd slept in his bed?

"I'll start by taking you out to breakfast—to *the* best damn breakfast joint in all of Shadyside," he smiled a broad smile. "And then we'll head over to my campus office and start working on your applications?"

"Applications?"

"Yes, your applications."

"What applications?"

"Your English grad school applications, dummy," he laughed a conspiratorial laugh as if I were in on the joke. "There's no way I'm going to let you go back to law school after what the so-called law did to you and everyone else who got shipped to Vietnam." He looked at me contritely. "Point is, you've already taken your English GREs so all we need to do is figure out where you want to go and begin the process. There's a good chance I'll know somebody at some of the schools where you'll apply. Whatever, we can have some fun with this and have you ready to move on with your life."

"Hold on a damn minute." There was more hostility in my voice than I'd expected. What was I mad about anyway? My girlfriend for sleeping with someone else while I was stuck in Vietnam. Being unemployed? Having spent a year of my life in Vietnam and two in Uncle Sam's Army while the rest of my generation let their freak flag fly? At a war that was still waging.

Kirkpatrick looked crestfallen. Shit, man, this was *my* life we were talking about, not his.

"Look, I know you mean well," my hands were sweating, "but I'm not even sure if I want to go to graduate school in

English. Sure, I'd like to hide out on a college campus and grow my hair and keep my beard and get high and get laid and flip the world the bird...but I'm not sure I'm ready for it."

"Ready for what?" Kirkpatrick interrupted me.

"Ready for school...or studying...hell, for filling out the applications even."

"Giving up, are we?" he gave me a cold stare. "Just like the old Doug Bradley."

Bingo.

* * *

Six hours and five grad school applications later, I was driving out of downtown Pittsburgh, heading east on the Pennsylvania Turnpike to my parents' apartment outside Philly. I was behind the wheel of my Aunt Kay's old 1967 Dodge Coronet 440 which she never drove. She'd handed me the keys to it when I got home from Vietnam three months ago. Because of Kirkpatrick's intervention, besides Philly, my possible destinations now included Denver, Boston, D. C., Storrs (Connecticut), Seattle...or wherever the hell I decided to go to grad school.

If I made it that far...

Aunt Kay's Dodge only had AM radio, so when I tuned into Pittsburgh's KDKA you guessed it—"Without You." Probably still blasting away in that Kirkpatrick's neighbor's apartment, zigzagging its way into Kirkpatrick's world. Seeing his face as I was leaving echoed in my head, unaware at that moment that I may have seen Kirkpatrick for the last time.

Passing a sign reading Philadelphia 269 miles, I punched the radio's off button and started singing "We Gotta Get Out of This Place." I kept on singing as Aunt Kay's old Dodge spirited me away from Harry Nilsson, high school, Kirkpatrick, and Vietnam.

Track 40:

KEY TO THE HIGHWAY

I glanced down at the odometer which read **18,747**. How in the hell had I amassed nearly 4,000 miles in less than three months? I ran the math in my head—Philly to Buffalo, 460 miles; Buffalo to Cleveland, 195; Cleveland to Philly, 430. Numbers appeared in my headlights. I wasn't even factoring in the bi-weekly trips to Rockville, Maryland, to hang out with George and Patti and their beautiful daughter Tara. Being there with the three of them, I felt sane and alive. Almost happy. It never occurred to me that it was because George and I were both Vietnam vets. I thought it was because he was my best friend. As the mamasans would say, *"same same."*

Still in the car. Still on the highway. Back into my past...

The Kirkpatrick interlude had left me shaken, bewildered. Once again I'd let him get the upper hand in our relationship—much like in high school—as I followed his lead on applying to grad schools north, south, east, and west. Why, exactly, I wasn't quite sure. But the more applications I filled out, the better I felt about getting back on a college campus, exhaling, not having to take orders from anyone, doing what the fuck I pleased.

Even more unnerving wasn't so much that I'd slept with Kirkpatrick, or I should say had fallen asleep in his bed, but that I'd seen him so brittle and vulnerable, curled up like a ball of discarded yarn on the floor of his apartment. Had everything between us changed because I'd finally observed what I'd only been thinking about who Kirkpatrick was? Did that even matter if I was sure of who or what I was?

The more I thought about it the more I figured we'd been building to that no-turning-back moment since that spring afternoon in the arboretum when he touched my leg and mussed my hair. Everything about me and him and high school and his Vietnam letters was snowballing, an emotional avalanche of dubious decisions and roads untraveled. I loved Kirkpatrick in my own way, but what I felt now was more like pity. He'd saved my life in high school, helped me appreciate nature, dig deeper into literature, become a better writer…maybe even a better person. And he never made a move on me, forced me to do anything physical. I owed the guy for all that.

But I'd have to live with the reality that my revered mentor, favorite teacher, all-knowing counselor, life guide was, in so many ways, a sad, sorry, hopeless homosexual who'd probably gotten himself kicked out of Thomas Jefferson High School for doing who knows what with whom. How had I missed it?

Was six years enough distance to see any of it more clearly? I'd been 16, 17; Kirkpatrick 22, 23. I had no friends, I was distraught, searching. He was my teacher and guide and...I groped for the word that fit. I'd hoped my years at college and in the Army, in a war zone no less, would give me insight, wisdom. Show me what it was like to be a man. All I had was an unending stream of lost highways.

Today's stretch of asphalt was taking me from my parents' apartment to see my old Bethany College roommate Dennis who was attending Law School at Boston University. Dennis and I were going to be roommates there back in 1969, but Uncle Sam and the draft got in the way.

I didn't begrudge Dennis his good fortune—if Vietnam had taught me anything, it was that life was a random accumulation of luck, good and bad. He'd written me a couple of letters, and I was curious to check out law school.

"So, Brads, why don't you come up here sometime, hang out for a while?" Dennis encouraged me over the phone one cold winter afternoon. "It's not like you've got anything else going on."

Was that a dig or what? But Dennis was right. Plus, I needed to get more distance from the Kirkpatrick fiasco.

From the Boston outskirts, I'd head to Nantucket, more of my English-major self trying to retrace the steps that Ishmael took before he boarded the Pequod and set sail in search of Moby Dick. If Ishmael could have an epiphany, or two, why not me?

Nantucket was also home to Teddy, an old fraternity brother of ours, and his wife. Taking a ferry to an island made the whole Massachusetts excursion seem exotic and mysterious.

Best of all, I'd taken my own music with me. No more radio miasma of "Without You" and "Precious and Few." I loaded the cassette player with tapes I'd purchased in Vietnam—*Tea for the Tillerman, All Things Must Pass, Tapestry,*

John Barleycorn Must Die, Layla, Who's Next. Blue was in there too, the album that had brought me back home thanks to George. It reminded me how much more hopeful I'd been about coming home to America and to Gina and being free. It hadn't taken long for all of that to fade away. I was running out of excuses for what I was doing, or not doing.

The highway was slippery. If I could find a river, I could skate from here to North Scituate and over to Nantucket. Enough Joni Mitchell. I ejected *Blue* and popped in Derek and the Dominoes. As I approached the outskirts of North Scituate, Cape Cod wind and snow bore down upon me like a frosty monsoon.

"Good old Aunt Kay," I said to the steering wheel, picturing my elderly aunt's tiny Italian face, big glasses, and large, conspicuous Basile family nose. And always a big, big smile. She was my mom's favorite of her four older sisters. I think she'd bestowed that green Dodge Coronet 440 as much on my mom as me. The kind of thing Italian-American families do.

"Here you go, Chickee," Aunt Kay smiled when she handed me the keys to the vehicle with less than 15,000 miles on it, sounding like W. C. Fields in *My Little Chickadee*. "Have a ball!"

After my last look at the odometer, I took in the rest of the Dodge. Whoa. It looked like 4,000 miles of bad road and then some—the ashtray filled with remnants of cigarettes and joints, the front seat littered with Baby Ruth and Clark Bar wrappers, used Kleenex, and cough drop boxes. The cigarette lighter looked like a miniature nuclear warhead from all the marijuana roach bombs I'd snorted.

I turned up the voice of Eric Clapton: "I got the key to the highway/billed out and bound to go" and sang as Clapton's and Duane Allman's guitars twined in and out of each other. The sound of friendship.

What was I feeding off? Distance? Separation? Fear? Only thing I was sure of, thanks to the odometer that wouldn't lie, was that I couldn't stay in one place very long.

"That's normal," a long-haired Vietnam vet told me one day at the Pennsylvania State Unemployment Office. He had a patch over one eye which in a strange way enabled him to see more.

"Doesn't seem normal to me," I fidgeted. As a rule, I didn't talk to anyone at Unemployment, but this guy had walked up to me a couple weeks ago and asked if I was a Vietnam vet. Since then, we'd talked a little on days when we had to wait forever to have our names called.

"It's a simple fight/flight response," he said.

"Forget airplanes, I'm driving not flying," I joked, trying to change the subject.

"No, really, man, fight or flight is a learned response to a trigger, and lord knows we've had a shitload of triggers." His smile made me think he knew more about this than I did.

"Tate? Brian Tate?" a mechanical voice called out, and before I knew it the vet was gone.

Damn, I said to myself in the car as I neared the house Dennis shared with several other law students. Why didn't I ask that guy more questions? How can a person be a trigger? When can you learn a new response to substitute for the fight/flight thing? How do you *not* feel bad about the need to fight, or flee?

Which was exactly what I was doing—more fleeing than fighting in my case, except for the TKO fallout with Gina. "I don't want to fight or argue with you right now," I pictured myself saying to her quite calmly, conjuring her face in the rear-view mirror. Damn, wish I'd applied that calm approach when I got home and then paid to bring her back from Hawaii. The second try was worse than Honolulu. We were always arguing, loudly, over every damn thing. The way she looked at me the day I dropped her in Buffalo told both of us that we were finished as a couple.

Clapton brought me back to the road I was on. Jesus, I was averaging a thousand miles a month and still on the go. How in the world had I ended up in snowy New England visiting a guy I hadn't seen in nearly two years? All I could do was join Brother Clapton, adding gusto to the last chorus. Like him, I was on my way, roaming this highway until the break of fucking day.

I drove that mean old highway past Dennis's place and kept on heading into town.

I'd call him later that night from a motel and apologize for not showing up, blaming the weather. Brian Tate wouldn't have been the least bit surprised.

Track 41:

ON THE ROAD TO FIND OUT

The sign at the Nantucket harbor read simply—"*No ferry boats today."*

Dennis was beside himself with dread and panic as the missed Law School classes accumulated like so many parking tickets. It got to the point where he tried to hire one of the ornery skippers we drank beer with at the local watering holes to spirit him back to the Massachusetts mainland. But the old salts knew there wasn't a damn thing you could do about ice in the harbor. You simply had to accept it.

And wait.

And drink.

And listen to stories.

And drink some more.

I knew the ice would melt someday, but I kept wishing that maybe it wouldn't, that everything would remain stuck in place like the boats and the sailors and Dennis and the ferries in Nantucket harbor. If everything just stopped, maybe

I wouldn't get back behind the steering wheel in Aunt Kay's Dodge but rather skate along the ice back to Hawaii and Gina, to the best moments in Vietnam and the Army, to that beach in Nassau, to the concerts at Bethany, to Kirkpatrick, to my parents and my brother, and my first times hearing the songs that helped get me through all the rest.

Maybe then I'd be able to slide up and down and back and forth, fingers on a guitar string, notes on a scale. My boat, my life, would be suspended in a moment, and I could relive, examine, appreciate…

Understand?

Understand what I had done right, and done wrong in high school.

Understand what Kirkpatrick taught me, meant to me then, meant to me now.

Really hear what Smokey and the Miracles, Josh White, Jr., Dionne Warwick, and the Association were trying to tell me.

Understand what Vietnam had done to my heart and my country, to trust and the capacity to connect.

To me and Gina.

Understand why there was always music in my head, in my ears, and on my lips.

* * *

As I watched Dennis fret and stew, I knew he wouldn't be able to relate to my musings. That gulf between us had a lot to do with Vietnam, but there was something more. For two years, my daily actions had been dictated and controlled by the Army. For 365 days I'd lived in a war zone where you never knew just where the enemy was or when your number would come up. Dennis had spent a mere six months in the

Reserves and then a year and a half at law school, on his own terms. We no longer shared a common language. "No ferry boats today" spelled disaster for him, relief for me.

The one language we did share was music. When we were roommates at Bethany, I'd mixed ample amounts of Doo-Wop, Philly soul, and R&B in with the eclectic new music Dennis was turning me on to—Cream, the Doors, and Love. As we'd made our journey last week from North Scituate to Woods Hole to catch the ferry to Nantucket, I'd trumpeted the virtues of *Tea for the Tillerman,* and I was doing it again as we sipped beers gazing out at the forsaken dock.

"I'm telling you this cat is on to something." I turned up the volume on my portable cassette player, "And his fucking name is *Cat*."

Cat Stevens's voice filled the bar, at this hour of the morning, empty except for the bored bartender and us. "Well I hit the rowdy road/and many kinds I met there/And many stories told me the way to get there." I smiled and paused the tape.

"Hell, doesn't that describe us here in Nantucket with Teddy and Sandy and our newfound friends? The long nights and longer stories, the fishing legends, heroic tales, epic poems…"

Dennis stared at me with a quizzical look.

"Weren't your ears drowning in a motherlode of narrative," I free associated onward. "The voices and cigarettes and laughter mingling and overlapping like the Atlantic Ocean waves. A symphony of Coleridge, Melville, Woolf, Poe…Paul Revere, and…" I unpaused the tape, nodding as Cat Stevens talked about time ticking away and the road out there to discover.

Dennis was smiling. "You should do it," he said.

"Do what?"

"Go to grad school in English, dumb ass," he laughed. "Didn't you just hear yourself? It's like a goddamn thesis. I thought I was back at Bethany with Mr. Taylor or Miss McGuffie. Trust me, you'll never be that excited about anything in law school. Your heart's in English for sure. Makes me a little jealous."

* * *

Happily, for Dennis, the weather broke and the ice in the harbor cooperated, and we were able to ferry back to Woods Hole. Our hard-drinking bar buddies, most notably Teddy and Sandy, returned to life without a pair of wayfaring fraternity brothers who'd overstayed their welcome, drank their beer, and smoked their pot.

On the ferry, I recalled a line from *Moby Dick*. "*There was a fine, boisterous something about everything connected with that famous old island.*" That's what Ishmael says, looking back on Nantucket as he sails off with Captain Ahab on the Pequod to meet the whale or his fate or eternity. I nodded in agreement. There *was* a boisterous something about those long Nantucket nights, punctuated by song. Not just "Blow the Man Down" but genuine New England whaling ditties like "Rolling Down the Old Maul." Hell, we'd even sung the Beach Boys' smoothed-out version of "Sloop John B."

For a minute, I thought I spotted Teddy and Sandy's house from the deck. I'd recited some of my GI poetry to them one night while Dennis was asleep. Surprisingly, they seemed moved. Teddy especially. I'd had a fleeting thought that Kirkpatrick would've loved Nantucket and be pleased that he'd pointed me toward a graduate degree in English.

The more I tried not to think about what awaited me on the mainland, the more I realized that Nantucket had been a lot like Vietnam. Loads of uncertainty. A little mystery. Close quarters. Comradery, booze, and pot. I craved the company and friendship of men. I needed a place to shine and show off, music to sing and share. No wonder I was always driving to Maryland to hang out with George and sing along with Joni Mitchell and James Taylor.

"What were you saying?" Dennis interrupted my reverie.

"Huh? Did I say something?"

"Said or sang," he pointed out. "Something about clearing your mind out?"

"Cat Stevens," I smiled, taking a last backward glance at the receding island.

Music always had been my lifebuoy. From the Jive Bombers and Sam Cooke to Smokey and the Miracles and Junior Walker, Joni Mitchell to Cat Stevens…

I dropped Dennis off and headed south toward Pennsylvania, silence in the car, music in my head. Home, like tomorrow, was a place I'd need to discover. Like Ishmael's destination in *Moby Dick,* it couldn't be found on any map—*"true places never are."*

Track 42:
VISIONS OF JOHANNA

I'd been having visions since Nantucket. Some real, others imaginary. Bob Dylan would have known the difference. He was my wingman guru, riding shotgun as I stepped on the gas from Philly toward Pullman, Washington, home of Washington State University, my grad school destination.

February's Massachusetts had morphed into Maryland and an Ides of March last-ditch attempt in D. C. to resolve things with Gina, that ended, as Ides always do, bloodlessly. April, come she will, had me and Dennis circumnavigating Florida with several spring-breaking coeds from Washington University which wasn't in the state or capitol but in St. Louis. May days in Martha's Vineyard with one of the girls from April. June, I changed my tune to head counselor and basketball coach, full-court pressing Hurricane Agnes and young Jewish campers in upstate Pennsylvania.

Letters, letters, stacks and stacks of letters to grad schools hither and yon. Lots of acceptances. Back and forth correspondence with an up, and mostly down, Kirkpatrick who encouraged me to "go go go." An unexpected epistolary connection with Dr. Charles Blackburn, chair of the English Department at Washington State University, who seemed intent on my becoming a WSU Cougar.

And so I did.

September 1972, and I'm listening to Dylan's *Blonde on Blonde*, barreling between the Detroit suburbs where I'd spent an evening with my sister-in-law's parents, to Minneapolis and a rendezvous with former USARV IO REMF Mike "Shirt" Goldstein, "Visions of Johanna" confounding me with peddlers, fiddlers, and Madonnas.

And then something made me pull over as I crossed the Illinois state line heading north.

Car idling, I grabbed the Vietnam-purchased Pentax camera next to me on the front seat and took a picture. And another. And another. Why? What made me pull over there and then? I hadn't pulled off the Interstate upon entering Ohio or Indiana or Michigan or Illinois. But here I was documenting the entrance to Wisconsin.

Was it because I'd never seen a welcome sign like this? Giant, pinkish-red cedars framed in a square with a large wooden outline of the state inside. Immense white letters diagonally across the state design that said, *"Welcome to Wisconsin."* It could have been hewn from a forest of trees by Paul Bunyan himself.

Or maybe Bob Dylan made me do it. The young Mr. Zimmerman haled from nearby Minnesota and had spent some time in Wisconsin. *Blonde on Blonde* had been doing a number on my head ever since my first encounter, thanks to a hippie fellow camp counselor named Rick.

"It doesn't get any better than this," Rick had said, passing me a joint as he flipped the tape on a hot summer night, the campers all snug in their beds. Was he talking about the dope or the music?

"Flat out genius," he declared as "Leopard-Skin Pill-Box Hat" gave way to "Just Like a Woman." He was right. Dylan delivered the perfect antidote to my post-Vietnam blues, balls-in-the-wind barreling toward the motorcycle accident that had laid him up for more than a year. From folk and protest to hard rock and Baudelaire, Dylan expanded, extended his world in ways I needed to. Wanted to. Maybe he was sending me a direct message in "Visions of Johanna." Was I talking myself so seriously, bragging of my misery?

Like Colonel Brock, our commanding officer in Vietnam, "Shirt" had attended the University of Wisconsin during the turbulent '60s. The two of them sang the praises of college life at Madison. Was that why I'd stopped?

I had a family connection too—my dad was stationed at Truax Field in Madison during World War II. In a late 1943 phone call conversation that passed into Bradley family lore, he told my mother he loved Madison and its friendly people and wanted to move there after the war. On that same phone call, he made the mistake of telling my mom there were ice boats on Madison's Lake Mendota, prompting her to inform him in no uncertain terms that she would *never* live in a place where the lakes froze solid. Never ever. My dad relented.

Or maybe it was the future beckoning to me. But Wisconsin? Really?

* * *

The sun was still shining when I got to Shirt's house in Minneapolis. Guess I'd been hauling ass. After updates on who knew what about whom from our Vietnam days, we took off in Shirt's parents' station wagon for a nearby lake, puffing on some good weed along the way. Shirt liked to talk even more than I did, so I was content to let him unload. He rambled on about work and politics and women, the Twin Cities, the war, and living at home with his folks. Eventually, Steve Warner's name came up, and we both had lumps in our throats.

"Dylan grew up here, didn't he?" I asked, trying to lift the gloom.

"Nah, he's from the Iron Range way north," Shirt corrected me, "but he went to the U for a while. Lived in Dinkytown."

I didn't want to admit I had no idea what Dinkytown was, so I shifted gears. "Don't you think *Blonde on Blonde*'s the greatest double album ever made?" I asked enthusiastically.

Shirt seemed puzzled. "Which album's that? The one with 'Like a Rolling Stone'?"

"Great song," I nodded, deciding to forgo a Dylan 101 lecture. But *"how does it feel?"* screamed in my head as I thought about how I'd abandoned Kirkpatrick during the summer of 1965, probably around the time when Mrs. Beale and her army of outraged mothers were getting him kicked out of TJ. And the "Mr. Tambourine Man" afternoon when Kirkpatrick told me he tried to commit suicide…

"Go get the tape," Shirt elbowed me. We were back in his parents' basement, swapping stories and passing joints. I was feeling the day's long drive and dreading the 2,000 miles I still had to go to my life as a WSU English major.

"What tape?"

"The Dylan album you're crazy about. Let's give it a listen."

"Jesus, Shirt, that'll take more than an hour…"

"So what? You said it was the best ever. Come on."

We listened to *Blonde on Blonde*, pausing for multiple repeats of "Stuck Inside of Mobile with the Memphis Blues Again" because Shirt swore Dylan switched the lyrics once and said, "stuck inside of Memphis with the Mobile blues again." Never happened, but it didn't stop Shirt from making me run the tape back.

"It's like goddamn Vietnam," Shirt announced as I was nodding off.

"Living in your parents' basement?"

"No, dumbass, that song. And the one about Joanna."

"Jo-hanna," I corrected him.

"Whatever. In Mobile-Memphis he talks about having no sense of time. And about the price of going through all those things twice. Isn't that our biggest fear, being sent back to Vietnam?"

I was surprised Shirt had been listening that closely. Must've been the dope. I was too far gone to keep up with him.

"And in Joanna, he talks about the night playin' tricks when you're trying to be quiet. When was there a night in Vietnam that didn't play tricks on us? Shit, on guard duty we were trying to be quiet. Didn't always work."

Silence. We were both back in Vietnam, out on the perimeter, wondering if that thing we thought we saw in the dark was a Viet Cong sapper or a mirage. A ghost? A vision of Johanna?

Jarred wide awake, knowing I wouldn't sleep at all, I told Shirt the story about pulling off the highway when I entered Wisconsin. Taking the pictures, and my speculations as to why. He took it all in.

"How did you feel?" Shirt asked.

"What do you mean?"

"When you pulled over, how did you feel?" Jesus, I hadn't thought about that, but Shirt's question hit a nerve.

"Liked I belonged there," came a response from somewhere inside me.

And it was true. The place was beckoning me to a home I'd never known.

Track 43:

TRACTION IN THE RAIN

I was still two years away from that Madison rendezvous when I pulled into Pullman, Washington, on a crisp fall day in mid-September 1972. Everything I owned was in Aunt Kay's Dodge Coronet 440, my most prized possessions being the Vietnam-purchased stereo equipment, a crate full of favorite record albums, and dogged-ear copies of *Ulysses, Catcher in the Rye, The Great Gatsby,* and *Bury My Heart at Wounded Knee.*

My WSU pen pal Charley Blackburn wasn't on hand to greet me, but he was the reason I was where I was. After that Kirkpatrick grad school push in early winter, I'd applied to English grad programs countrywide, including a couple in both Oregon and Washington. Flunked first-year geography by not locating Pullman right next to damn Idaho, but I was probably under Charley's spell as he wrote me long, friendly, and reassuring letters about joining the WSU English department. My acceptance came too late for me to get a TA position, but Charley helped land me a job as assistant head resident of Rogers Hall, a deal that included room and board, in-state tuition, and a small stipend. Given the fairly shitty GI Bill, compliments of Uncle Sam, the Pullman package made sense. Plus, World War II veteran Charley Blackburn seemed to get me and my post-Vietnam predicament.

And so there I was.

Disaster doesn't do justice to the depth of my rude awakening. The Rogers Hall head resident was a Casper Milquetoast type who seemed fearful of me; the guy who'd held my position the year before had walked on water; and bearded and burned-out me was deluged with late night calls and visits from drunk, stoned, or weepy, wet-behind-the-ears freshmen. As far as I knew, there wasn't another Vietnam vet within 500 miles. And to top it off, my introduction to English grad school was a course entitled "Bibliography of Bibliographies" taught by a guy who would've made a drill sergeant do pushups.

As far away from home as I'd ever been, except for Vietnam, I was lonely with a capital L. Maladjusted thanks to the Army, Vietnam, and America. Longing for love and as horny as the hundreds of students I was babysitting. Even poor old Charley Blackburn couldn't get me though this, which is why I drove across the state and ended up alone in a Seattle motel near the University of Washington campus in early October. Purpose? Figuring I'd find some way to end it...or confront my purposeless-ness? Whatever the motivation, all the aspirin and booze and other shit I took didn't do the trick, so I woke up alive on a bright and sunny Saturday morning, albeit with a very, very bad headache. Opted to head out to the Olympic Peninsula and maybe jump off a ferry or off a cliff when I ran into a guy I'd met at WSU just a week or two earlier. He was going home to see his brother who was on his way back from Vietnam. Irony? Divine intervention? The two of us hiked, smoked a few joints, and went to see *Andromeda Strain.* Crashed at his place that night and drove back to WSU. Not refreshed, but not dead either.

Probably wasn't a good idea to be reading Sylvia Plath's poetry or reading about Sylvia Plath's aftermath. Or constantly reciting Thomas Wolfe's line, *"O lost, and by the wind grieved, ghost, come back again."* Or listening to "Traction in the Rain" from David Crosby's solo album *If I Could Only Remember My Name.* Something about his haunting voice, the modulation, the questions that seemed to align with me and my lost status, questions about gaining any traction in the rain, how hard it is to understand.

Understanding indeed...I'd dropped acid with Dennis and his roommates outside Boston that previous February, and my only comfort was the fireplace in the living room as I slowly regained my body temperature. I was still tripping, very much alone even though I was surrounded by a room full of strangers, except for David Crosby and his sad voice.

All I could think about was following Crosby's advice about "getting out." Since that night, whenever I got cold or incredibly low, I'm back by that fire, back there listening to Crosby's melancholy melody.

I rebounded, albeit briefly, from that Seattle death trip. Even started to enjoy grad school because I ended up doing my boot camp bibliography on "Fiction and Non-Fiction Personal Narratives of the U. S. War in Vietnam." The post-Vietnam "renaissance" of fiction, poetry, and memoir was still years off, so my spelunking was breaking new ground, and healing me a little in the process. I became a fan of John Sack's *M*, David Halberstam's *One Very Hot Day*, and Bernard Fall's riveting first-hand report *Hell in a Very Small Place*. I dug deeply into the personal narratives of doctors in Vietnam—*365 Days* by Dr. Ronald J. Glasser and *12, 20, and 5* by Dr. John Parrish. Wept and cursed while I read *Winning Hearts and Minds*, a collection of riveting poetry by Vietnam vets like me.

But my research could only take me so far, and I'd return to my "apartment" in that dormitory every night, alone, bitter, and displaced. Not very long before a knock on the door or a call from one of the floor monitors or the head resident would interrupt me. So, I debated ending things again. If I was going to go through with this, I would need to get serious. Didn't Plath put her head in an oven? There was a kitchen next to my Rogers Hall "penthouse." Or why not mimic what my old mentor Kirkpatrick had tried way back when, himself mimicking Papa Hemingway? But the Army and Vietnam had turned me off to weapons forever, so I kept on wondering, Thomas Wolfe and his ghosts and David Crosby and other songs echoing throughout those western Washington days and nights.

Even a trip home to Philly for Christmas with my family couldn't lift my soul. They freaked out about my hair and beard—hadn't had a haircut or shave since 'Nam—so I humored them by going to the barbershop...but resisted telling them what else I wanted to dispose of.

Tried to put on a happy face after I arrived back in Pullman, hoping that a couple evening seminars would cut down on my tedious dorm time. Helped a little but not a lot. Eventually, it dawned on me that another huge part of my problem was that I wasn't social chairman or DJ anymore. Since my high school days, I'd spent a lot of my time entertaining audiences with music. Did that in spades at Bethany, and even in Vietnam with the tunes I shared and listening sessions I choreographed. Now, I was an audience of one. No others to wow or woo. Nobody to impress or delight.

No relief, no direction, no woman…and we were still killing Vietnamese over there, still launching grenades at one another back here. A big fucking difference an advanced degree in English would do to help put an end to all that.

Maybe that's why I drove out to nearby Kamiak Butte every chance I got. Rain or snow. Cold or colder, I'd drive the 15 or so miles on Highway 27 because…because the place called to me. I heard voices there in the wind and from the ground, voices of the land's indigenous ancestors expecting to be heard. They got louder the closer I got, but I wasn't sure what the message was or why they were calling to me.

Given my topography ignorance, I wasn't sure why the place was classified as a butte. But I had read up on its namesake, Chief Kamiakin of the Yakima tribe. Good of us to name a landscape after him as we hunted him down, took his land, and broke his spirit. I felt like he and his struggle were with me on the butte, but that only made me feel sadder, worse. Made me despise my country more.

On a take-your-breath-away cold late February day when something, or many things, had gone wrong, I had to get away from Pullman and Rogers Hall and the English Department and my misery, so I drove hard and fast to Kamiak Butte. I was shouting and crying as I drove, pretty much deciding that there wasn't any use in continuing this sad Doug Bradley song that I was singing. No fucking traction in the rain, or the snow, for me, so I abandoned the car just below the parking lot and started to hike the 3,000 or more feet to the top. The light out there can do crazy things and this day was the craziest. Sun bouncing off the snow, picking up some of the Palouse Valley's burnished yellows. As the sun dipped, reds, oranges, and purples simmered off the rocks. An occasional animal-shaped cloud gave the whole thing a dream-like quality.

I was listening, watching, waiting. Not a whisper of wind. And then something gripped me, grabbed me hard and tight. Wouldn't let me move. Blinded by the barrage of light, I started to feel the presence of dead Indians. The ground was crying. The sky too. And me, tears freezing on my cheeks. The light was somehow painful, but I couldn't look away. Something—the land, the sky, the death, my own misery—sighed, and I knew this was it...my spirit was too broken and I was ready to give myself up to despair. Wasn't that the message from Chief Kamiakin?

Next thing I knew I was standing at the door of Charley Blackburn's house. His tiny, cheery wife Alice answered, and as soon as she saw the look on my face, she called for her husband, who was sitting at the dinner table with his two children. She pointed me toward the basement stairs, and I descended to their family room with Charley behind me. My teeth were chattering, I was having one of those crying jags where you can't get your breath and get the words out. And the ominous Kamiak Butte vision lingered.

For the life of me, I can't remember that conversation, if it even was a conversation. All I know is that Dr. Charles Blackburn, the man who'd brought me to Pullman, Washington, in the first place, saved my life that evening. Whatever he said or however he looked at me or just his presence got me off that cliff.

I didn't know it then, but I would never be that low again. A couple weeks later, good old Charley invited me and Wes Ross, another grad school Vietnam vet—news to me—to his home to show slides from our time in Vietnam and talk about our year at war with him and several of his English department colleagues and spouses. Maybe that was something else I saw on Kamiak Butte that late February afternoon? My own war, my own possible death, giving way to a new life?

The rest of that semester got better. I got a TA-ship for the following fall, kept decompressing from Vietnam through my studies—I even wrote a paper about Coriolanus, a returning soldier who had a very bad case of PTSD—for my Shakespeare class. And a few Washington State women began to find me interesting…

I made fewer trips to Kamiak Butte. But I kept the place in my head, and in my heart, appreciating how the Yakima, Palouse, and Klickitat peoples that once roamed there had provided some much-needed traction to my coming home from Vietnam.

Track 44:

PEACE LIKE A RIVER

Home began with that "Wisconsin Welcomes You" Kodak moment in September 1972. The crucible for it all was Pam Shannon, my spouse of almost 50 years, the mother of my children, my partner in grandparenthood. She loves music almost as much as I do. Unlike me, Pam has perfect pitch and a fabulous singing voice. She sojourned in Pullman, Washington, in fall 1973, won my heart, and brought me to Madison, Wisconsin, where we've lived since 1974.

The Grateful Dead, Allman Brothers, Marshall Tucker, and Tchaikovsky's Violin Concerto counterpointed our early days and nights together in that tiny town nestled in western Washington wheat country. Nearby, we could hear the "three forks" of the Missouri Flat Creek, Dry Fork, and the South Fork of the Palouse River converge and roll on.

Having Pam in my life and being able to shed some of my Vietnam skin made remote Pullman tolerable. Better than tolerable. Little did I know that I was mere months away from my "homecoming" in Wisconsin. We fell deeply in love and just let life flow on in 1973-74, taking us and my Vietnam hangover with it.

Whether writing papers or grading them, music was always playing. Not as much Dylan now with Pam and her Grateful Dead albums in the picture. We still avoided commercial radio. And on late nights, Pam asleep and my fingers on the typewriter keys, I'd listen to "Peace Like a River," a lesser-known Paul Simon song. His sweet voice observing peace running through the city like a river counterpointed my "three forks" location. And his repetition of *being up for a while* sure suited my late nights and early mornings. Still, if I ever got too far down the grad school or Vietnam stream, Pam would tether me home.

I kept in touch with my parents, my brother, George, and Patti, who now had two little girls, by long-distance calls. Around Christmas, I sent holiday greetings to old friends. Then, in January 1974 I saw the familiar typeface and return address—*W. J. Kirkpatrick, Apartment 31, 4825 Centre Avenue, Pittsburgh, Pa*. It had been months since we'd last communicated, and what our last exchange was about, I sure as hell couldn't remember. Maybe I'd told him about falling in love with Pam?

Holding Kirkpatrick's letter, I thought about how much my relationship with him consisted of paper and words. We'd done more communicating, soul searching, and sharing, even arguing and fighting, in letters than in person, especially in the years after Thomas Jefferson High. Those letters had accompanied me, from Athens, Ohio, to Pittsburgh; Athens to Bethany; Pittsburgh to Vietnam, Pittsburgh to Philly; and now here to Pullman, Washington. Why had I held on to all of them, even the nasty notes Kirkpatrick had left in my high school locker? Were they part of my graduate education too? When would I be able to take *that* final exam?

For some reason, I hesitated. Maybe getting a letter from Kirkpatrick wasn't such a good thing. Pam was asleep in the other room, probably dreaming about Wisconsin. What did I know about this guy anyway? I'd seen him like once in the past decade, and I wasn't any surer what that was about—the two of us—than I'd been in high school. What exactly had gone down between us? Between him and others? Did any of that even matter now? Part of me yearned for finality, closure, much like I wanted to get past Vietnam.

I opened his letter.

"*Dear Dube,*

Glad to hear from you. Life rolls along through the bleak midwinter. I am presently in love with nobody and have had no sex of any kind for about six months. I'm still liable to tumble into bed with almost anybody, but haven't looked for anyone recently. Of course, this is quite different from your own hetero-masturbatory sex with your kept woman daily."

A "Fuck You" erupted inside me. That did it. He doesn't even know Pam and throws her under the bus. I was done with Kirkpatrick once and forever. Why keep reading? He closed with "*Hope you're enjoying all those orgasms.*" I crumpled the paper and threw it on the floor. No wonder this asshole was alone and unloved. He was incapable of being happy for someone else, someone he even, supposedly, loved. I may have been sitting in a tiny apartment in Pullman that night in early 1974, but another me was mired at Thomas Jefferson High School, encountering Kirkpatrick for the first time outside my hall locker, Lou Christie's "Two

Faces Have I" marking the occasion; being consoled by him outside his classroom after I'd written my revelatory short story about my blackballing, "Be Fair" by the Galahads accenting my despair; talking and drinking coffee with me and my mom in our kitchen, "People" by Barbra Streisand whispering in the background; sitting next to me in my basement as he told me about his attempted suicide, "Mr. Tambourine Man" blocking out his words; that morning in Pittsburgh just two years ago, "Without You" blaring from the apartment across the hall...

Now this bullshit. From the professor of love who saw life and beauty in flowers, in nature, in poetry, in literature, in other people. Fucking guy was selfish and jealous. Like I'd been in high school. There wasn't a song I wanted to mix with what I was feeling now.

"Damn you Bill Kirkpatrick," I shouted into my past.

"You okay honey?" came Pam's voice from the bedroom.

"I'm fine. Just pissed at my students for not following the assignment," I lied.

"You coming to bed soon?"

"Yep, be in shortly."

"I'm gonna be up for a while" Paul Simon's voice came from somewhere in the apartment, or in my head. Which I shook when I repeated the line, "Nowhere to go but back to sleep."

The water was still flowing in and around Pullman, but I was gonna be up for a while, trying to put an end to the nightmare that is W. J. Kirkpatrick.

Track 45:

RIPPLE

The unreeling I'd started in grad school was the beginning of my floating downstream from Vietnam. Ripples in a much larger pond, I reckoned, as I listened to the Grateful Dead in our tiny apartment next to the University of Wisconsin campus. Thanks to Pam, I'd developed a much deeper appreciation for Jerry Garcia and his merry band. At first, I hadn't really listened to what they were saying, distracted by marijuana or endless solos, but I'd grown to appreciate their landscapes, stories, and quirky characters.

As I listened to "Ripple" and Jerry sing about how he'd take you home if he knew the way, I thought about how unlikely it was that I'd landed in this rebellious, anti-war, hotbed. But Madison would be the place that would bring me back, become my home.

No sooner had Pam and I landed in town than I saw an article in the local paper about a fledgling operation called Vets House. Created *by* Vietnam era vets *for* Vietnam era vets, the grassroots non-profit was trying to make a difference to the guys who'd been ignored, ostracized, or vilified by their country. With a shoestring budget but a team of committed volunteers, Vets House helped former GIs find jobs, upgrade their less-than-honorable discharges, and access their VA benefits—even if they were incarcerated. Helping these guys deal with their shame and guilt wasn't in anyone's job description, but it was a central part of the Vets House mission.

From the first day I set foot in the storefront operation on South Park Street, I knew it was where I belonged—two run-down houses next to a car wash, filled with old sofas, chairs, desks, lamps, filing cabinets, and a couple of beds. A burly fellow with a big smile greeted me, introducing himself as Navy veteran Steve Schoch, and bid me "welcome." "Southbound" by the Allman Brothers was playing somewhere, and I exhaled.

"You here about the job?" Steve started to hand me an application.

"Uh, yeah, sure," I stumbled. "I saw the article in the paper and…"

"Some good press for Vietnam vets for a change," Steve shook his head. "Best way to rehabilitate a vet is with a good job. I take it you're a vet?"

"Army. Long Binh, 70-71," I replied, adding "71Q20" as if my military job specs would mean anything.

In the next room, several other guys were filling out applications on clipboards amidst a clutter of crammed wastebaskets, reams of paper, and cans of paint. Steve explained that Vets House had just received a contract for $15,000—their first major outside funding—from the state unemployment office for a job placement specialist and had decided to split it into three part-time positions.

"We'll get more bang for our buck that way," he nodded, "because we know all three of you will work more than 20 hours a week."

Did Steve just say *we*? Was that a sign I was going to get the job? I filled out the application. Later, I dropped off a neatly typed resume. New to Madison, knowing nothing about the town's employment scene but giving a damn about my fellow Vietnam vets, I was hired anyway.

Hours were long, funds were sparse, and stress sometimes got the better of us. Disagreements raged around just what kind of organization we should be—"Our only By-law should say 'no By-laws,'" contended Steve Barnes, one of the founders—and inter-office dynamics, especially where women were involved. We were all working through our own post-Vietnams, and even though that's what we were helping vets deal with, we didn't spend that much time helping ourselves. But just when it looked like we'd all come to blows, we'd get up and walk across the street to the Rustic Tavern, a dive bar, where we'd drink and smoke and joke about what we'd just come near to blows about.

With Pam bottled up in law school, Vets House became my professional school. I made straight A's in finding jobs for unemployed vets, securing donations and grants for programs, and debating with my co-workers about how to run a nontraditional organization, learning to navigate a new town's media, jobs, and politics as if I'd lived there forever. Since I was writing the Vets House press releases, I became the guy being interviewed on local radio and TV.

Songs wafted up and down the Vets House halls, mixing with intense conversations and typewriter clatter. Sometimes I'd listen with Steve Barnes and Dan Naylor, Vets House co-founders who'd both served Uncle Sam but not in Vietnam. Dan leaned toward soul and country, while Steve was inclined to progressive rockers. No Deadheads here.

"When I left for Germany," Steve confided in me one day, "it was the Beach Boys and stretch Levi's and penny loafers. When I got back it was Led Zeppelin and drugs. Everything changed, and it takes a helluva long time to catch up."

Weren't all of us vets trying to catch up?

Women had changed a lot too, and Madison was ahead of the curve with several women in positions of power locally, so we needed to get our shit together and treat them as equals. Easier said than done with all the testosterone on the premises. The first time Pam visited Vets House she ripped up a *Playboy* calendar she saw prominently displayed in one of the offices. Eventually, we began hiring women like Dawn Sears and Carolyn Emmerson as job placement specialists and therapists, not just receptionists. Maybe we were learning and growing?

Mindful of Vets House burnout, I took on a job teaching English at a two-year UW campus nearby. I encouraged my freshman students to read Ken Kesey's *One Flew Over the Cuckoo's Nest* as if it were a substitute for Vietnam.

Everything in my life was still swirling around Vietnam, but now rather than prompting waves of despair or anger, it was lifting me up. The key was helping guys who'd had it worse than I did. Helping them to get back on their feet served as my own therapy.

* * *

"Would you hear my voice come through the music? Would you hold it near as it were your own?" "Ripple" reminded me of that Robert Frost poem from college, which reminded me of being an English major which took me back to TJ and Kirkpatrick and back around to "Ripple."

I grabbed a pad and scribbled a few lines about how "Ripple" was about the relationship between the singer and the listener who the singer hopes, in turn, will become the singer…Once an English major, always an English major.

I wrote a haiku about Pam's smile. Then a short poem about Vietnam entitled "Pledging Allegiance." A short story I titled "Malaria" about me and my father before I left for Vietnam. It would take me the next forty years to get my Vietnam story down on paper.

Ripples.

* * *

I've always loved teasing out threads and connections between unlikely sources. Robert Frost and Robert Hunter. The Crests and the Brooklyn Bridge. Buffalo and the Bahamas. Laura Nyro and Adrienne Rich. D. H. Lawrence and e. e. cummings. Charley Blackburn and Bill Kirkpatrick. Maybe that's why I carried Kirkpatrick's letters with me, thinking someday I'd find something in them, a strand that sheds light on what I'd been seeking from Kirkpatrick all those years ago.

I think part of me knew that someday I'd write my way deeply enough into that story to discover whatever it had to say. All these years later, I see the story, our story, differently. The letters have helped, but listening to Dylan and the Beatles and "Without You" and re-reading D. H. Lawrence and Shelley helped too. They've all made me realize I loved

Kirkpatrick but was afraid to say the words. I was scared because I thought people would assume there had to be something deviant about that kind of love. That hesitancy, no it was more like fear, came through more in the Vietnam and post-Vietnam letters because by then Kirkpatrick had come out as…whatever it was he was. I was too frightened to ask or to understand or to give him anything in return.

Whatever it was Kirkpatrick had wanted me to grasp had, on some subterranean level, worked. I'd learned to love men, with the guys I'd been with in Vietnam, George at the top of that list. I didn't sleep with them, but I loved them. Hell, I even danced with a bunch of them on a night in Vietnam when we were stoned and our bodies just had to move to the music. Wasn't that love Kirkpatrick style?

Add the Beatles and Dylan to the Doug Bradley blend, my passion for literature and poetry, the fact I was an English major and a writer…well, I had Bill Kirkpatrick to thank for all that. Maybe there was still time to find him and say thanks.

Track 46:

THANK YOU, ANYWAY (MR. D.J.)

Having played "the platters that matter" and spun the discs at sock hops, mixers, and dances all through high school—not to mention my Bethany social chairman chops—convinced me that I was *the* one and only member of the TJ Class of 1965 who could get the 50th reunion music right. There was something magical about the number 50 and that all of us who'd made it this far were nearing 70. The songs we listened to back then had helped define who we were and who we would become. They'd definitely defined the Vietnam and post-Vietnam me. If I could weave a musical spell in the 1960s, could I do it again now?

So I reached out to the local planning committee in early 2015 and faster than you could say, *"sugar pie, honey bunch"* I had the DJ job. As I assembled the playlist, I began by clustering the songs by my class's freshman (1961-62), sophomore (1962-63), junior (1963-64), and senior (1964-65) years. Then I put together a mega playlist that mixed all four years together. Then I asked my classmates for requests. Finally, I revisited the broadcasts of some of the Pittsburgh DJs from 50 years ago—Terry Lee, who provided music for young lovers for our Saturday night make-out a-thons and Porky Chedwick, "Pork the Tork," the maestro of Doo-Wop and R&B.

Listening to all that music transported me to my TJ days which was both a good thing and a bad thing. The good was that it helped me remember what it was like to be young, to dream and hope, to learn and be in love. With Carla. With Kirkpatrick?

The bad was recalling the Class of '65 fortieth reunion ten years earlier, 2005, when the high school ghosts of Carla, and Kirkpatrick, came calling.

* * *

Thanks to the internet, Bart Foster, one of my TJ classmates, had located me in 2004 and began to lobby me to attend our 40th class reunion. I resisted, not sure I wanted to reconnect to that part of my past. But in the end, I relented, not just because Foster was wearing me out—indeed he was—but also because I hoped maybe, just maybe, Kirkpatrick, Carla, or both, might show up. By the summer of 2005, I'd convinced myself that the reunion would help me understand what I'd missed 40 years earlier but also what I'd learned.

Pam was helping our UW college-attending son Ian move into a new apartment that summer weekend, so I flew back to Pittsburgh, and my past, solo. The night of the reunion gathering, my heart skipped a beat when I spied Carla Bonner's nametag on the registration table. Jesus, what if they played

"High on a Hill"? Would I ask her to dance? Would she say yes? Would we waltz back in time, to 1964 and 1965, and fall head over heels in love again?

Get a grip.

I made a point of walking by the registration table all night. Carla's nametag sat there, the only Class of 1965 registrant who was a no-show. I pictured Carla's mom breathing a sigh of relief since I never was serious enough to be a contender for her daughter's heart.

I'd urged the 40th Reunion organizers to reach out to Kirkpatrick. I could've tried to get a hold of him myself, but I was still pissed at him for that 1974 letter. Why hadn't I mellowed in the thirty years since? I was happy being a father and husband; a son and a brother; a communications professional with the University of Wisconsin, an aspiring author. Kirkpatrick deserved some credit. Maybe more than just a little. Hell, the least he merited was an invite to the reunion of a Thomas Jefferson High School class that was his as much as ours.

By the time I worked my way up the invitation chain-of-command, it was too late. But maybe Kirkpatrick would make a surprise appearance? He thrived on drama back in the day, so why not now? He knew about the event, Shirley, one of the local reunion planners, informed me, but hadn't committed to coming.

"Mr. Kirkpatrick's an English professor at Westminster," she proclaimed, seemingly unaware Westminster was about an hour away in New Wilmington, PA, not across the pond in London.

Didn't matter. Once I reunited with my Class of '65 classmates, I found out how contentious the idea of a Kirkpatrick invite was.

"I wouldn't want that fucking guy here," Pete Starr hotly announced to a group of us huddled together that first night in Rumerz Sports Bar. Several graying heads nodded in agreement.

"Why?" I asked in honest bewilderment.

"He's an asshole and a jerk and..." Starr and a handful of others spat out. I heard terms like *creep, fairy,* and *queer*. I exchanged a glance with Carol Davies, one of my TJ classmates, who, like me, supported a Kirkpatrick appearance.

"He was the best teacher I ever had," she and I said in near unison. "He opened up so much to us in English and Creative Writing," Carol continued. "And what about the great plays he directed and all the college prep help he gave us and..."

A groan from the back of the room came via Bob Revis as he made a masturbation gesture with his hand. A flood of newly arrived Class of '65 alums redirected the conversation and Kirkpatrick's name never came up again. Nor did Will Beale's. I let it go.

For a little while.

With my curiosity piqued and the Internet omniscient, I located Kirkpatrick several months after the 40th reunion. He was indeed teaching English at tiny Westminster College. Or I should say *had* taught there, because what I found was his obituary. William J. Kirkpatrick had passed away in early 2006 at age 64. That hit me as lonely and sad. Really sad. The college's website included worshiping comments by Kirkpatrick's Westminster students, reminiscent of accolades TJ kids like Carol Davies and I would've offered. There was some reference to his suffering from depression and an announcement of a scholarship in his name. I promised myself I'd contribute. But by the time I revisited the Westminster website a few years later, everything about Kirkpatrick was gone.

So, once I decided to return to TJ ten years later for our 50th class reunion, was I doing it for Kirkpatrick? Or simply to perform my last rites as a high school DJ?

* * *

In the process of assembling all the 50th reunion playlists, I was doing a lot of Doug Bradley processing. All that 1961-65 music reminded me just how much I didn't know then, how immature and lonesome and downright anxious I was. The blackballing, JFK's assassination, the beginnings of Vietnam…as much craziness as anyone could handle. I mean, "Eve of Destruction" came out the summer after we'd graduated for Christ's sake. But as oblivious as we were to much of that mayhem, we had Kirkpatrick to put it into perspective, often using music to play counterpoint.

Knowing I'd accumulated far too many songs for the two hours I'd been allotted, I started to doubt my playlist would resonate with any of my classmates. I'd moved away from the Pittsburgh area 49 years ago, and I was a Vietnam vet to boot. Maybe Dylan and James Brown and the Supremes weren't really all that popular in Pittsburgh anymore?

Maybe nobody else remembered Porky Chedwick?

And then the planning committee, now aware of my Vietnam vet status, asked me to put together a mini playlist to honor the veterans who would be in attendance. They wanted me to play "Anchors Aweigh" and "The Halls of Montezuma" but I knew better, having spent years collecting the music-based memories of hundreds of Vietnam veterans for my book *We Gotta Get Out of This Place*. The vets would much rather hear "These Boots Are Made for Walkin'," "Detroit City," and "We Gotta Get Out of This Place."

In the end, I skipped the military hymns. But just before I cranked up the good stuff, some tipsy blowhard on the planning committee commandeered the microphone to orchestrate mass picture-taking. Chaos ensued, and it took forever to get back to the music. To make things worse, I overheard a theatrical rendering by Shirley James about Kirkpatrick's having begged her to find him a job at the college where she worked. She set the scene of the phone call, established Kirkpatrick as her sad, hopeless suitor, and for the climax revealed that Kirkpatrick had played the suicide card with her. She made fun of his helplessness. Pissed all over his memory.

By the time I finally got to perform my DJ duties, I was in a funk, wondering why Kirkpatrick had been so desperate and helpless with Shirley, much like he was with me that one time. I guess maybe he needed us more than we needed him.

I was more confused than ever.

"Great tunes, Dube." I looked up to see Les Hollinger, one of our more fit and successful classmates, in front of me.

"Oh, hi Les. Thanks. How's it going?"

"Great. Jane and I are having a ball. We might even come back for her 50th next year." Les's wife was a year behind us. I'd had a mad crush on her my freshman year. One of many.

"Too bad your wife couldn't join us."

"Yeah, she would've liked meeting you, Jane, and some of the others," I replied.

"You ever hear from Carla?" Les shifted gears.

"Funny you should ask. Bart asked me to reach out to her to see if I could get her to come tonight. She lives off the grid in New England somewhere."

"You obviously didn't convince her to come."

"Nope. But we had a good conversation. She seemed glad to hear from me which made me feel good about calling her. Her life's been kind of sad at times. She seemed to choke up when I reminded her how much I genuinely liked her in high school."

We were getting near the end of the evening, so I was cueing slow songs like "I Only Have Eyes for You," "High on a Hill," and "We Belong Together." Shirley James walked by and waved at us. Les waved back. I turned away.

"What was that about?" Les asked.

"Whaddya mean?"

"Did something happen with you and Shirley?"

"Us? Nah." I did not want to go into a whole Kirkpatrick thing again.

"Did you hear what she said about Kirkpatrick?" Apparently, Les did want to go there.

"About his asking her to help him get a job?"

"No. Kirkpatrick's saying he'd commit suicide if she didn't get him a job."

"She's full of shit," I countered.

Les grinned. "She did have a big mouth in high school."

"Not sure if you remember," Les quickly changed the subject, "but a bunch of us TJ grads went to Ohio U the fall of '65. Kirkpatrick was there, in grad school. He hung out in our dorm, looking sadder and shaggier as the semester wore on. Next thing we knew, he was in England on some kind of scholarship, and we never saw him again."

I remained silent.

"Might not surprise you," Les continued, "but when Kirkpatrick would visit our dorm and strike up a conversation, he always talked about you. You and Will Beale. I guess you were his favorites."

Meaning what?

It was time for the last song, the last dance, the goodnight kiss. I decided to play a golden oldie called "Thank You Anyway, Mr. DJ" by a sad sack singer named Lou Johnson. It was always the last song Terry Lee played on "Music for Young Lovers" when most of us were nestled in the backseats of our cars with our arms around someone we wanted to believe we were madly in love with. I remembered the story of the song better than the lyrics, about a guy who was devastated after a break-up and wrote a letter to the local DJ, begging him to play the favorite song when he and his girl were still together...

"But I know now she, she just doesn't care." Poor Lou Johnson sounded so damn distressed. And so was I, haunted by the ghost of W. J. Kirkpatrick. What had I missed, or misunderstood? Maybe I hadn't missed, or misunderstood anything, maybe I was just a lonely, friendless dreamer when Kirkpatrick reached out to me in 1963, took me by the hand, and became my friend, my cheerleader. He never asked for anything more, anything physical. I doubted anything ever happened between him and anyone else. He just wanted a world with room for a D. H. Lawrence utopia where men could love men as well as women, where we could all love each other. Sex got in the way, or at least it seemed to for Kirkpatrick. So he turned to platonic love and new ideas and unsullied nature and romantic poetry. He'd let me be a part of that, of him. I'd responded with jealousy, possessiveness... and maybe even fear. Of what, I'd never know...

I looked up to see a face that I suddenly remembered from 50 years ago. How had I forgotten this? Kirkpatrick's younger sister had been in our class! And there she was, dancing in front of me. I jumped from my seat and ran out onto the dance floor. Her name? Rosemary?

"Rosemary, hi Rosemary." She stopped dancing and looked at me like I was drunk. Her husband seemed annoyed.

"Great tunes," she smiled at me. "But I'm not Rosemary."

"Sorry if I forgot your first name," I sputtered, "but aren't you Bill Kirkpatrick's sister?"

She and her husband both laughed.

"That happens all the time. I'm Pat Fields. Used to be Pat Marchall... This is my husband Bob. Rosemary Kirkpatrick and I still get confused even today."

Had I struck gold? "Of course. Sorry, Pat. Hi, Bob. Is she here?"

"No, I haven't seen her. Not in years. She and her husband live in central PA somewhere and never come back here. Sorry."

Momentarily frozen, I debated tracking down Rosemary Kirkpatrick. Not much of a debate, really, as I realized I didn't want to turn her life upside down with questions about her dead, older brother. I glanced back at the dance floor filled with 68- and 69-year-olds, slow dancing, imagining falling in love like they had a half century before, all of us 17 or 18 again, the memories stirred by the music, bringing them back to that moment, that time, that *them*.

That me.

So many moments. So many songs. So many times. From "World on a String" to "Chain Gang," "Kansas City" to "Wild Horses." Philly, Ohio, Pittsburgh, Vietnam, Pullman, and Madison. Music. Yesterday. Today.

I smiled, fulfilled, at least for the moment at peace. I was where I was always meant to be, past and present, playing the music that mattered.

Coda:
REMEMBER ME

    I've always been the DJ, inviting others to join me in what I'm feeling in a song. Even today, in the midst of multiple national and international meltdowns that appear unending, no sooner do I get out of bed than I fire up one of the Spotify playlists my son Ian has sent. Thanks to him I know who Mount Joy, Fruit Bats, and Hippo Campus are. And if she weren't so busy with her demanding work and two busy children, Summer would be joining in, adding her newly found love of Zach Bryan and country to the family soundtrack. Pam tolerates all of it, punctuating the brief silences with Bonnie Raitt, Gilbert and Sullivan, or classic Broadway show tunes. The days of Bobo the Oboe are long gone, thankfully.
    My penchant for soundtracking almost every occasion—be it a dinner with friends, a university lecture, my children's weddings, or my high school and college reunions—even my parents' memorial services—has helped keep me alive… and something resembling sane.

* * *

What I learned that night at the TJ 50th reunion, and every day since, is that music saved my life before, during, and after high school and college. For sure with Vietnam and returning home. My way of coming full circle—and the genesis of my ultimate Vietnam catharsis—centered on songs and memory. Sound familiar? My children, Summer and Ian, helped facilitate this breakthrough, because they'd both been students of Craig Werner at UW-Madison. So, when I ran into Craig at a 2004 Christmas party at the Vet Center in Madison, we immediately began sharing our favorite songs from the Vietnam era, talking about what music had meant to us, especially to soldiers, during that tumultuous time. Before long, we were surrounded by other vets who were anxious to share their own memories about the music they'd listened to in 'Nam and once they got back to the U.S. It didn't take long for me and Craig to realize that we were hearing stories that wouldn't have been shared without music as the hook. So, we decided to use music as the foundation for a very popular course we taught about the Vietnam War at the UW. And eleven years after that initial Vet Center conversation, *Rolling Stone* named our book, *We Gotta Get Out of This Place: The Soundtrack of the Vietnam War,* **"the best music book of 2015."** The interviews, the songs, and memories shared by veterans didn't just help bring them home—they brought me home too. I'd been writing and speaking about Vietnam ever since I got back, but *We Gotta Get Out of This Place* was *the* story—the stories—I needed to help communicate. I had finally—finally—made it all the way home from the war.

***

Summer married Brandon Strand on 11/2/13 and Ian wed Mary Rowley on 4/14/18. Love the linear math in those dates. Music filled the air at both weddings. Jerry Butler's "Moon River" played when Summer and I had our father-daughter dance, a special moment I will hold on to forever. For one night, "Moon River" had replaced "You've Got Your Troubles" as our song.

And Ian? He's more like his father, so he orchestrated the music for his and Mary's wedding. All of it terrific. Danceable. And for the two of us he included "Queen of the Slipstream" by Van Morrison, a haunting melody that has linked our souls for more than twenty years. Our music-memory library is, of course, different than mine with Summer, but nonetheless indispensable. From "Swing Low Sweet Chariot" which I sang to him to that catchy song by the Proclaimers about walking 500 miles to "Shimmer" by Fuel and the Dave Matthews band everywhere in between. We lost each other as most fathers and sons do during teenage testosterone days, but we came back stronger than ever, belting out "Read My Mind" by the Killers and "Codes and Keys" by Death Cab for Cutie at the top of our lungs. His Spotify playlists, which always have at least one Mt. Joy and Caamp tune on them, have kept me going when I've lost my bearings, which has happened too much lately.

When Jack Bradley passed away in May of 2009, I closed his memorial service with "Begin the Beguine" by Artie Shaw and his orchestra, a big band send-off to a big band lover, a flawed, fragile man who instilled in me a love and appreciation for music. And little Lucy, my mom, who passed away in 2018 at 99, exited to the strains of "My Ideal," another old

Big Band tune that my golden-throated World War II veteran dad would sing to her. They're together again, dancing in the dark to songs from "Music for Lovers Only" by the Jackie Gleason Orchestra. All those sounds humming away in my head all these years.

Something else had been humming in my head, which is probably why I'd returned to TJ in 2015 to spin that last platter, Lou Johnson's woeful "Thank You Anyway."

* * *

Unfortunately for Summer, she turned 40 during COVID, so the major celebration we had planned, like everything else in Wisconsin and America and the world at that time, was voided by the pandemic. She did promise me that I'd have access to the microphone that night, and I intended to tell the story of the two of us and our "You've Got Your Troubles" moment. And how we got her little brother to bounce around the room to "Born in the USA" when he wasn't yet a toddler. How she and I danced together to "Moon River."

But while the music keeps playing, Summer's 40th birthday party never happened. Maybe we'll try this when she turns 50, if we're all still here and the planet isn't completely off its moorings.

In the meantime, I get to marvel at my four grandchildren and the worlds they're shaping and engaging. Music and rhythm and song are part of the mix, and I can only hope that Tess, Bo, Lu, and Teddy can keep a song in their hearts and a smile on their faces. And, hopefully, a kind memory of their grandpa who adores them.

At moments like now when I sit back and reflect on all of it, life becomes a single symphony, one long song about who I am and was and will be. Music didn't just help me on this journey of discovery. It *was* the journey. The songs are foreground, not background, they and I are permeable, inseparable.

All of the music flows together. I can go online and lose myself in the arias of my Italian ancestors and their ancestors, my father's jazz and big band music, the Hip Hop and Indie rock my kids know, Pam's Gilbert and Sullivan, the grandkids' "Baby Shark," and anything by Taylor Swift, and, endearingly, "Remember Me" from *Coco*.

I hold on to all of it, and to them, and the memories. Which is how I got here in the first place. From the leaky bedroom in that rundown Philly row house to my brother Ron's record collection to all those high school mixers and sock hops and the Bethany concerts to Vietnam to Pullman to Madison and *We Gotta Get Out of This Place* and back again.

It took me this long to realize that the gift Bill Kirkpatrick gave me was the courage to find myself in words, to discover and lose and recover my *voice*. This book is, these tracks are, a way of thanking him.

The memories and the music, the melody that connects the singer and the song, are one together.

As my Italian ancestors, the pull that is family, would remind me, "*Da Capo*." Yes, indeed, *from the beginning*. Or here near the end. At both points you find music. And story. And family. The surety and elasticity and connectivity of music and memory and family in their beginnings and endings.

Here they are, here I am, adrift in those musical moments when the sound hits my ear, strikes my brain, pierces memory…

And I ask, remember me.

– FINIS –

ACKNOWLEDGEMENTS

Let me begin by thanking you, the reader, for your interest in my story, my memories, and my music. I hope you've enjoyed the journey as much as I have. And maybe discovered something about your own soundtrack along the way…

Family, words, friends, and songs are at the heart of *Tracks* and are my pillars. All of my extended **family**—past, present, and future—enrich my life. My parents Jack and Lucy and my brother Ron got me going. My spouse Pam, my daughter Summer, my son Ian, and their spouses Brandon and Mary, keep me centered and loved. And there's a host of Basiles, Bradleys, Shannons, Strands, and more who have always been in my corner. They have never wavered in their support of me and my writing. Last, and definitely not least, my grandchildren Tess, Bo, Lu, and Teddy give me hope and make me smile even when the world is off-kilter.

All the terrific teachers I've had during my life have inspired me with their **words** and taught me how to discover, and apply, my own. Foremost among them were Bill McTaggart, John Taylor, and Charles Blackburn. They're no longer with us, but they live on in me and my writing. I thanked them then and I thank them now.

Fortunately, **friends** have been abundant in my life, and they, too, have been a boon to me and my writing. At the top of that list is Craig Werner, my *We Gotta Get Out of This Place* co-author. More than just a brilliant friend, he is a one-of-a-kind teacher, scholar, writer, and music aficionado. Craig's insights, contributions, and encouragement have enhanced this book greatly. For years, he and I were members of the Deadly Writers Patrol. Our fellow members—Tom Deits, Steve Piotrowski, Tom Helgeson, Howard "Doc" Sherpe, Bruce Meredith, Dennis McQuade, Rick Larson, and Wyl Schuth—helped these music-memories become better stories, and, eventually, this book. Along the way, a host of other friends, some of whom are mentioned in *Tracks*, have helped in ways large and small, among them my men's breakfast group and my men's book club. My designer, Maegan Hart, and my publisher, Jodie Toohey, and my marketing assistant, Theresa Hunt, fall into the friends category as well given their skill in bringing *Tracks* to the finish line. There are far too many other friends and supporters to spell out, but you all know who you are and that I am immensely grateful.

Finally, there are the **songs** that fill these pages, reverberate in my mind, and expand my world. I was so lucky to grow up in a time when music was readily available, meaningful, and was so honest and genuine. My deepest thanks to the men and women whose musical talents have put a song on my lips and in my heart.

I'm still here, the music plays on, and the memories come rushing. There are many more tracks to unpack and remember. Maestro, if you please…?

Doug Bradley, Spring 2025

ABOUT THE AUTHOR

Doug Bradley is an author, educator, and veteran who spends his time in Wisconsin and Arizona. He spent his early years in *American Bandstand*-ed Philadelphia listening to his aspiring vocalist father croon big band songs and his older brother show off his falsetto with street-corner Doo-Wop groups. After two years in Ohio, Doug and his family landed in the gritty suburbs of Pittsburgh where DJs like Porky Chedwick and Clark Race helped local artists like the Skyliners, Marcels, Del-Vikings, Vogues, and Lou Christie move up the pop charts. While Doug endured his share of ups and downs at Thomas Jefferson (TJ) High School outside Clairton, he amassed a superb 45 RPM record collection and spun the platters at countless TJ dances and sock hops. A first-generation college student, Doug was awarded a scholarship by tiny Bethany College in nearby Bethany, West Virginia, where he served as social chairman from 1967-69, bringing 19 prominent singers and bands to Bethany, among them Count Basie, Smokey & the Miracles, Jefferson Airplane, Dionne Warwick, the Association, and the Fifth Dimension.

After graduation from college in 1969, Doug was drafted into the U. S. Army in March 1970. He served as a combat correspondent for the U. S. Army Republic of Vietnam headquarters at Long Binh, South Vietnam, from November 1970-November 1971. After completing his M. A. at Washington State University, Doug relocated to Madison, Wisconsin, in 1974 where he helped establish Vets House, a storefront, community-based service center for Vietnam era veterans. He has been writing and advocating on veterans' issues for more than five decades.

Professionally, Doug spent more than 30 years working for the University of Wisconsin in communications; media and public relations; marketing; and local, state, and federal stakeholder relations. For eight years he and UW-Professor Craig Werner taught a highly popular course at the UW entitled "The U. S. in Vietnam: Music, Media, and Mayhem."

He has blogged for PBS's *Next Avenue* and *The Huffington Post*, taught at UW-Madison, Baldwin-Wallace University, Edgewood College, and Arizona State University, and is the author of three books grounded in the Vietnam experience, including *DEROS Vietnam: Dispatches from the Air-Conditioned Jungle, Who'll Stop the Rain: Respect, Remembrance, and Reconciliation in Post-Vietnam America*, and co-author of *We Gotta Get Out of This Place: The*

Soundtrack of the Vietnam War, named the **Best Music Book of 2015** by *Rolling Stone* magazine. Doug has been happily married to retired attorney Pam Shannon for 49 years. They are the parents of two grown children and four grandchildren.